THE LIFE AND TIMES OF

LAST MINUTE REILLY

Ted Brack is a retired head teacher and lifelong Hibs supporter. His book *There is a Bonny Fitba Team*, chronicled half a century of supporting Hibernian Football Club and reached No 5 in the Scottish bestsellers chart. Ted co-authored *Pat Stanton's Hibernian Dream Team* and his latest book, *There's Only One Sauzée*, documents the highs and lows of Le God's time at Easter Road.

THE LIFE AND TIMES OF
LAST MINUTE REILLY

LAWRIE REILLY

WITH TED BRACK

BLACK & WHITE PUBLISHING

First published 2010
This edition first published 2011
by Black & White Publishing Ltd
29 Ocean Drive, Edinburgh EH6 6JL

1 3 5 7 9 10 8 6 4 2   11 12 13 14

ISBN: 978 1 84502 347 8

Typeset by Iolaire Typesetting, Newtonmore
Printed and bound by CPI Cox & Wyman, Reading

CONTENTS

ACKNOWLEDGEMENTS

I think it is fair to say that I have had a wonderful life. My football career was a source of success and satisfaction. When I retired I did well in business. I have a marvellous wife and family and I have been lucky enough to achieve quite a lot during my lifetime.

I had never, though, written an autobiography. Until now, that is! In my eighty-second year, I embarked on a journey down memory lane as I recalled growing up in Edinburgh in the 1930s, playing for the greatest football team in the world when they were at their best, and starring and scoring goals for the country I love.

I enjoyed the experience of writing my life story and I am delighted with the final result. I would like to thank my co-author Ted Brack for the excellent job he has done in putting my thoughts on paper so accurately and readably.

My dad supported me greatly in becoming the footballer I did. The scrapbooks which he meticulously compiled throughout my career have proved a great help in writing this book and I appreciate his doing this as much now as I did at the time.

He kept cuttings from the *Scotsman*, *Daily Express*, *Daily Mail*, *Daily Mirror*, *Daily Record*, *Weekly News*, *People*, *Sunday Express*, *Sunday Mail*, *Sunday Post*, Edinburgh's two evening newspapers of the 1940s and '50s, *The News* and *The Dispatch*, and other journals whose correspondents I have been unable to identify. The articles and reports add excellent period flavour to my recollections and I thank all the newspapers in question for helping to jog my career memories.

I would also like to thank my son Lawrance for his support in compiling this book. Most of all though, I want to record my appreciation of my wife Iris, who was there for me throughout the writing of my memoirs just as she has always been there for me in every other area of my life.

Lawrie Reilly

As a boy growing up in Leith, I heard all about the Famous Five and the successes of the team which that illustrious forward line spearheaded. When I was old enough to start attending Hibs matches, I was privileged to watch Lawrie Reilly, at the end of his career, play with Joe Baker, who was just starting out on his.

I stood on a wet, windswept Easter Road terracing and paid tribute to Lawrie in his testimonial match, and joined 2,500 others in packing the Usher Hall for the rally to mark his retirement in 1958.

In later life, I got to know Lawrie as a person as well as a footballer. When I published a book chronicling fifty years of supporting Hibs, Lawrie along with Pat Stanton gave me great support in launching the book and by doing so contributed to its subsequent success.

I was honoured when Black & White Publishing asked me to co-author Lawrie's autobiography. Our collaboration proved to be a pleasure and a privilege for me. The process of creating Lawrie's memoirs was much enhanced by having access to the superb collection of cuttings which Lawrie's father John maintained throughout his son's career.

Lawrie, thank you for the opportunity to help you put together your life story. Thank you too for your marvellous career, which provided a Hibs fanatic like me with many wonderful memories and huge pride in the great football club which we both support.

Ted Brack

We would both like to thank everyone at Black & White Publishing for their help and support in producing this book.

FOREWORD
BY SIR TOM FINNEY

Lawrie Reilly and I have been great friends for over sixty years and in addition to our general love of football we had two things in common.

The first thing is that we both loved playing at Wembley Stadium. In fact Lawrie scored there five times in five appearances for Scotland. The second thing is that we both remained loyal to a single club throughout our careers. I stayed with Preston North End and Lawrie only ever played for Hibernian.

I loved playing for England against Scotland but towards the end of a game when Lawrie was in the Scottish team and the ball came into the English penalty area I always had the feeling that we might hear that mighty Scottish roar for a goal. They didn't call him 'Last Minute Reilly' for nothing!

Lawrie Reilly was very special and he is without doubt one of the greatest players that Scottish football has ever produced.

I wish Lawrie every success with his long overdue autobiography.

August 2010

INTRODUCTION
BY HUGH MCILVANNEY

Nostalgia has long been the natural refuge for anybody intent on praising Scottish football. There is obviously something sad about finding the present such a barren, dispiriting landscape that we Scots have to bolster our sense of deep identification with the game by looking back across the decades. But at least we can be sure that the consolations provided by our past are solid and genuine, free of reliance on romantic distortions or self-serving revisionism.

In the area of collective performance the record is, admittedly, less than breathtaking. Scotland teams have always been restricted to the most parochial versions of glory – occasionally banjoing England hardly compensates for uninterrupted failure to progress beyond the first stage of the World Cup finals – and club success outside our borders has been noticeably limited, though the European Cup Winners' Cup victories of Rangers in 1972 and Aberdeen in 1983 were immensely admirable and Celtic's European Cup triumph in 1967 was historic for reasons even more important than its significance as British football's breakthrough into the ranks of continental champions. The sweetest, most enduring distinction of the Lisbon final was that the might of Helenio Herrera's Internazionale of Milan was convincingly and exuberantly overcome by players all born within 30 miles of Celtic Park.

What they accomplished was, of course, testament to the genius of Jock Stein, the Big Man who forms with Sir Matt

Busby, Bill Shankly and Sir Alex Ferguson the extraordinary quartet that is the ultimate representation of Scotland's unrivalled capacity (the claim is irrefutable on a per capita basis) for supplying football with outstanding managers. However, the almost miraculous feat of dominating Europe with a group of men drawn from a small corner of a small country also resonates down the years as a reminder of how fecund Scotland once was as a breeder of footballers capable of competing effectively against the best. And the example of the Lisbon Lions doesn't obscure the reality that, until the current era of deprivation loomed in the 1980s, the geographical spread of productivity was wide, with the eastern side of Scotland never in danger of lagging behind the western hotbeds of football in delivering players of the highest quality, the kind who deserved to be rated with the most gifted contemporaries operating in the same positions anywhere in the game. Aberdeen gave us Denis Law, Fife sent out Jim Baxter, and the flow of exceptional talent from Edinburgh effortlessly stood comparison with Glasgow's output.

If I am asked to name the true elite of Scottish players I have seen in an experience of watching football that stretches back to the years immediately after the Second World War, several Edinburgh-born figures are inevitably prominent on my list. There has to be a place for Willie Woodburn, who was so comprehensively equipped to be authoritative on the ground and in the air that it is impossible for me to believe that Britain ever produced a better centre-half. Woodburn's devastating flaw was the explosiveness of temperament and consequent violence that caused his career to be curtailed by a *sine die* suspension imposed in 1954 and not lifted until three years later, when he was 37 and beyond thoughts of a comeback. But when I recall him at his imperious peak the image is of somebody whose abilities would have made him a worthy ally for the finest central defenders I ever saw, Franco Baresi, Franz Beckenbauer and Bobby Moore.

That other son of Edinburgh Graeme Souness was also inclined to invite disciplinary sanctions but his intermittent transgressions never threatened the soaring arc of achievement that was his on-field career or, in my view, blurred his right to be regarded as the most influential midfielder to emerge in Scotland in the last 70 years. A powerful case might be made for such as Baxter, Dave Mackay or Bobby Murdoch but none of those marvellous players had, I feel, quite Souness's range of assets. His combination of profound understanding of how best to have an impact on the shaping of a football match and the level of technique needed to implement his minute-by-minute analysis, with all of that backed up by an uncompromising physical presence, enabled him consistently to have a vital effect in the most demanding competitive environments and it was automatic that team-mates' performances were raised by having him around.

Clearly, when reflecting on Edinburgh's connection with manifestations of extreme excellence in Scottish football, the attention is grabbed by the Hibernian team that won the national league championship three times in five years between 1948 and 1952 and lost out to Rangers only on goal average in 1953, and the focus on their deeds is bound to tighten on to the Famous Five forward line that was the wonder of the age. Only two of the five were actually born in the capital (Bobby Johnstone originated in Selkirk, both Willie Ormond and Eddie Turnbull in Falkirk) but that pair would constitute a substantial honour for any birthplace. Gordon Smith in his Easter Road prime was a winger of such grace, fluent skills and goal-making and goal-scoring penetration that no amount of club prejudice could prevent the majority of fans throughout Scotland from acclaiming him. After his long service to Hibs, he was so successful in brief spells with Hearts and Dundee that by the age of 38 he had become the only player ever to win league titles with three different clubs. Any roll of Scotland's greatest footballers that did not include Smith would be laughable.

And the same can be said, emphatically, of the other Edinburgh-born member of the Famous Five, the man who is the subject of this book and who, more than 50 years after his career was prematurely ended by injury, still magnetises superlatives in the minds of those of us who saw him at work. Lawrie Reilly occupies a special place in my personal pantheon of Scottish players, which is scarcely surprising, given that the early seasons of his development as a brilliant centre-forward coincided with the period of my youth when enthusiasm for playing football was accompanied by a hunger to see the leading performers of the day in action. As a 14-year-old glad of the adult solicitude of a family friend, I was on the Hampden terraces among the crowd of more than 143,000 who watched Hibs largely outplay Rangers in a 1948 Scottish Cup semi-final but lose to a Willie Thornton goal. Reilly and his team-mates had balm for the disappointment, since Hibernian were league champions that year. They would be supreme again in 1951 and 1952, by which time he had started his run of seven consecutive seasons as their top scorer. In taking the 1951 title, Hibs finished 10 points clear of Rangers in the table and struck 14 goals more than the Ibrox men did over 30 matches. In the 1952 league campaign Hibs accumulated 92 goals to Rangers' 61.

Theirs was an exhilarating attacking style that neutrals would travel far to witness, which was just what a boyhood pal and I did when enduring a wearisome journey in a lurching double-decker bus from our home town of Kilmarnock to Motherwell on October 14, 1950. The reward was a demonstration of relentless aggression that saw Hibs slaughter Motherwell 6-2, and the one small regret for this devoted admirer of Reilly was that he scored just once. In the equivalent fixture in 1952 he claimed four goals as Hibs stormed to a 7-3 win, but by then I was doing National Service. Making my dubious contribution to the defence of the realm did not, however, stop me from getting to Wembley on April 18, 1953, so I was on hand to cheer perhaps the most notable example of the late and momentous interventions that generated the legend of Last Minute Reilly. Scotland, trailing 2-1 in spite of an earlier goal by their ubiquitous, constantly probing centre-forward, had entered the final 20 minutes against England with 10 men after injury removed another of my favourite players, the wonderfully talented Sammy Cox, and rescue seemed impossible until, with (according to the match reporters) just 10 seconds of the hour and a half remaining, Reilly stunningly conjured up his second equaliser of the afternoon. His overall scoring record for Scotland was prodigious, 22 goals in 38 appearances, a strike rate of 61 per cent, and for his one and only club he had hit the net 234 times in league and cup games before physical problems obliged him to retire at the age of 29.

Yet statistics cannot convey a fraction of how dramatically impressive Reilly could be on the pitch. Nor can a simple cataloguing of the formidable weapons he deployed against defenders. Of course, he had an incredibly sharp positional sense and a concentrated and unflagging alertness to any opportunity to hurt the opposition; he was technically adroit, with the assured economy of touch and swift deadliness as a finisher to exploit the chances created by his intelligent movement and his brisk elusiveness in the face of challenges; he was strong and brave and endlessly energetic, harrying adversaries into vulnerability. But it was the way all his telling attributes came together in a dynamic amalgam that so often made him an unsubduable plunderer.

There was a time when Scots had the luxury of indulging in calculated understatement when saluting the best of their footballers and the man celebrated in this book warrants reversion to that tradition. Let's just say that Lawrie Reilly could really play.

PREFACE

I am a very fortunate man. My life has been blessed.

I was brought up in a close-knit family home which was united by an affection for Hibernian Football Club. As a boy, I dreamt of playing for my heroes in green and white and I managed to realise that dream.

I am a proud Scotsman and always had a burning desire to represent my country. I achieved that ambition too.

I played my football at a time when the great game was very different from what it is now. Every season had a definite shape. We didn't start far too early like they do these days with their pre-season friendlies and European qualifying matches in July. In sport, as in life, quality is better than quantity. We used to finish our season in early May and start the new season in August. There was a full three-month close season and this meant that when the new campaign got properly under way, the fans were absolutely desperate for action and flocked to games full of enthusiasm.

Our preparation usually consisted of taking part in five-a-side tournaments. They were great fun and really popular. Then the Edinburgh Select, made up of a mixture of Hibs and Hearts players, would take on a top English team at Easter Road or Tynecastle on the first Saturday in August.

The season proper started after that with the League Cup. Teams were in sections of four and the winners of each section qualified for the quarter-finals. The quarters and semis were played in September and the final took place at Hampden in October. It was the first trophy to be won each season and, in my time, was fiercely contested and highly prestigious.

International football was really big in the 1940s and '50s as well. The main event was the Home International Championship. Scotland would play Wales and Ireland in the autumn. Then there would be a delay until the following spring when we would meet England in what was usually the match to decide the outcome of the championship. The contest with the English was always considered the game of the season.

We also played a few international friendly matches. The World Cup only really started to assume prominence in 1950. We didn't have to play European countries to qualify during my playing career. First or second place in the Home International Championship was enough to take the British teams to the World Cup finals.

Then, as now, the League Championship was the most important honour that any club could win. There were sixteen teams in the league and we played each other twice. This thirty-match campaign was really exciting and every game was meaningful. The Old Firm were still the teams to beat but most other teams were able to compete with them far more than they do now. The fans really savoured our meetings with Hearts, which always took place at the same time. We would play each other in one of the early league fixtures and then again on New Year's Day. The Ne'erday derby was one of the highlights of the season.

European club competition didn't start until 1955 and even then there was only one competition. That was the European Cup, of course, and Hibs had the honour of being the first British team to take part in it.

Hibs also blazed the trail in undertaking end-of-season tours abroad. They were great fun and enabled all the players at Easter Road to learn from highly skilled Continental players. We definitely developed our own games through doing this.

I loved every minute of my career and it was only when I retired that I really appreciated just how privileged the life of a footballer is.

On retirement I entered the world of business and devoted more time to playing golf. I was lucky enough to be successful in both those fields. I also have a wonderful wife who continues to enrich my life.

My son Lawrance has been a source of great pride and pleasure to me since his arrival in the world more than fifty years ago. I also have a stepson, a stepdaughter, four grand-daughters and two grandsons, all of whom I love dearly.

So, as you see, I've done pretty well. I've enjoyed success within and outwith football. I had the good fortune as a young man to travel the world and be paid to do so. I have also been a 100 per cent Hibee for all my life. I have played in triumphs and witnessed disasters but there has always only been one team for me. That team is the pride of Leith, Hibernian FC. The Hibs may drive me mad at times but I will always support them and they will always have a special place in my heart.

There is one thing I haven't done, though, and that is write my life story. By the time this book comes out, I will have celebrated my eighty-second birthday, so it is probably fair to say that this autobiography is more than overdue.

Football has changed beyond all recognition since my playing days. Some players these days earn 100 times more in a week than I was paid per year. It doesn't make them better players, though. Gordon Smith, my boyhood hero, long-term colleague and lifelong friend, had to make do, like me, with a wage of less than £20 per week. He was world class though, simply the best player I ever played alongside.

People often ask me if the story about Gordon running down the touchline at Easter Road keeping the ball up with his head is true. It is. It happened during a match against Third Lanark and he ran virtually the full length of the field with the ball under perfect control. Not one Thirds defender tried to foul him either. They were probably mesmerised by Gordon's skill. I know that his team mates and the Hibs support marvelled at his talent on a regular basis.

I am not exaggerating when I say that some players who get picked for Scotland nowadays would have struggled to get a game in the Hibs team in the 1950s. I am simply stating a fact. Take Dougie Moran as an example. Dougie had to leave Hibs to get first-team football. He went to Falkirk and won the Scottish Cup. He was then signed for Ipswich Town by Alf Ramsey and won a league championship medal with them. That's how good he was, but he never came close to making himself a regular in the Hibs first team.

In fact, Hibs were so good at that time that they were odds on to win every match they played. Fans who liked a bet used to place their money on Hibs winning by more than two goals. It was the only way they could get a decent return from the bookmakers.

I accept that there are some tremendous players around in world football today, though. I think Lionel Messi might even have made the Easter Road first team in my day. There again, I am not sure which member of the Famous Five would have had to make way to accommodate him.

I don't grudge the modern players their wealth or celebrity status one bit. Good luck to them is what I say. I know that if I had played in the twenty-first century I would have been a millionaire. There again, I would probably have had to leave Easter Road to make the really big money and that is not something I would have wanted to do.

I have no regrets, and many, many treasured memories. Writing this book has enabled me to share these memories with you. I derived great pleasure from recalling so many great players, matches and occasions. I hope that older readers will enjoy reliving some magical moments and that those who are a little younger will be able to discover just how good both Hibs and Scotland were in the not-so-distant past.

I was famed for scoring last-minute goals and I suppose I have taken my time in committing my career highlights to print as well. However, as the old saying goes, better late than never.

Enjoy.

1

A WEE HIBEE FROM GORGIE

I was brought up on the wrong side of town. Our family lived in Bryson Road, deep in Hearts territory, but there was no doubting where the allegiance of the Reilly family lay. We were Hibs supporters through and through. My love for Hibs wasn't only a family thing though. I loved the green and white strip from the minute I set eyes on it. It just appealed to me. I'm not sure why but I thought it was the best strip around. As a matter of fact, I still think that is the case even now.

Our family was not rich in the material sense but there was a wealth of love in the Reilly household. My mum Jean and my dad John were tremendous parents. They taught me the correct values in life and were always there to support me. I had one sister, Rita, who was three years older than me. Like all brothers and sisters we had our fair share of scrapes but most of the time we got on really well.

My dad was a small man. He was just over five foot six. He was a man of principle, strict but fair. He had a fiery temper and if he thought that someone was in the wrong, he wasn't slow in letting them know. My mum was a real homemaker but loved her football. She went to all my games, which was unusual for a woman in those days.

Mind you, the person in charge of the famous Hutchison Vale Boys' Club when I was young was also a woman. She was Ma Bryson, a well-known and redoubtable character in Edinburgh juvenile football circles. My sister Rita came to all my matches as well and she never seemed to mind the amount of attention my football got. To be honest, I think she was proud of me.

My grandad lived in Stockbridge. His name was Bernard but he was known as Barney. Barney Reilly has a real Irish ring to it and our family was originally from County Cavan. We used to visit Grandad Reilly regularly. He always sat in a chair by the fire and, whenever I was in his house, he never moved from that position. I am sure that he did move around the house at other times but he never did when we came to visit.

My dad had been a good footballer himself. He played for the Stockbridge club Raeburn, who played in green shirts. Once, when Raeburn were playing in a cup final, I was enlisted as mascot and had to run from the centre circle to the goalmouth to hand a lucky horseshoe draped in green and white ribbons to the goalkeeper. As I ran towards him, I slipped and fell, no doubt to the amusement of the crowd. Undaunted, I jumped up, completed my task and left the field to a round of applause.

My dad worked on the railway as a guard on the goods van. This entitled him to free rail travel and his bosses used to let him take me along for the ride. The benefit of this was that I was able to watch Hibs play at every ground in Scotland before I even signed for the club.

Dad and I saw some great matches and in no time at all I had found myself a hero. He was the Hibs outside right, the one and only Gordon Smith. I couldn't believe how good Gordon was. I idolised him as a boy and when, as an adult, I became his teammate, I still idolised him.

Two matches which stick in my mind were against Rangers at Easter Road. In the first one, the Rangers and Scotland goal-keeper Jerry Dawson was hit by a bottle thrown from the terracing behind the goals at the bottom of the slope. I remember the police going into the crowd and dragging out the man who had thrown the bottle. Dawson, meanwhile, was carried off on a stretcher. After this incident, the game went dead, as if a sense of shock and disgust had settled over the whole ground.

I remember the other game for much happier reasons. Hibs beat Rangers 8–1, with Bobby Combe scoring four goals. That's how good a player Bobby was, yet in later years he couldn't force his way into our Famous Five forward line. As often as not, Bobby played in the half-back line or filled in as a forward when one of the Five was missing. He was brilliant that day and so, of course, was the great Gordon Smith. Matt Busby, the legendary Manchester United manager, also played as a guest for Hibs at that time but he wasn't in the team on that famous occasion.

As a wee boy, I thought that it was the norm for Hibs to beat Rangers 8–1. If only I had known! Another game I remember vividly was the Southern League Cup Final at Hampden. Hibs beat Rangers by six corners to five in front of a huge crowd. A decision had been taken before the match that if the teams were level on goals at full time, then corners would count. With the match locked at nil–nil and each team having five corners, Jimmy Caskie forced another corner for Hibs. Our fans went wild and the players mobbed Jimmy. It was the only time in my life I have seen over-the-top celebrations at the winning of a corner. It was the corner which won the cup.

When I was twelve years old, I was walking along Ardmillan after a Hibs–Hearts derby game at Tynecastle and who should walk past me but the great man himself – Gordon Smith. Gordon had just changed after the match and was heading for the nearest bus stop to catch his bus home. I can't quite imagine passing Wayne Rooney at a bus stop these days but that was then and this is now. Anyway, I walked up to Gordon and invited him back to my house for his tea. He looked a little taken aback but politely declined my invitation like the gentleman he was. In later years, of course, Gordon was a regular visitor to my home.

I attended North Merchiston Primary School before moving on to Boroughmuir for secondary education. The football teacher at North Merchiston was Bob Pryde, who came from Arniston. He and my dad got on really well. No matter what shift he was on, my dad usually managed to get from work to Meggetland for my school matches. He and Mr Pryde used to stand together on the touchline and shout advice to us.

I'll never forget the first time I was chosen for the school. But then again, maybe I wasn't actually selected. Mr Pryde gathered all the boys in his room and started to call out the names of those who were in the team. When he shouted out 'Reilly', I jumped up and grabbed a strip. What I didn't know was that there was another boy in the school with the same name. He insisted that Mr Pryde had meant him when he read out the players' names. He may have been right but I didn't stop to argue. I took the strip home, played the next day and never missed a game during the rest of my time at the school.

One of the first school matches my mother watched me in was at the Meadows. She had only just arrived when I had to go off with a badly cut knee. I was taken to the Royal Infirmary and stitched up, but if Mum thought that this football game was a bit rough for her wee boy she never said as much and I was soon back in action.

My sister went to Darroch Secondary which was a football school, but although I was the footballer in the family, I ended up at a rugby-playing school. It was a great school, though, and I was very happy there.

I only played two games of rugby for Boroughmuir. In both games, I scored all our points. I gave rugby up, though, for the very simple reason that I only had one pair of shorts. I played football for the Boys' Brigade and my boys' club on Saturday afternoons so if I had played rugby in the mornings I had to turn up for the football in soaking, muddy shorts. Sadly, the rugby had to go.

I also played cricket for Boroughmuir – I was a bit of a sporting all-rounder! I remember one game against Holy Cross, which was the school that Pat Stanton and Jimmy O'Rourke went to, when I scored forty-seven not out. The teacher in charge made me declare at that point because he didn't want me to get the chance to get big-headed if I scored a half-century. Jimmy

Wardhaugh, the great Hearts inside forward, played cricket for Holy Cross. He might even have been playing in that match. I was no Ian Botham but I was a fair player. My son Lawrance is a decent cricketer as well. His highest score is seventy-five, so that's one he's got over me!

Jimmy Wardhaugh was a great player and a really nice man. When he retired from football he went to work for the *Daily Express*. The *Express* had a staff football team and Jimmy used to play in it. They used Jimmy's old Scotland jerseys for their team strip. He had won eleven caps and had ten jerseys with number ten on the back and one with number nine. Jimmy wore that one and let the rest of the lads wear the others. It was a nice touch and typical of the man.

When I started secondary school, World War II was already in full flow. When the air-raid sirens went off, everyone in our tenement gathered at the foot of the stair as it was considered safer to be at ground level. It was probably a bit scary for the grown-ups but for us youngsters it was just a great adventure. The mums and grannies used to provide sandwiches and flasks of tea and we had a picnic inside while the bombs went off outside. There was never a direct hit on Bryson Road but I remember a bomb falling in Dalry. When that happened, my dad and I agreed that it was a pity that the pilot's aim hadn't been slightly out. Then he might have hit Tynecastle instead!

Another sport I was into was boxing. My dad started a boxing club at railway premises in Gorgie Road. It was called the LMS, which stood for London, Midland, Scottish which were the three main railway lines. I wasn't a bad boxer. I liked to land blows on my opponents but it wasn't as much fun when they hit me back. I didn't fancy too many bloody noses, so my interest in the noble art was fairly short-lived.

My reputation as an exponent of the noble art did me no harm at school, though. Because the other children knew that I had a bit of experience in the ring, they tended to show me respect when any fights were taking place in the playground. I didn't want to get involved in these scraps and I usually didn't need to because my schoolmates never tried anything on with me.

Actually, there was one time, but only one time, when I did get involved in a fight. One of the hardest boys in the school, Jackie Glen, challenged me to take him on after school. I didn't want to, but I didn't want to appear a coward either, so I was waiting for him when he came out at home time. A crowd gathered round us and we went at each other. We slugged it out toe to toe for a while then Jackie decided that he had had enough. That was fine by me and it was also the end of my fighting career at school. The perception of me as someone who could handle himself was increased further by this encounter and I didn't have another moment's bother.

My dad liked his boxing but football and Hibs were his main loves. At that time Hibs had a player called Ginger Watson. One day my dad and I travelled back from an away match on the same train as the Hibs players. When we got off at Haymarket some of the players were walking along the platform beside us. I called over to Watson, 'Hey, Ginger'. He wasn't too happy and gave me a ticking off. He left me in no doubt that for a youngster like me, the correct form of address was 'Mr Watson'. My dad was not best pleased and he made it clear that he wouldn't have his boy spoken to like that. Ginger Watson was a tough footballer and not a person to be trifled with. However, he backed off that day when my dad stood up to him. My dad was not an aggressive man but he didn't take a backward step when he believed he was in the right.

I remember another time when my dad showed his courage. I was out playing football with my friends and noticed that a man and a woman were sitting on the wall opposite the house. I didn't recognise them but I sensed that there was something wrong. Then I heard the family whistle. My dad used to whistle in a certain way when it was time for Rita and me to come in for our meals or for the night. When I played for Scotland at Wembley in 1949, my dad gave his whistle and I was able to pick out my family in a crowd of 95,500. On this occasion, my dad was coming back along the road from work. He motioned to Rita and me to go into the house but stayed outside himself.

We didn't see what happened next but my mum did. The man went for Dad, who used his boxing skills to put him on the ground. It turned out that there has been a dispute at work and that the man had come up to our house to 'sort out' my dad. In the event, he got more than he bargained for. Maybe some of my famous fighting spirit on the football pitch was in the genes.

I was playing plenty of football and it became obvious to me very early on that I was blessed with natural speed and an eye for goal. When I was fourteen, I was good enough to sign for Murrayfield Athletic at under-twenty-one level. Despite playing with men, I was more than able to hold my own.

Murrayfield was a happy club. All the players' girlfriends used to come along and support the team and there was a real family atmosphere. My parents and my sister attended our matches as well and through this connection Rita met her husband. One of my teammates, Jim Marshall, took a shine to my sister. They started going out together and ended up being very happily married. So that was one thing which the Reilly family had to thank Murrayfield Athletic for.

I was being watched playing for Murrayfield by a man called Harry Reading. Harry was Hibs groundsman and also ran a team called Edinburgh Thistle. Thistle wore green jerseys and played a lot of their matches at Easter Road. They were one of the top secondary juvenile teams in the country. Harry gave me the chance to sign for his team and I didn't need to be asked twice. What a team we had. In one season we won seven trophies. We played fifty-five matches that season and I managed to score no less than 106 goals. Again I was playing in an under-twenty-one team and again I was years younger than my teammates. This didn't deter me though. I just loved playing and scoring goals.

Three of my teammates at Edinburgh Thistle also went on to play for Hibs. Jim Souness was a winger who played for both

Edinburgh teams and Pat McDade was a left winger who seemed destined for the very top but didn't quite fulfil his potential. Then there was Archie Buchanan. Archie was born in the same month as me. We became great pals and played together at Easter Road for many years.

Secondary juvenile football was incredibly popular in the mid-1940s. When Edinburgh Thistle played Port Glasgow in the Scottish Cup Final at Easter Road, no fewer than 9,200 spectators came through the gate. They paid a total of £452, so, on average, they each paid around one shilling in those days, which is the equivalent of 5p now. They got value for money as well, as we beat the Glaswegians 3–1. They hadn't lost for forty matches but they were on the receiving end that day. A certain Lawrie Reilly managed to score Thistle's second goal.

In another cup competition we drew 4–4 with Portobello Renton. Two of Portobello's goals were scored by someone called Cropley. I wonder if he was any relation to the great Alex Cropley who graced Hibs' Turnbull's Tornadoes side in the 1970s?

We drew that match but we shouldn't have done. I missed a penalty in the last minute. When we got back to the dressing room, I expected to be on the receiving end of some criticism. Instead, it was quite the reverse. Some of the lads in the team started hugging me and jumping all over me. I couldn't work out what was going on until someone explained that the replay would be at Tynecastle. Half of our team were Hibees and the other half were Jambos. It was the maroon sympathisers who were congratulating me instead of criticising me. They were just delighted to get the chance to play at their club's home ground.

We won the replay and I scored two goals so everything ended well. I got two more in the last game of the season. It was the final of the Manclark Trophy (I have no idea where the name came from) and we beat Inveresk Athletic 6–3. I was delighted to bag a hat-trick. Inveresk came from Musselburgh and there was another team from the Honest Toun in our league. The goalkeeper for this

Musselburgh side was Lou Goram, none other than the father of Andy, who played for Hibs and Scotland in the 1980s. Lou was a fine keeper and also ended up at Hibs for a while before moving to England.

Every time Edinburgh Thistle won a trophy – and we won plenty – Harry Reading took the team back to his house for a celebration party afterwards. Harry's wife used to look after us really well. She and Harry had no children of their own and I think that, in some ways, the Thistle players were like family to them.

The success of Edinburgh Thistle was starting to attract attention and a lot of senior scouts were watching our games. I was obviously catching the eye of a few of them because an article appeared in the Edinburgh *Evening News* which said, 'It is as certain as anything in football possibly can be, that Lawrie Reilly will join Willie McCartney's talented band of youngsters.' McCartney was, of course, the Hibs manager.

McCartney was a flamboyant character who was always expensively dressed and never went out without a flower in his buttonhole. This habit earned him the nickname of 'The Buttonhole Boss'. He had a booming voice and a commanding presence and was more like a show-business impresario than a football manager. He lived in a big house in Corstorphine.

Reading that Hibs were after me made me feel great. Then things went quiet on the Hibs front, before taking a turn for the worse. The newspapers reported that the Hearts manager David McLean wanted to sign me. My dad was having none of it. As soon as he heard of Hearts' interest, he contacted Harry Reading at Edinburgh Thistle and Harry got in touch with Willie McCartney. Fortunately McCartney wasted no time in signing me and, at the age of sixteen, I realised my greatest ambition which, of course, was to play for the Hibs. When I signed, Hibs chairman Harry Swan told the press that he expected me to be the next Hughie Gallacher – a real honour as Gallacher was a member of the Wembley Wizards and one of Scotland's greatest centre forwards. No pressure there then!

9

I received the princely sum of £20 for signing on at Easter Road. When Gordon Smith had signed in 1941, he had been given £10, so, with my tongue firmly in my cheek, I used to kid Gordon in later years that I must have been twice the player that he was!

I was sixteen years old and had realised my dream of signing for the Hibs. Naturally, I dreamed of a great career ahead of me but little could I have known just what an amazing adventure I was about to embark upon.

2

HEARTACHE AT HAMPDEN

My first season at Easter Road was 1945-46. It was the first season since the end of the war so there was a great deal of optimism around. People were just pleased that the fighting was over, even though life at home was no picnic. Large parts of the country had been devastated by German bombing, food and clothes were rationed and a lot of people had lost loved ones. Despite this, there was a strong spirit of new beginning in the air. There had been a lot of suffering and there was still a great deal of austerity. Maybe that was why people had decided to enjoy themselves while they could.

The most popular form of entertainment was sport. Football grounds were absolutely packed every week, as men back from the Forces tried to escape the rigours of war by once again taking up the support of their favourite football team.

I was sixteen and a part-time player with Hibs so I thought I would have to wait quite a while for my first taste of big-time action. I was wrong. In those days, one of the traditional curtain-raisers to the season was the Rangers Sports. Eighty thousand fans would turn up at Ibrox to watch the top athletes of the day such as McDonald Bailey and Arthur Wint. Most of all, though, they went to watch the Rangers' Fives. This was a fiercely contested five-a-side competition which attracted all the top teams in the country.

On Friday 3 August, I received a telegram from Willie McCartney telling me to report to Leith Central Station next day to travel to Glasgow. Mr McCartney must have thought that my eye for goal and turn of speed would be just right for the five-a-side format.

I can't remember how we did on my first appearance at Ibrox, but I know that we usually did really well in five-a-side tournaments at that time. In later years, our team was normally Eddie Turnbull, who took on the role of goalkeeper/defender, John Paterson, Gordon Smith, Willie Ormond and myself. We hit it off as a combination and lifted a few trophies. We used to get excellent prizes such as canteens of cutlery or armchairs. We also got cash prizes on occasion.

I remember one year when we won the Rangers' Fives in great style. Our success pleased us no end but it didn't go down too well with the Rangers support. What really enraged them most of all was Eddie Turnbull bringing the ball out of defence, stopping, sitting on the ball and gesturing to the Rangers players to come towards him and try and get it. World War II hadn't long ended but Eddie's actions almost provoked the start of World War III!

I began the season proper in the reserves and it didn't take me long to attract attention in the press. One journalist wrote, 'Lawrie Reilly is an apprentice painter. He is putting plenty of colour into his football.' Like a lot of players in these days, I had a job outside football and trained at Easter Road in the evenings. The thinking was that if you didn't make it as a player, you would have something to fall back on. I was totally determined, though, that I most definitely would make the grade with Hibs.

I soon played my first match at Hampden. In those days, as now, the national stadium not only housed international matches but was the home ground for Queen's Park. Nowadays, the Amateurs are a low-profile, lower-league side but back then they were a highly rated top-division team. When Hibs played them in a reserve match, I got my first taste of action on the pitch which I would come to know so well in the years ahead. We won 10–3 and I scored my first Hibs goal, but it was a strange experience. The massive ground was virtually empty and my biggest memory of that match is the eerie atmosphere. At one point, the ball went into the terracing and, as there were no ballboys, I had to climb over the wall to collect it and climb back over before taking the throw-in.

My first-team debut wasn't long in coming. On 13 October 1945, just a few days short of my seventeenth birthday, I played my first league match for Hibs against Kilmarnock at Rugby Park. I was selected at inside right and my winger was my hero, Gordon Smith. I felt like I had gone to heaven and that when I had got there I had discovered God himself playing outside me.

My only thought was to give Gordon plenty of the ball and I certainly did that. Every time I got possession, I passed out to the great man on the right. I probably ignored better-placed colleagues in other positions at times in my eagerness to ply Gordon with the ball, but it didn't matter to me that day because there was only one thing on my mind – 'feed Gordon Smith'.

We left Ayrshire with a 4–3 win, thanks to a fifty-five-yard wonder goal from Sammy Kean. The *Evening News* report of the match stated that, 'Young Reilly emerged successfully from his experience and will be the better for it.' The reporter added, 'Gordon Smith was again the best player on view.' Maybe my service had something to do with that!

Just before Christmas, I was back at Hampden, but this time I was on first-team duty. Our centre forward Jock Weir had been sold to Blackburn Rovers and I was given my first opportunity to play in my best position and prove that I could be his long-term successor. As it turned out, the game was abandoned because of fog with just ten minutes left and Queens one goal in front. They weren't best pleased and the press weren't overjoyed about my performance either. One reporter stated, 'Whether Lawrie Reilly will be a long-term success is problematic.'

My manager sprang to my defence and when Willie McCartney spoke, people paid attention. He was a charismatic character whose views carried a lot of weight. This time he declared, 'Don't worry about Reilly. This boy is going to be a good player.' That did a lot for my confidence, I can tell you. I welcomed this boost from the boss but I didn't really need it because I knew within myself that I could play and I never doubted that I would make it.

McCartney was an expert talent-spotter. He signed some great players for Hibs and generally managed things well. In the main, though, he left training and team talks to Hugh Shaw and Jimmy McColl, his two assistants. Hugh and Jimmy had both been top players for Hibs and they really knew the game. Mr McCartney had never played at a high level but he knew the game too.

I was being selected in all the forward positions at that time. I suppose the manager wanted to develop my game by giving me a variety of experiences. One happy moment was teaming up on the left wing with my old Edinburgh Thistle teammate and great pal, Archie Buchanan. It seemed like no time since Archie and I had been playing juvenile football together. Now, here we were partnering each other in the Hibs first team!

My first senior goal at Easter Road was against Queen of the South. I felt great when the ball hit the net and the moment was made all the sweeter because Gordon Smith supplied the pass which allowed me to finish off the move.

It was a good job that I had done something right that day, because I didn't get off to the best of starts. Our chairman, Harry Swan, came into the dressing room before the match and issued the team with some tactical instructions. Mr Swan was small in stature but large in self-belief. He had never played football but that didn't dent his confidence. When he had finished his team talk, I perked up with, 'Why are you telling us how to play the game, Mr Swan? You've never played football yourself.' As soon as I spoke, I knew that I had made a major error. One minute the thought was in my mind, the next the words were out of my mouth and there was no taking them back.

The chairman was furious and immediately sought out my dad. He told him that I had given him a 'mouthful of cheek' and instructed him to deal with me after the game. I don't think Mr

Swan ever really forgave me for my youthful outburst. I may have been indiscreet but I was also right. He knew a great deal about business but a whole lot less about football.

When I had played a few more games for the first team, I realised that the chairman's dressing-room visits were a regular occurrence. I found out too that no one paid any attention to what he said. As soon as he had closed the dressing-room door on his way out, Mr McCartney would say, 'Right lads, just ignore everything that he said.'

He would encourage us players to speak our mind though. During his half-time team talks, he would often invite us to tell him what we thought about the way the game was going. He was years ahead of his time in that respect.

I loved life at Easter Road. I couldn't get in there for training quickly enough. Our team spirit was terrific and there was a non-stop flow of banter. We used to stretch a net across the dressing room and play a game of badminton with a shuttlecock and table tennis bats. When somebody came into the dressing room, we would shout, 'Get out of the way, you're spoiling the game.'

I did most of my training in the evenings since I worked during the day. I was an apprentice painter and decorator. I worked for my Uncle Armstrong's company and he paid me the princely sum of fifteen shillings per week, which equates to seventy-five pence in today's money. My uncle was a Hearts supporter but I didn't hold that against him. He lived in Gorgie Road, just a stone's throw from Tynecastle. I was still living in Hearts territory myself, of course, and signing for Hibs didn't exactly make me popular with some of the local residents. I got the occasional bit of stick as I went about my daily business but I can honestly say that it never bothered me.

Another advantage of serving an apprenticeship was that it made you exempt from call-up to the Forces. One of my teammates at Easter Road was Johnny Cuthbertson, who worked in a government department. One day he came up to Archie Buchanan and me at training and told us that he had found out that young men born in October 1928 were to be exempted from call-up as there was a glut of recruits. That meant that Archie and I definitely didn't have to join up. It also meant that the only uniform I ever wore was that of the Boys' Brigade when I played football for them as a boy.

As soon as I knew that I didn't have to go into the Forces, I gave up my decorating work and went full-time at Easter Road. That probably made a bit of a difference to my weekly income, as I was only earning £3 to £4 per week as a part-time player.

At that time I was playing a lot of my first-team football at outside right, filling in for Gordon Smith when he was away with Scotland on international duty. In those days, when international matches took place, a full programme of league fixtures went ahead as usual.

My right-wing displays were obviously attracting attention elsewhere as Bolton Wanderers came in with a bid for me. They tried to entice me to sign by telling me that I would be playing in the same forward line as the great English goal-scorer Nat Lofthouse. In another ploy to get me to move, they pointed out that I was only getting selected on the right wing because Gordon Smith was away. They told me what I was already well aware of when they said, 'You'll never displace Smith on a permanent basis.' I knew the truth of that but I also knew that my long-term ambitions lay at centre forward and not on the right wing. More importantly though, I had no intention of leaving Hibs for Bolton Wanderers or anybody else. My heart was well and truly at Easter Road and that was where I was going to stay.

Funnily enough, I did displace Gordon once, when the Scotland selectors chose me on the right wing in front of him for an international. I played and Gordon was the travelling reserve in those pre-substitute days. I don't know what they based their team selection on but it puzzled me then and it still mystifies me to this day. I was also chosen in front of Willie Ormond for the left-wing berth in the Scotland team on occasion as well. I am not sure what Gordon and Willie made of these selections, but they never said anything to me and it never affected our friendship.

When season 1946-47 came round, it was obvious that we were starting to build a seriously strong team at Easter Road. This was confirmed by no less an authority than Bill Struth, the Rangers manager. Struth has legendary status now and he was a towering figure back in the 1940s. Writing in the Rangers handbook in the summer of 1946, he stated, 'Hibs are the team most likely to challenge Rangers' supremacy.' To say Struth was a disciplinarian is an understatement. The ex-Hibs goalie Ronnie Simpson told me a story about his dad, Jimmy, who had once played for Rangers. One day when Jimmy reported for training, Bill Struth called him into his office and said, 'Somebody saw you in Sauchiehall Street yesterday and you had your hands in your pockets. Rangers players don't conduct themselves in that manner. Make sure you don't do it again.' Can you imagine how a modern player would react to being spoken to like that?

In that same handbook, the Rangers reserve team player-manager, Dougie Gray, who had been a top full back in his day, had an opinion to express on me. Remembering how I had given him the runaround in a reserve game the previous season, he wrote, 'I have unpleasant memories of trying to catch up with the boy. The kid has come on a mile.'

As the season got underway, I was also getting regular mentions in press reports. One reporter said, 'Young Reilly is making many friends. This boy is really good.' This was after I scored four goals in a reserve game against Celtic which we won 7–0. In another report I was described as 'another coming Gordon Smith'. I couldn't have had higher praise than that. I got press praise of a different kind after another match. I had torn my shorts and changed them for new ones and the journalist covering the match wrote, 'Reilly managed to slip into a second pair of shorts without having to leave the field!'

I was getting some first-team experience too, but I was picking up my fair share of injuries. One very wet day we beat Morton 2–0 at Cappielow and the ball was really heavy. The balls in these days were always heavy, but being completely sodden, this one was particularly so. During the game I had headed it so much that I gave myself concussion. Most of the game was a blur and at the end I tried to go into the Morton dressing room instead of our own and one of the Morton players had to take me through to the Hibs changing room. When I regained my senses, I was delighted to discover that we had won the match.

In another game, I broke my finger and injured my knee. However, the match programme of the time reports that I was confidently expected to return from both injuries 'in a couple of weeks'. They obviously made us tough in those days.

I also played in the derby match at Tynecastle, which was the great Tommy Walker's last match for Hearts before he signed for Celtic. Unfortunately for us, Tommy signed off with a victory, as Hearts beat us 1–0. Tommy was a thorough gentleman who successfully managed the Jam Tarts when his playing career was over. He is best remembered for the penalty kick he scored for Scotland against England at Wembley in 1938 to earn us a 1–1 draw. It was a windy day and the ball kept blowing off the spot, which would have fazed a lot of players – but not Tommy. At the third time of asking, he dispatched the ball into the corner of the net to send the tartan hordes who packed Wembley into delirious celebrations. While all this was happening, I was out playing football in the street with my pals. My mum and dad were listening to the game on the radio. When the penalty was awarded, my mum opened the window to tell us. We stopped playing and stood and listened as Mum gave us a running commentary on one of the most famous Wembley moments.

Hibs were getting progressively stronger. Four of the Famous Five were now at the club. As well as Gordon and myself, we had Willie Ormond on the left wing and Eddie Turnbull at inside left. Eddie impressed everyone with his all-round play when he joined up at Easter Road but his most striking talent was his ability to hit the ball with great power. At that time there was a character in a children's comic with a rocket shot who was called 'The Cannonball Kid'. That soon became Eddie's nickname at Easter Road.

As I have mentioned we had a great team spirit at the club. Our left half Sammy Kean was the life and soul of the dressing room. Sammy was an ebullient character who was always up to something. He wasn't the only one. I remember one day when the team set off on tour and we made the first part of the journey by train. The management and directors were also on the train with their wives. Hugh Shaw was manager by that time and he had boarded the train wearing a brand new, stylish trilby hat. He put the hat in the luggage rack and went to sit with his wife further down the carriage. A few of us were playing cards and Mr Shaw's hat fell on the card table. Jimmy McColl threw the hat back up onto the luggage rack. A few minutes later, to everyone's annoyance, the hat again fell into the middle of our game. Jimmy picked it up once more and threw it up towards the rack. Unfortunately it flew straight out of the window and disappeared into the distance as the train raced on. The window wasn't even open all that wide and Jimmy probably couldn't have got the hat through the space available again if he had tried 100 times.

However unlikely it was, he had indeed thrown the manager's new hat out of the window. Needless to say, Jimmy was mortified, while the rest of us were helpless with laughter. McColl then had to deliver the bad news on the hat front to the boss. It's fair to say that while Mr Shaw was less than pleased, his wife was absolutely furious!

Another great character was Jimmy Cairns. He hailed from the Falkirk area like Eddie Turnbull and Willie Ormond and travelled to Easter Road with them every day. Jimmy was hard as nails and appointed himself my minder on the park. If an opponent got rough with me during a game, Jimmy wasted no time in sorting him out.

On another tour, we were travelling by ship. One night we had gathered for a game of cards and all the usual players were there except Bobby Johnstone. We assumed that he had decided to have an early night but Jimmy decided to go and get him out of bed to join the game. He went to what he thought was Bobby's cabin and opened the door. All he could see was a shock of black hair showing above the covers which convinced him that he was in the right room for wee Bobby. He pulled off the sheets and shouted, 'Get oot your bed, ya wee black-haired bastard.' To his horror, he discovered that he was in the wrong cabin and lying in the bed was the wife of one of the directors!

We were progressing well in the Scottish Cup in 1946-47 and beat Rangers at Easter Road in a quarter-final replay. Even though the game was played on a Wednesday afternoon, 50,000 fans turned up to cheer the Hibees on. The match programme for that game reported that Bobby Combe had returned from the Forces. In the quaint language of the day, it also stated, 'Combe, who took unto himself a wife recently . . .' Bobby's wife May was a lovely lady. The last time I spoke to her she was in the stand at Easter Road watching her grand-nephew, Alan Combe, the Hibs supporting goalie who has played for Dundee United and Kilmarnock.

We reached the Scottish Cup Final that year and our opponents were Aberdeen. Even then, in 1947, it was forty-five years since Hibs had won the Scottish Cup. We were determined to lift the trophy and were confident that we could do it. I just wanted to make sure that I played in the game because at this time I still wasn't a regular in the side. The competition for places had increased as well, because Willie McCartney had paid a record sum to sign inside right Leslie Johnston from Clyde. Johnston's arrival meant that for the first time, in a friendly match against East Fife, Hibs were able to field a forward line of Smith, Johnston, Reilly, Turnbull and Ormond. The Johnston, of course, was Leslie not Bobby.

The week before the Scottish Cup Final we played Celtic.

Gordon Smith was on international duty and I took his place. We won 2–0 and I scored and played really well. One match report went so far as to say 'Little Reilly was immense.' I wasn't taking anything for granted, but I thought that I had a great chance of playing. I knew Gordon would come back in but I thought that I might manage to keep out one of the other forwards.

When the big day came, I was one of twelve players who travelled to Hampden. In those days, of course, there were no substitutes so we all knew that one of us was going to miss out. Before getting on the train for Glasgow, we posed for a photograph in the station. I am smiling in this photograph but I certainly wasn't smiling when we reached the stadium.

When we entered the dressing room, Willie McCartney pinned the team sheet up on the wall and the name which was missing was mine. While the rest of the players started to change into their cup final strips, I sat bitterly disappointed. Johnny Cuthbertson had been selected at centre forward. 'Cubby' was a wholehearted player who got his share of goals but he wasn't a great footballer and, in my opinion, he most certainly wasn't a centre forward.

What really saddened me was that neither Mr McCartney nor Hugh Shaw pulled me aside and explained why I had been left out. To this day, I have no idea why I wasn't chosen for the final, having played so well against Celtic the week before. I was devastated not to be picked and it took the edge off what should have been a really special day.

We started the game in great style and Cubby tapped home a rebound from a couple of yards out to give us the lead in the very first minute of the game. We peaked too early, though, and didn't play well. Despite Jimmy Kerr, our goalkeeper, saving a penalty, Aberdeen fought back to win 2–1. Hibs' Hampden hoodoo had struck again and to this day, it hasn't been overcome. Would the jinx have been broken that day, if a certain L. Reilly had played centre forward? Who can say? I certainly thought at the time that I could have made a real difference if I had been on the field. Looking back, the manager was possibly right to prefer an experienced player to an eighteen-year-old. I just wished he had found time to have a quiet word in the ear of a young player who suffered a massive disappointment on that dark day sixty-three years ago.

Hibs did finish the season on a high, though. We won the three competitions which were played for in reserve-team football in those days. We won the Reserve Team League, the Second Eleven Cup and the Reserve League Cup. In the final of the League Cup, our last game of the season, we beat Rangers 3–0 and I managed to score the second goal, so my season ended on a bright note.

We knew we had a top team and plenty of talent in our reserves. Season 1947-48 promised a lot and for everyone at Easter Road, it just couldn't come quickly enough.

3

TEENAGE TITLE WINNER

I was really looking forward to the start of season 1947-48. I was eighteen years old and delighted to be a Hibs player. I had already played first-team football in a number of positions but my aim as the new campaign approached was to make the centre forward berth my own.

These hopes took a bit of a knock when the club signed Alec Linwood from Middlesbrough. Linwood was an experienced centre forward and also a very good one. His signing told me that Hibs didn't yet consider me the finished article and that I would have to scrap to get a place in the team in any of the forward positions.

I soon got to know Alec Linwood and I really liked him. One day, not long after he had joined up at Easter Road, when we were doing a stretching routine together in training, I asked him who he thought was the fastest player on the books. I thought he might say that I was because I was pretty nippy, as was Gordon Smith. As I expected, he named Gordon; then he surprised me by nominating himself. I hadn't considered Alec all that quick but I soon discovered that he was right. He didn't look all that pacy but that was deceptive as his long stride ate up the ground. When we did sprints in training I could never keep up with Linwood and I very soon got used to having a view of his backside as he powered away from me and the rest of the group.

We did a lot of running in training in those days. The accepted wisdom back then was that if you didn't see the ball during the week you would be hungry for it come a Saturday. That was ridiculous, of course, and conveniently ignored the fact that the less you practise with the ball the more your touch loses its polish.

We used to do countless laps of the Easter Road pitch. We would start at the bottom end of the ground, run to the halfway line, walk across the field and then sprint back down to the bottom of the pitch. There was a pronounced slope on the pitch in those days, of course, so it was a whole lot easier coming down the hill than it was racing up it for the umpteenth time.

Before the season proper got underway, we set off on a five-match tour of Scandinavia. I can tell you that was a tremendous experience for a wee lad from Bryson Road. We won our first four games and scored twenty-eight goals in the process. I was only selected for one of those matches and made a point by scoring four goals in a 7–0 victory – 7–0, that's a score that has a nice ring for Hibs supporters! Anyway, I must have impressed the media because the next day's *Evening News* said, 'Reilly touched such magnificent form that his inclusion in the Easter Road first team cannot be long delayed.'

The whole team came in for praise in one of the local newspapers called *Dagbladet* which published this fulsome tribute: 'Thank you Hibs. Your exhibition last night left us breathless. Your name will live in Norwegian football for years. Your first-class football and sportsmanship brings pride to your country.' I finished off my time in Norway by looking up my cousin who had married a Norwegian and moved to Stavanger.

We then moved over the border to Sweden to play their champions Norrköping. Norrköping were a top side and had won sixty of their last sixty-six matches. They had 21,000 supporters inside the ground and we knew we were in for a tough match. We had no idea just how tough!

I came up against many referees who did the Hibs very few favours in my time, but none of them, in my opinion, came close to the man who controlled (and I use that word advisedly) our game in Norrköping. We lost 3–1 against a very good team, but it's fair to say that the man in the middle significantly influenced that result. He awarded the Swedes two penalties and chalked off a perfectly good Hibs goal. He then rounded off his perform-ance by diverting the ball into our net for Norrköping's third goal. The ref would no doubt have claimed that ball went in off him accidentally. We definitely saw it differently!

We got home in time to fit in a few of the pre-season five-a-side tournaments which were so popular just after the war. We won the first two, the Police Sports and the Press Gala, and beat Hearts on the way to both our successes. In the first tournament we took four goals without reply off our local rivals. Gordon Smith notched up a hat-trick and I was delighted to score the other. No fewer than 14,000 fans turned up to watch the second tournament which shows how popular 'fives' were at that time.

When the papers previewed the season, they highlighted our forward line and claimed that it would be worth £50,000 on the open market. That might not sound like much now but it was a veritable fortune in 1947. There was only one problem with the articles in question. They all left me out of our front five and selected Alec Linwood instead.

It was the custom back then to list each club's playing staff on the eve of the upcoming campaign. In this list, each player's height, weight and previous club were given. I weighed in at ten stone seven pounds in those days (I am not much more than that now) and, at five feet eight inches, I was taller than quite a few of my colleagues. It just shows how much smaller people generally were at the end of World War II during a time of food rationing. In fact, only one player on Hibs' books at that time was a six-footer. The tallest player we had was a certain S. P. Waldie, who had signed from Inverness Caley and was exactly six feet in his stocking soles. Big Simon was a footballing centre half and a lovely lad. He stayed with me for a while when he first came down from the Highlands.

We made a great start to the season by winning 2–0 at Pittodrie on a Wednesday night. There were no floodlights in those days but that didn't stop 40,000 Aberdonians turning up in natural northern light to see their team outplayed. According to the next Hibs match programme, 'The weather, like the match, was brilliant and a scorcher.' Our goals came from Gordon Smith and Eddie Turnbull and I can remember the Aberdeen fans clapping both of them. Were they a particularly sporting crowd or were fans just generally less partisan in those days? I am not sure – maybe they were just really impressed by the quality of our football and broke into applause spontaneously. Whatever prompted them to do it, I can't see it happening nowadays.

I got a chance at centre forward when we met Queen of the South at Easter Road and banged in my first senior hat-trick as we won 6–0. The match report said that 'by snatching chances like a veteran, Reilly had made himself the hat-trick hero of a one-sided game'.

Hibs then sold Leslie Johnston back to Clyde. He had been the club's record signing but had never really settled. Although the club lost a little money on the deal, chairman Harry Swan assured supporters that we hadn't 'dropped a packet'. Johnston was replaced by a near namesake in Bobby Johnstone, who came to us from Selkirk. Little did we realise when wee Bobby signed on at Easter Road that the last member of what was to be an immortal forward line had joined our club. Bobby had caught Willie McCartney's eye when we beat Selkirk 11–2 in a friendly. He must have done something right to show up well in a match which his team had lost so heavily.

I wasn't a regular in the team yet but got back in for a game against Queen's Park at Hampden when Gordon Smith was injured. We were locked in a struggle with Rangers to win the league and every game was vital. We managed to win 3–2, thanks to a late rocket shot from Eddie Turnbull which, according to the next day's report, he 'smote with power and superb direction'. The goalkeeper who couldn't keep out Eddie's winner was none other than Ronnie Simpson, who signed for Hibs twelve years later, before moving on to win the European Cup with Celtic in 1967.

A 2–1 defeat to Rangers at Ibrox was a blow. I was back at centre forward that day but was marked well by Willie Woodburn. 'Big Ben' and I were to become friends and colleagues in the Scotland team in years to come. His nickname had nothing to do with a certain London clock; it came from a trip Rangers made to Portugal, where they played Benfica. After the game Willie partook over-enthusiastically of the post-match hospitality and had to be helped to bed by his teammates. Even though the match had been played in Lisbon, he kept repeating that 'Benfica was a great place' – with all the emphasis on the first syllable. Hence the nickname, which he retained for the rest of his career.

Although Willie got the better of me that day, I did give him a few tricky moments. In fact I felt that we should have had a penalty. I burst into the Rangers box and three Rangers defenders converged on me. Between them they bundled me over and as I hit the ground I waited for the referee's whistle. That proves that I was still young and naïve. Unsurprisingly the referee did not award a penalty and I was to find out over the years that it took something really special to merit a spot kick against Rangers at Ibrox. Mind you, being brought down by three players at once is a bit out of the ordinary.

More praise came my way when I was described in the press as 'one of the most promising propositions ever picked up by Willie McCartney and that is saying something'. Not long after that my football teacher at North Merchiston Primary School, Bob Pryde, became President of the Scottish Schools Football Association. The report describing Mr Pryde's elevation to this prestigious position also noted that he had 'produced many fine players, the latest being L. Reilly (Hibernian)'.

Alec Linwood was still keeping me out of most first-team matches, though, but that didn't stop the Portobello Branch of the Hibs Supporters' Association inviting me along to their annual dance in the local town hall. Five hundred fans turned up and asked me to auction a bottle of whisky. This was as close as I ever allowed myself to get to a bottle of the hard stuff as I have been a lifelong teetotaller. Even in later years when I became a publican, I always preferred pouring drinks to consuming them.

The next day's *Daily Mail* revealed that I had stayed out until 1am! It also printed a photograph of me sitting on the fans' shoulders holding aloft the bottle of whisky before handing it over to the successful bidder. The headline was 'Supporters welcome "Transfer" '.

There was transfer talk of a different kind just a few weeks later. While Hibs continued their quest for the league title, Hearts were struggling to avoid relegation. There was a lot of specula-tion that we might do them a good turn by loaning them a couple of our players to help them stay up. Harry Swan confirmed that talks were taking place and that such a move was a possibility. Imagine my consternation when the press then reported that the two players who were being considered for loan were Johnny Aitkenhead and myself. In the event, nothing came of it and I state categorically now, some sixty-two years later, that nothing ever would have come of it. If Mr Swan had asked me to move to Hearts, he would have got a very direct and completely negative response. I just wouldn't have considered it.

If our neighbours were having a hard time, we were going great guns. Half way through the season, Hibs' three teams had scored a total of 215 goals between them. The first team had notched half a century, the reserves had gone ten better than that and the third team had hit the net no less than 105 times. We had a great chance of winning the league for the first time in forty-five years and we knew it. As usually seemed to be the case in those days, Rangers were our main rivals, but we definitely felt that we had a great chance of seeing the championship flag being raised at Easter Road.

But our feelgood factor was to be struck a massive blow. In February, Hibs manager Willie McCartney died suddenly at the age of only fifty-nine. Mr McCartney took ill during our Scottish Cup match with Albion Rovers in Coatbridge. Harry Swan arranged for him to be driven home before the end of the match and tragically he passed away at home later that evening after suffering a heart attack.

'The Buttonhole Boss' was a larger-than-life character. Like Jock Stein in later years, his presence dominated any room he entered. He had managed Hearts for sixteen years and had signed two of their greatest-ever players in Tommy Walker and Alec Massie. It was considered sensational when he resigned his post at Tynecastle and even more of a sensation when he moved across the city to Easter Road. It was a bit like the Maurice Johnston move in later years, but without the religious connotations.

As his obituary declared, Willie McCartney 'revolutionised Hibs and transformed their fortunes'. The tributes to our manager also stated that, 'No manager had a better flair for spotting young talent. He knew how to blend his captures.'

Another paper was of the opinion that 'The best way for Hibs to perpetuate their manager's memory would be to win the league and the Scottish Cup.' We were well placed to do the first of these but sadly, even now, all these years after the loss of one of Hibs' greatest ever managers, we still haven't managed to win the cup.

Unsurprisingly, the boss's funeral at St Bernard's Church was packed with mourners. The turnout was so large, in fact, that 200 people were left outside and unable to gain entrance. We players were all present and six of the team carried Mr McCartney's coffin. There was a great sense of sadness and shock around the club and for a time football was the last thing on our minds.

Of course, Willie McCartney would have to be replaced and there was talk of Matt Busby becoming our new manager. He had played for Hibs during the war and had become very popular with our supporters. Mr Busby was now in charge of Manchester United, though, and I don't think that he would have left Old Trafford to come to Easter Road, even though he definitely had a lot of affection for Hibs. He seemed to have a soft spot for me as well and was a real father figure to me over the years. If he came to watch a Hibs match, or if we were playing down south, he would come up afterwards, put his arm around me and offer me advice and encouragement. He made it clear that he thought highly of me as a player, which meant a lot.

Harry Swan didn't waste any time in appointing Willie McCartney's successor. He promoted from within and gave the job to our trainer Hugh Shaw. Hugh had played for Hibs with distinction in the 1920s and had been part of our team when we lost two successive Scottish Cup Finals to Celtic and Airdrie in 1922-23 and 1923-24. He had returned to the club as part of the backroom staff in 1934 and was made trainer by Willie McCartney in 1936. Now he was our manager and he was to be supported by two other fine former Hibs players in Jimmy McColl and Sammy Kean.

We were all still shocked by the loss of our inspirational manager but our new boss got our minds back on football and made sure that we were fully focused for the run-in to the end of the season. With eight games to go, we were still trailing Rangers by one point. We had also played two more games than them. Our second and third teams, however, were miles ahead in their leagues. It was the top team which mattered, though, and we still believed that we could pip Rangers for the title. They had tough games coming up and we were sure that we could win the matches which we had left.

All this success was attracting the attention of top English teams and there was a lot of talk of bids coming in for some of our players. Harry Swan responded to this by saying that Hibs would sell those that they could afford to part with, but would be holding on to the players they intended to keep. He added, 'That includes Lawrie Reilly. He is progressing at fire-brigade pace. Remember his name!'

Our confidence that we could win the matches we had left was justified as we went on a run that saw us win six games in a row. This was championship form but we still needed Rangers to drop points. They were used to having things their own way and now the unaccustomed pressure began to tell on them. They lost and drew games which they should have won and we pulled in front of them with only two games to go.

When we beat Motherwell 5–0 at Easter Road in the second-last game of the season, we only needed one more point to secure the title. I was delighted to be back in the team due to an injury to Willie Ormond. I didn't manage a goal but I played well. I got a real boost when my name was announced in our line-up before the match and a great cheer went round the ground. It's nice to know that you are popular.

Gordon Smith scored an outstanding goal with a brilliant half-volley from a cross from Alec Linwood, but Eddie Turnbull went one better. Eddie scored a goal that was contender for goal of the season. The *Evening News* described it like this: 'Turnbull bored in and hit a shot whose progress no one could follow until it smacked against the back of the net.' Twenty-five thousand Hibs fans were inside Easter Road for this crucial victory and I am sure that they were almost all delighted with what they saw. One supporter clearly wasn't happy, though, as the next day's newspapers reported that, 'One small man was escorted from the scene of his discontent by two large policemen.'

But he was in a minority of one, as everyone else inside the ground knew that they had witnessed history in the making. We now needed just one point from our last game at Dundee to win the league. It would be the first time in almost half a century that Hibs had lifted the title. Surely we couldn't throw it away now?

As luck would have it, the same Motherwell team which we had just thrashed went on to beat Rangers and, as they could no longer match our points total, Hibs had won the league. It was a magnificent achievement and a wonderful sensation to know that we were the best in the country. Great credit went to both our recently deceased manager and his successor, who had stepped so ably into the breach when Mr McCartney had passed away. We were delighted that Motherwell had done us such a big favour, but there was a slight sense of anti-climax that we hadn't won the title on the park ourselves.

For that reason, we really wanted to finish the season in style by winning our last game at Dens Park, but we caught Dundee at their best and they beat us 3–1. I did manage to get on the scoresheet but that didn't stop me being disappointed that we hadn't managed to end such a great season on a high. I suppose you could say that it was typical of Hibs to win seven games in a row and then manage to lose the last game of a triumphant season. Dundee were highly motivated to beat the team which was about to be crowned champions and we possibly subconsciously relaxed but they were too good for us on the day. It would have been much better if we had finished our season with a victory but it wasn't to be.

Our defeat opened the door the merest theoretical crack for Rangers. If they managed to beat Hearts at Tynecastle in the last game of the season by twenty goals to nil, they would win the league championship on goal average. That was never likely to happen of course. Harry Swan went on the record to say that if Hearts did indeed lose the game by that margin, Hibs would never again set foot inside Tynecastle.

The impossible didn't happen and the Hibees were crowned champions of Scotland. It was a great, great feeling. We were all asked by the press to say how we felt. Gordon Smith was as eloquent as ever when he said, 'Considering that we have had to play without two or three of our key players all season, it makes our achievement all the more meritorious.' I proved myself a pretty good prophet when I declared, 'I think we can do it again, with a bit of luck.'

A number of functions were organised to mark our achievement. At one of them, local dignitary Sir William Darling rechristened our club when he referred to us as 'The Edinburgh

Nibs'. Maybe it was just our pen name! Lord Provost Andrew Murray did better at a civic reception when he said, 'We congratulate your directors, manager and players and rejoice with your supporters.'

As well as our top team winning the First Division, our reserves won their league and both their cups and the third team also captured their flag. It was a season of glory but it didn't end without regret. We all felt sad that Willie McCartney hadn't survived to enjoy the success which he had done so much to create. On a personal note, I had just failed to play enough games to qualify for a league winner's medal, so to my deep disappointment I had to do without. I had taken part in eight or nine matches, had scored a few goals and had definitely played my part but I had nothing to show for it. I made a promise to myself that the next time Hibs won a trophy, Lawrie Reilly would be well and truly established as a first-team regular. I then determined to make that happen the very next season, when we would do our best to defend the League Championship which we had fought so hard and played so well to win.

4

A WINNER AT WEMBLEY

We entered season 1948-49 as proud champions of Scotland but before we got down to the serious business of defending our crown, we were off on another of our summer tours. Hibs were definitely trailblazers in this area. Most British clubs gave their players the summer off but Harry Swan had other ideas. He believed that taking us abroad would widen our horizons. We would play against new players and come up against different styles of play. As people and as footballers, we could only benefit from this.

He was right too. Our summer tours were great experiences. I still look back on them now with fond memories. So, in 1948, we were off to Belgium. We took the train down to London where we took in a show. We went to the Hippodrome Theatre to see the Vic Oliver Show. Vic was a famous bandleader at that time and the big band sound was highly popular in the 1940s. Again for young lads like us from backgrounds which were not full of the expensive things in life, going to a top show in a well-known London theatre was something special.

We then took the ferry to Ostend to play our five matches in Belgium and again experienced some refereeing which was interesting to say the least. It seemed like most of the Continental officials operated a simple rule – 'Give the home team everything no matter how doubtful, and give the Hibs nothing.' We played five matches, won one, drew one and lost the rest.

While we were there, our hosts presented Gordon Smith with a cake to mark his birthday. Very thoughtfully, they had placed a figure of a footballer on top of the cake. Unfortunately he was wearing a maroon jersey. You can imagine the sort of comments which some of the lads made about this. One of them suggested that I should use my decorating experience to paint it green. I said that I would give them an estimate and let them see if they could afford it.

In our last game, the light was closing in as we approached full time, so the referee called for a white ball. This was a first for us as back home we only ever used brown or orange balls. These were made of a leather casing with a bladder inside. The bladder was blown up through a valve which was then tucked into the case. To complete the operation, the case was laced up. To put it mildly, these balls were heavy and in wet weather, of course, they became heavier still. The Belgian ball was light, easy to see and a pleasure to play with. We were the first Scottish team to use the white ball, so once again the Hibs were ahead of their time.

When we returned home, we set about the task of holding on to our status as league champions. We were dealt an early blow when Willie Ormond broke his leg. Willie would be a real miss and it looked like my hopes of becoming Hibs' first-choice centre forward would have to go on hold for a while longer as I would have to fill in for him on the left wing.

The Scottish League flag was unfurled at Easter Road before our first home game which was against none other than our greatest challengers at that time – Rangers. We hammered them 0–0! We played them off the park but just couldn't put the ball in the net.

At that time, the *Sunday Mail*'s main writer was Rex Kingsley. He said that we had superior speed and skill and displayed slick and exciting ball play. He also thought that we had 'weaved pretty patterns'. We didn't manage to score, though, which was a rare occurrence for our forward line at that time. As the teams came off at full time, the Rangers fans jeered Gordon Smith. That just showed how much they feared, respected and secretly admired Gordon. Gordon simply clasped his hands above his head like a boxer acknowledging the crowd after winning a fight. That soon put their gas at a peep. There was a crowd of 47,000 inside Easter Road for this match, so support for Hibs had never been greater.

We were soon into our goal-scoring stride and beat Hearts 3–1 at Easter Road in the first derby of the season. I didn't score but I was generally considered to have been the man of the match. As the *Evening News* put it, 'Reilly was the boy of the afternoon and oh what a boy!' I was to discover throughout my career that we found Hearts more difficult to beat than any other opponents, even Rangers, so it was great to get a win against them. It was even better to have played so well. As a real Hibs supporter, beating our city rivals probably meant more to me than it did to a lot of the other players. I certainly went home a happy young man that night.

When we played Albion Rovers next, I scored a hat-trick but we carelessly allowed them to come back from 4–1 down to draw 4–4. Shades of Hibs and Motherwell and that infamous 6–6 draw in 2010.

I must have been playing well because the papers now started to mention me for international recognition. In those days, as well as full internationals, the four home countries and the Republic of Ireland also played league internationals. For these games, the selectors who picked the international team – because there was no team manager at that time – could only choose players who were with Scottish clubs. All forms of international football were hugely popular then. The games drew massive crowds and the results really mattered. A famous win put a spring in the country's step and a bad defeat caused nationwide depression.

The press were recommending that the selectors should take a look at both Archie Buchanan and me. We were both approaching our twentieth birthdays and playing well. I would have been hugely flattered to be capped by Scotland but I couldn't really see it happening so I just put it out of my mind.

I always believed in my ability as a player but I was never big-headed. On this occasion though, my modesty was to be misplaced. Hibs had arranged to play Manchester United in a memorial match for Willie McCartney. I left the house to catch a bus to the game as usual. As I was standing at the bus stop, a supporter approached me and told me that I had been chosen to play on the left wing for the Scottish League against the League of Ireland. I couldn't believe it and wanted to race back to the house to let my mum and dad know the good news. I was scared, though, that if I did that I would be late for the match, so I headed for Easter Road. As I made my way through the streets to the ground, every supporter seemed to want to congratulate me. It was an unforgettable experience.

Manchester United beat us 1–0. We used a white ball for the first time in a match in Scotland and 30,225 turned out to watch a great game which we were unlucky to lose. The proceeds went to Mr McCartney's widow and it was estimated that through gate receipts, programme sales and donations from other clubs, she would receive a cheque for around £5,500. If you think that you could still buy a decent small flat in Edinburgh for under £1,000 in 1970, that must have been an awful lot of money back in the late 1940s.

At this time I was again attracting attention from English clubs and this brought a few reporters to our door to get the Reilly family reaction. As always my dad gave it to them straight. His message was simple and direct: 'If Lawrie plays for any club other than Hibs, I'll disown him!'

When I made my international debut I had one of my Hibs teammates for company, but it wasn't my pal Archie Buchanan. I was joined by Bobby Combe. We won the match 5–1 and Bobby and I did Hibs proud by each scoring two goals. The star of the night, though, was Jimmy Mason, the Third Lanark inside forward. Jimmy was a typical Scottish inside forward of his time. He was small, could dribble, score goals and was a superb passer of the ball.

I scored within fourteen minutes and, to be honest, wee Jimmy laid it on a plate for me. I got another in the second half and could be well pleased with my first game in the dark blue of Scotland. The game was at Ibrox and 57,000 fans cheered us on. One of the next day's reports, in the old-fashioned language of the day, referred to my Emerald Isle roots when it said, 'The Easter Road youngster with the Irish nomenclature made an excellent impression.' I don't think you would get phraseology like that in the tabloids these days. I knew that I had played well though. I also knew that Jimmy Mason's prompting had contributed greatly to my performance and I made up my mind that I would repay the compliment to Jimmy next time we played together.

I had obviously impressed the watching Matt Busby because he told journalists after the game that 'this boy is going places.' The only place I was going after the game was right back to Easter Road, because we had a big game coming up against Celtic.

I was probably only picked for the League of Ireland match because Willie Ormond was out injured so I really appreciated it when Willie sent me a good luck telegram before the game. I carried my good form back to club football and got another goal when we beat Celtic 4–2. The *Pink News* said that interest in the game was so high that the ground was full half an hour before kick-off, with great queues still waiting outside. We gave the fans a treat. Charlie Tully was Celtic's top man and he was at his best that day but was still outshone by the one and only Gordon Smith. Gordon scored two goals and led the Celtic defence a merry dance. He was magnificent.

My goal was the climax of a four-man move. Gordon started it, Johnny Cuthbertson carried it on and Bobby Combe supplied the killer pass. The match report states that I 'enticed Miller the Celtic goalkeeper out and placed the ball in the corner of his net with the skill and coolness of a veteran'. That will do for me since I was still only nineteen at the time.

Willie Ormond was back from injury now and I found myself

on the right wing. Gordon Smith had switched to centre forward which was where I really wanted to be. However, I got two goals from outside right when we beat Morton. We played with ten men because Davie Shaw, one of football's gentlemen, got sent off and I got heaps of press praise again. How about this – 'Reilly wrote his name all over this game. What power, what pace, what a shot!' That performance convinced the national selectors to award me my first full cap against Wales at Cardiff. All season, I had played on one wing or another but for this match, I was chosen at centre forward. I was delighted, excited and nervous in equal measure.

Once again the press were back at our family's door looking for quotes from my dad. Again he gave them one. He told them of how he had taken me as a fourteen-year-old to Easter Road on one training night and demanded to see Hugh Shaw who was the trainer at time.

When Mr Shaw had appeared to see what this stranger wanted, my dad had said, 'This is my son Lawrie. He is showing a lot of promise at football and if he makes it as a footballer, I want to make sure that he plays for nobody else but the Hibs.'

Whether this visit and conversation had anything to do with the club later signing me I'll never know, but my dad had once again nailed the Reilly family colours firmly to the Hibernian mast.

It was a time of double celebration for me because just before I travelled to Cardiff for my full international debut, my girlfriend Kitty Cruickshank and I announced our engagement. We were both nineteen, which might sound a bit young to people today, but remember in those days a lot of people left school at fourteen. By the end of your teens, you were considered all the man you were going to be.

Kitty and I had both attended Boroughmuir Secondary School. We were in the same year, in fact, and were almost the same age. Kitty had come into the world just five days before me so I was marrying an older woman! We hadn't really known each other at school and we had met properly at the YMCA at Watson Crescent, just along from my house in Bryson Road, after we had both left school. We were both sixteen at the time. Coming from the west side of the city, Kitty, unsurprisingly, was from a Hearts-supporting family. Her dad had even taken her to Tynecastle, but I never held that against her. When we married later, Kitty was quite happy to go to Easter Road with my mum and dad and cheer on both her husband and the Hibs.

The Scotland team stayed in Reading before travelling over to Ninian Park for the match. The ground was full to bursting, with a crowd of 60,000 and the singing of the Welsh supporters was something I'll never forget. Before and during the game they created a wall of sound as they sung their national songs with tremendous passion.

I was joined in the Scotland team by two of my Easter Road colleagues in Hugh Howie and Davie Shaw. At full time, we were all able to reflect on a 3–1 victory and I had the added satisfaction of reflecting on my first full international goal. I headed in a cross from Howie on fifteen minutes to open the scoring so I had taken just one minute longer to open my account than I had against the League of Ireland. It felt great, of course, to score goals for my country. In all honesty, though, I was having difficulty taking everything in. Here I was, not yet twenty years old, and banging in the goals for Scotland. I was a lucky lad and I knew it. I was also aware that I wouldn't be progressing the way I was if I wasn't talented. I was never a big-head but I didn't believe in false modesty either.

When I returned to league duty, our first port of call was a visit to Fortress Ibrox. It was no fortress that day because we scored four goals in the first half and ended up 4–2 winners. Gordon Smith was at his peerless best with two goals, the second of which was a thirty-five-yard shot described as 'One of the bonniest ever seen at Ibrox'. I don't suppose that the Rangers fans would have thought that it was too bonny.

My reward for scoring in a winning team in Cardiff was to be dropped when the selectors announced the team to meet Ireland in Scotland's next game. My place went to Billy Houliston of Queen of the South and the newspapers were not impressed. Their opinions ranged from 'The selectors have done the dirty on Reilly' to 'They've done Reilly wrong'. I covered my disappointment and sent Billy a telegram of congratulations. He wasn't a great footballer but he never stopped running and gave defenders a torrid time. Scotland beat Ireland 3–1 in front of 93,000 at Hampden and Houliston got two of the goals, so both he and the selectors would have been feeling good that evening.

As 1948 came to an end, Hibs' form was on the wane. We were losing and drawing games we should have won. This pattern carried forward into 1949 as we contrived to lose 3–2 to Hearts at Tynecastle in the Ne'erday derby.

What a sickener that game was. We played well but missed chances and found ourselves 2–0 down. Alec Linwood had been transferred to Clyde shortly before the game and I allowed myself to think that my time to become Hibs' regular centre forward had finally come. It hadn't though. Hibs had unearthed yet another promising youngster. This one had an unusual name – Angus Plumb. Angus was at centre forward at Tynecastle and I was back on the left wing. We both scored to draw us level and we let slip opportunities to win the game. In the final minute, we had cause to rue these misses as Willie Bauld back-heeled the ball to Alfie Conn, who drove it home. He celebrated by swinging from the crossbar and was then 'almost slapped unconscious by his deliriously happy teammates'. If I had got near him, he would have got a different kind of slap.

If Conn's last-minute winner wasn't a big enough shock, I had another one just around the corner. Newcastle United and Derby County came in with bids for me. The Geordies offered £17,500 but Harry Swan knocked them back with the words 'even £20,000 wouldn't interest us'. It wouldn't have interested me either, because I had no intention of going anywhere.

When Hibs played St Mirren, Bobby Johnstone made his

debut. It was a great day for Bobby but not such a good day for the club because we lost the match and the defeat effectively ended our hopes of retaining our league title. That was depressing, but I didn't stay down for long because I was recalled to the Scotland team for the match against England at Wembley.

The game against the 'Auld Enemy' was the highlight of every season. Scots fans saved for two years to make the trip to Wembley and the ground was always a sea of tartan. I was chosen at outside left and Billy Houliston retained his place at centre forward, but we were huge underdogs as the England team contained players of the calibre of Frank Swift, Billy Wright, Stan Matthews, Jackie Milburn, Stan Mortensen and Tom Finney.

Our pre-match base was the Oatlands Park Hotel in Weybridge and we were quietly confident. When we walked out onto the immaculate Wembley turf for the game, there were 95,500 people in a sunlit stadium. We lined up to meet the Duke of Edinburgh and his young wife Princess Elizabeth. As we stood waiting our turn to shake hands with the royals, I heard a familiar sound. It was my dad giving his whistle. I was able to pinpoint exactly where he was and wave to my mum and him. To be honest, I can't remember what the duke and princess said to me or what I said to them. They probably said, 'Good luck', and I more than likely replied, 'Thanks very much.'

We didn't need any luck as we played brilliantly, although my match didn't get off to the best of starts. I lined up directly opposite the great Matthews or 'The Wizard of the Dribble' as he was known. I had heard all about him of course and knew just what a special player he was. Being the determined character that I was, I set myself to show him that I meant business right from the start. When England kicked off, the ball went straight out to Matthews. I didn't hesitate and launched myself into a ferocious tackle on the great man. He saw me coming, swerved past me and left me lying on the ground. I felt foolish and resolved to concentrate on my attacking duties for the rest of the game.

Our goalkeeper, Jimmy Cowan of Morton, played the game of his life and broke the hearts of the English forwards. I was able to lay on a goal for wee Jimmy Mason and I felt good about that. Jimmy had created my first international goal against the League of Ireland and now I was able to pay him back. Billy Steel got the second and I scored the third with a diving header from a cross from Willie Waddell. Waddell played for Rangers, of course, and was fast and direct. He wasn't in the same class as Gordon Smith, though, and it was ridiculous the number of times that Gordon was overlooked so that the selectors could make room for Waddell. When people used to ask me to sum up the difference between Willie and Gordon, I would say that when Gordon crossed the ball for you to head, he was so exact that he would make sure that the lace of the ball was facing away from you when you met it with your forehead. Neither Willie nor any other right winger in Scotland could match that level of precision.

Willie had a great game at Wembley this day, however, and it was some feeling for me as I flung myself horizontally at his cross and bulleted it past Swift in the England goal. 'Big Swifty' was a top keeper who became a journalist when he retired and sadly lost his life in the Munich air crash of 1958.

Even though that goal came very early in my career, I consider it one of my best. It is still talked about today and looking back on it gives me almost as much pleasure now as scoring it did at the time. Jackie Milburn got a late consolation goal for England but nothing could stop us Scots recording a historic victory.

It is no exaggeration to say that we were treated like national heroes. The newspapers went into overdrive with headlines like 'Wembley Heroes should be decorated' and 'Once there was the Wembley Wizards. Now we have the Wembley Warriors'. They were kind to me too with 'The Toast is Lawrie Reilly' and 'Reilly was a Wembley Star.'

I had gone into the big game against England with the good wishes of everyone at Hibs. Manager Hugh Shaw sent me a telegram which I have to this day. Addressed to 'Reilly, the

Scottish Team, Wembley Stadium, London' it read 'Remember Bannockburn. Hit them hard and apologise on Sunday. The best of luck from all at Easter Road. – Shaw Hibernian FC'

The Scotland team selectors invariably made changes from game to game but not after this special triumph. When the side to meet France at Hampden was named a few weeks later, exactly the same eleven players were announced. We won again, 2–0 this time, and 125,000 supporters packed the old ground to hail the men who had won at Wembley.

Hibs' season came to a tame end with defeat by Third Lanark. We had put a good run together but it came to an end at Cathkin. Our goalkeeper that night was Tommy Younger, who was to have a great career at both club and international level. Tommy was described as 'Hibs' boy goalkeeper who kept the score down in the first half.' He was less successful in the second half and our league campaign petered out.

We did manage to win a couple of friendlies, though. We travelled to Dumfriesshire to play Nithsdale Wanderers. We won 8–1 and our forward line read Smith, Johnstone, Reilly, Turnbull and Ormond. It was a significant moment in Hibs' history although we didn't know it at the time. This was the first time that the players who became known as the Famous Five played together. We were all on the scoresheet except Bobby Johnstone and a large crowd turned up at Sanquhar to 'see Gordon Smith make some dazzling runs, Hibs play lovely exhibition football and Wembley hero Reilly prove a great attraction'. We then travelled to London and trounced Tottenham Hotspur 5–2, which was no mean feat.

So ended what had been a momentous season for me. I was still a few months short of my twenty-first birthday but I had a lot to look back on. I couldn't do this at my leisure, though, for I had been chosen for Scotland's close-season trip to the United States of America and I was about to set sail for New York in the ocean liner the *Queen Mary*.

5

TRANSATLANTIC TOURIST

To a twenty-year-old lad from the west side of Edinburgh, the prospect of travelling to America on the world's most luxurious ship was almost unimaginable. Life in Scotland then was fairly hard. Food and clothes were rationed as the after-effects of the war continued to grip the country. My tenement home was clean and comfortable but was nothing like the surroundings I would experience on the *Queen Mary*.

We travelled by train to Southampton and embarked there. We got a great send-off and soon got used to life at sea. A large number of SFA officials were with us and needless to say they were travelling first class. Not surprisingly the players were in tourist class. Newcastle United were also aboard the ship and both their players and directors were in the first-class section of the boat, so a club team was travelling in better conditions that the Scottish international team which had just beaten England and France.

That didn't worry us in the least as we were having a great time. I was rooming with Bobby Evans of Celtic. Bobby and I got on really well. At that time he was an attacking right half but he later became a centre half. He was playing in that position when he left Celtic towards the end of his career to join Chelsea.

We had the time of our lives on the *Queen Mary*. There were daily table tennis matches and training on the sports deck. The ship also had a really well-equipped gym. One day when we were kicking the ball around on deck, I sent it into the ventilator shaft. The force of the suction there burst the ball into a thousand pieces. I wasn't allowed to forget that one, I can tell you.

We used to listen to the ship's band at night and when they went off for their break one night, one of the lads suggested that we take over the bandstand so we did exactly that. Jimmy Brown, the Hearts goalkeeper, picked up the trumpet, Billy Houliston played the piano and Jock Govan, my Hibs teammate, sat down at the drums. Jock wasn't content with just playing the drums, he threw the sticks up in the air and caught them every time. Our impromptu concert went down a storm.

The biggest attraction when we were at sea was the food. At home, due to rationing, a small portion of mince and tatties or stew was the norm. On the 'Queen' there was plenty of everything. Steaks, chops, chicken and fish were all readily available. Given the chance we would probably have pigged out but the team doctor made sure that that did not happen. Dr McMillan did not want us to make ourselves ill by eating too much rich food too quickly so he controlled our diet and made sure that our transition from eating a little to eating a lot was gradual rather than sudden.

There was no such monitoring of what the Newcastle players ate though. They could have what they liked and big Frank Brennan, their Scottish centre half, was the champion in the eating stakes. Frank was a real character with a massive appetite. One day he set the record for the trip when he consumed seven eggs with his cooked breakfast. One of the chefs on board was a Scot and when our doctor wasn't around, he used to slip us extra portions so we didn't do too badly either.

Something else which was much more readily available was clothing. At home, you were limited to what you could buy because you could only use the clothes coupons issued to you. To give you an idea of how short of things to wear some of us were, Johnny McKenzie, the tricky Partick Thistle right winger, travelled with only the demob suit which he had been given when he left the army after the war. Johnny put his army training to good effect by laying his suit trousers under his mattress every night. The next day, they always had a perfect crease again.

The Rangers players considered themselves to be the leaders in the sartorial stakes. They had brand new blue blazers with navy and white piping. They looked like college boys and were never done preening themselves. The rest of us gave them constant stick. The two Celtic men in the party, Bobby Evans and Alec Dowdalls, the trainer, kept telling everyone that they were having new blazers shipped out and that they would be waiting for them when we reached New York. They were indeed there and were very smart. They were green with the Celtic crest on the top pocket. The first time they sat down to dinner in these new jackets, Bobby and Alec were acting like they were royalty. Bobby then asked someone to pass him the tomato sauce. It was thrown across to him but the lid wasn't properly closed. Imagine Bobby's face when he caught the bottle and the sauce squirted out all over the new blazer he was so proud of.

There was also a fantastic swimming pool on board the *Queen Mary*. When the weather was calm, you could have a great swim. Unfortunately when it was choppy, which it was a lot of the time, the ship's motion sent all the water to one end of the pool. The water overflowed at one end and hardly covered the bottom of the pool at the other.

Mind you, the pool was full the day wee Billy Steel decided to throw Willie Woodburn in. Billy was a tricky inside forward who had left Dundee for Derby County. What he lacked in height, he more than made up for in self-confidence. Billy was the ultimate cheeky chappie, but none of us really believed him when he said that he was going to chuck big Woodburn in the pool. Much to our amusement and Willie's fury, wee Steely did exactly as he had promised. He was a strong character and he sneaked up behind the Rangers centre half and tipped him full-force into the water. This gave some of the rest of us the idea to repeat the dose with big Geordie Young. George was our captain and he was a man mountain. This didn't stop him hitting the water, though. Mind you, the next day's paper reported that it had taken eight of us to overcome the struggling Young and deposit him fully clothed into the pool.

What a welcome we got when we docked at New York. I stood there wide-eyed and drank it all in. There in front of me was the famous New York skyline which I had seen so many times in films. The docks were full of tug boats and ferries which moved out of the way to let us through. On the quayside were thousands of expatriate Scots who cheered us to the echo. There were quite a number of pipers and the familiar skirl of their music made us feel at home. There was also a girl I had known at school called Margaret Yates. Margaret's family had emigrated to the States and her father worked in a chocolate factory. There she was on the quay to meet us and in her hands was a large box of her dad's delicious produce.

It was nice to see Margaret and her dad but I think the rest of the boys were more pleased to make acquaintance with her box of chocolates.

The trip wasn't all about pleasure, though. We had business to attend to, in the shape of a number of games. The first was to be against an American Select at the Triboro Stadium. The pitch was a far cry from Wembley. It was small and covered in dock leaves. Training was difficult because the temperatures were in the eighties. Two days before the game, the heavens opened and there was forty-eight hours of torrential rain, which meant that the game had to be rearranged for later in the trip.

This meant that we played St Louis first. We hammered them 6–0, but I didn't play. I had caught a stomach bug and felt really unwell. There was tension before the game when the home team's officials said that they wanted to field three substitutes. This was unheard of at the time and George Graham, the SFA secretary, refused to play the game. In fact, he threatened to call off the tour there and then. To say the secretary was a strong-minded character would be an understatement. He dug his heels in and the Americans had to give way. The game was played under floodlights, though, which was a first for all of us.

After the game, George Graham had expected a full banquet to be laid on for the Scotland team and officials. All St Louis provided was beer and sandwiches, which was fine by most of us. It wasn't acceptable to our autocratic secretary, though. He led us out in high dudgeon and marched us to a nearby restaurant where we sat down to an excellent formal meal.

Back in Edinburgh, when word got out that I hadn't played against St Louis, a rumour began to sweep the city that I had broken my leg. The rumour became so strong that Harry Swan, the Hibs chairman, had to issue a statement to the press confirming that I was unwell and that my leg was definitely in one piece.

Our next match was against Belfast Celtic and I missed that too as I was still feeling the effects of my bug. In the event, I was really glad that I did miss the match. Belfast Celtic were a decent club side (they went out of existence over fifty years ago) but no more than that. They approached the game like a cup tie and we treated it like a stroll in the park. We made and missed numerous chances. They had two, took them both and beat us 2–0. That did not go down well back home or in the American press. The organisers of our tour had financed it thinking that we would be a great draw for the public as we had just beaten England and France. We would be less of an attraction now, after losing to a club side.

The Belfast lads didn't hold back with their tackling. The press called it 'over robust' which was strong language by the reporting standards of the day. Our right winger was Willie Waddell of Rangers. Willie was a top player. He was fast, direct, a good crosser and could score goals. He was no Gordon Smith, though – and yet, time and again, he was picked ahead of Gordon by the SFA selection panel. It was scandalous. Anyway, in this match, Willie took exception to the tackling of the Belfast left half O'Flannaghan and the pair of them exchanged blows. This led to a lot of the other players joining in and a mêlée developed like the one that took place at Easter Road when Graeme

Souness marked his debut for Rangers by splitting open George McCluskey's leg.

It took the referee two minutes to restore order and the next day's press report described what had happened as 'a distasteful spectacle'. After the game, Waddell denied that he had punched O'Flannaghan, but that certainly wasn't the way the press had seen it.

Next up was the rearranged game against the American Select. I was delighted to be fit again and to be back in our team for a 4–1 win. I didn't score but the match report said, 'Reilly gave the attack more directness without reducing its level of skill.' That was nice – and so was a gift I got from the groundsman. I split one of my boots and he gave me a brand-new, top-quality pair to wear. At full time, he said that I could keep the new boots if I let him have my torn old boots and I had no problem agreeing to that one.

We played Kearney next. They were popular with the local Irish community and wore Celtic strips. They gave us a tough game but we came through 3–1. I got a really good goal and the press went to town the next day. How about this: 'Reilly gave the crowd a real thrill with a first-time crashing shot from an Orr pass for the Scots third goal. The crowd cheered him for fully five minutes.' That kind of thing could easily have given me a big head! My goal was laid on by Tommy Orr of Morton. Tommy was a really nice man and a very good player. His son Neil played for Morton and West Ham and then joined Hibs when Alex Miller was manager.

During the Kearney match the temperature was over eighty degrees in the shade. It was really unpleasant and uncomfortable. Most of our team stripped down to their socks and boots and took cold showers at half-time. Sammy Cox, the Rangers full back, and I sneaked oranges onto the pitch for the second half to combat dehydration.

We were having a tremendous time in the USA. We visited the world-famous Jack Dempsey's Restaurant. Dempsey, a legendary former world heavyweight boxing champion, was known as 'The Manassa Mauler', and his restaurant was where the rich and famous went to eat. We also got taken to the boxing stadium at Madison Square Garden where Jack Dempsey had fought some of his most famous fights. There was a real atmosphere and feeling of boxing history there.

We also went to see the world-renowned Brooklyn Dodgers baseball team in action. There was a tradition in baseball then (for all I know it might still be the case now) that if the ball was hit into the crowd and a spectator caught it, he or she was allowed to keep it. Imagine our excitement when the ball was cracked in our direction. As luck would have it, the ball was heading straight for our goalkeeper Jimmy Brown. Jimmy stood up and positioned himself perfectly and we all got ready to cheer. You can guess what happened next. Jimmy let the ball slip through his fingers to the ground. He never did that when he played for Hearts against Hibs, I can tell you.

Incredibly, the SFA had only chosen one goalkeeper for this transatlantic trip. If Jimmy had got injured, I would have been in goal. I used to take a turn in goals during training and, even though I say so myself, I wasn't bad. The thought of going between the sticks in a real match, and an international at that, petrified me though. Fortunately it never happened. If Jimmy had gone down hurt, I would have had to give him the kiss of life.

The SFA had given us a small money allowance for our trip but it wasn't enough. We went to George Graham and asked for more money. He said that he would give us an extra £50 each if we agreed to play an extra match when we moved over to Canada. We were more than happy to agree. In those days there were four American dollars to the pound so this was quite a lot of money.

I bought myself some great clothes. They were the type of thing which I would never have got back home, even if there hadn't been rationing. I also bought an expensive evening dress for my fiancée Kitty. When I bought the dress, an expatriate Scot from Edinburgh was standing nearby and we got talking. His name was David Linton, he was a Hibs fan and had moved to the States two years earlier. He still had a house in Edinburgh and when he heard that I was engaged, he offered to sell it to me. It was an intriguing offer from a complete stranger thousands of miles from home and it would have been a great story if it had come off. Sadly I felt the price was a bit on the high side so I declined. Nice of him to offer though!

We also visited the New York racetrack. That was exciting but certainly not profitable. Willie Thornton, the Rangers centre forward who fancied himself as a bit of a tipster, marked our cards but he didn't mark them very well. In fact, at the end of the day, even Willie himself had to admit that the only gee-gee left carrying Scottish money was G. G. himself, our SFA secretary, George Graham.

Then it was on to Canada. Just like in the USA, the Scottish players took the field one at a time. You waited until the man with the microphone called your name and then ran on to take the plaudits of the crowd. As I played on the left wing in those days, I was always announced last. The MC would call, 'And now let's hear it for the kid of the team. Please welcome from Hibernian, Edinburgh . . . Lawrie Reilly!'

I loved that and I also loved it when we won both our games in Canada. We beat the Toronto Maple Leaf Select 2–0 and I laid on our first goal with a 'beautiful free kick'. We took care of Eastern Canada 5–2 in the next game and I was back among the goals with a shot from 'The high-powered boot of young Reilly'. The Scots in the crowd were so pleased with our performance that they ran on to the field to mob us after the game and even followed us into the dressing room. They were high-spirited but meant no harm and nobody got hurt.

We continued our winning form into our last three games back in America. Philadelphia All Stars were weak and we took eight goals off them. I scored again but the star of the show was Willie

Waddell who played at centre forward and scored no less than six goals. I think Willie enjoyed that match more than he had the game against Belfast Celtic.

We then travelled to Fall River to play the New England All Stars. They had kicked Belfast Celtic off the park in a previous match and the Irish players had warned us to expect a 'rough house'. That is what we got, but it wasn't quite as bad as we had expected. We won 3–1 and then finished on a high by taking four goals off another American Select. Seventeen thousand turned out for this match, which was one of our better crowds. The crowds for most of the other matches had been poor, which had disappointed the tour's organisers.

Our defeat to Belfast Celtic hadn't helped draw the crowds but the truth was that most Americans weren't really interested in our form of football – or 'soccer' as they called it. It had been a wonderful trip and an amazing experience but we had been away for over a month and couldn't wait to see our loved ones again.

When we returned, I was wearing a smart trench coat and a natty trilby hat which I had bought in the States. When the press approached us, I was looking pretty smooth, even if I say so myself. Mind you, as the camera clicked, it passed through my mind that I was dressed in the style favoured by my manager at Hibs, Hugh Shaw. I covered myself by telling the reporters, 'If Hugh Shaw sees a picture of me in this, I'll be on the transfer list.' The quote was duly printed next day, as was my comment 'It's good to be home again.'

I would be meeting up with Hugh Shaw again soon enough as I set out to establish myself as the first-choice centre forward and to help the club regain the league championship title.

6

THE MAN IN THE MIDDLE AT LAST

So far, I had played most of my first-team football for Hibs on the wing, mainly at outside left. Similarly with Scotland, I was also seen as a left winger. I had made my debut for Hibs at inside right and had played almost all my football at Edinburgh Thistle in the centre of the attack. From that position, I had scored over 100 goals in a season and it seemed to me that someone who had a natural gift for scoring goals, which I clearly did, should be playing centre forward and leading the line. To date, I had been kept out of this position by players like Johnny Cuthbertson and Alec Linwood but as season 1949-50 dawned, I had hopes that I could make myself the number one man in the middle for Hibs and possibly even for Scotland.

The curtain-raiser to the new season was a bit of a novelty event. Hibs took on Hearts in a soccer tennis match in Princes Street Gardens. This really caught the imagination of the public and a great crowd turned out. We managed to win the game 3–2. which maybe shouldn't have been too much of a surprise as we played soccer tennis in training all the time.

Then it was into the League Cup qualifying games. At that time, teams competed in sections of four. They played each other home and away and the team which topped the section qualified for the quarter-finals. It seemed like Hugh Shaw agreed with me about what my best position was because he had started to pick me at centre forward. We were doing well as a team in our early games but I wasn't having too much personal success. In fact one reporter made the following evaluation of my prowess as the leader of the attack: 'Are Hibs really getting the best from this brilliant young player in this position? He is too good to be kept out but it is apparent that he is not a centre forward.'

However, in the next game we beat Third Lanark 4–2 and I scored a hat-trick. Matt Busby was at the game and was seen having a conversation with Hugh Shaw and Harry Swan after the game. The papers speculated on the conversation which might have taken place. They imagined Mr Busby saying: 'Would you sell Reilly to us?' and Mr Swan replying: 'Good night.'

I was enjoying being the man in the middle for Hibs and when we took six off Raith Rovers, I got one of my best ever goals. The match report described it like this: 'Reilly showed the great footballer he is by dribbling right in, even past the goalkeeper and walking the ball into the net.' Jack Harkness of the *Sunday Post*, who was a former Scotland goalkeeper and one of the main writers at that time, proclaimed, 'There's Nothing to Stop Hibs.'

That was more like it but we got a fright when we played Partick Thistle in the League Cup quarter-final. The tie was played over two legs and our early season form deserted us when we lost 4–2 at Firhill. I got one goal in that game and two more in the return leg at Easter Road when we won 4–0 to make our way into the semi-finals. Again the press were full of praise for me: 'Reilly scored and made goals which will long be remembered. Thousands left Easter Road swearing that he is the best centre forward in Britain.' Well, that was a bit of a change from what had been written just a few short weeks before!

That's why it is important not to take too much notice of journalists' predictions. When they get them right, they trumpet their foresight for months afterwards. If they get things totally wrong, they just ignore their original comments and completely change their mind without the slightest hint of embarrassment.

Our next match was against Hearts at Tynecastle. This was a time, bear in mind, when the Old Firm didn't dominate Scottish football the way they do now. Rangers were always powerful and definitely the team to beat, while Celtic were inconsistent, capable of brilliance but prone to bad days as well. Hibs, Hearts, Aberdeen, Dundee and Motherwell, among others, were able to beat the Glasgow giants and challenge them for the title. There was one significant difference between now and then. Until George Eastham of Arsenal went to court in the early 1960s, with the support of the English Professional Footballers' Association, to have the law on players' salaries changed, no club in England was allowed to exceed the maximum wage which was in force. This meant that you got the same money (around £20 per week) no matter who you played for. Rangers and Celtic couldn't cherry-pick the best players as they do now either, because they didn't pay any more than teams like Hibs, Hearts or Aberdeen did at that time. Players may leave the team they support for a huge hike in their pay packet but they won't make that move if there is nothing in it for them financially.

Hearts were a top side at this time, with their three inside forwards Alfie Conn, Willie Bauld and Jimmy Wardhaugh presenting a real danger to every team they came up against. For some reason, they always caused Hibs problems. They were good but we were definitely better. Yet we usually ended up losing to them. This game was no exception. In fact it was an absolute disaster. They beat us 5–2 and it could have been worse. After fifty-four minutes they were 5–0 up and they had missed a penalty. Bobby Combe and I eventually pulled goals back but that was little consolation.

Everyone at Easter Road was really depressed after that game, but I had no time to wallow in my despair as I was selected to play for Scotland against Ireland in Belfast. The World Cup finals were to take place in Brazil in the summer of 1950 and FIFA had invited the two top British teams to compete. The four home nations took part in a British Championship in those days and the matches were huge with the public. All we needed to do, then, was to finish at least second in that competition and we were on 'The Road to Rio' as the press had taken to referring to the fight for World Cup qualification.

Then the SFA took a hand. With no little arrogance and a complete lack of logic, they declared that Scotland would only go to Brazil if they became British Champions. Second would not be good enough for us. It was first or bust.

There was no lack of motivation, then, when we travelled to Belfast and we more than rose to the challenge. We overwhelmed the Irish 8–2 and I got my usual goal. I was back on the left wing as the Scotland selectors clearly didn't consider me good enough yet to play through the middle for my country. To be fair, Scotland had an embarrassment of riches in the centre forward position. Willie Bauld, as I have already mentioned, was brilliant. He could play other players into the game, was exceptional in the air and scored goals for fun.

Bustling Billy Houliston of Queen of the South was a menace to defences and although not a classy footballer was again a regular goal-scorer. Neither Willie nor Billy had been picked for this match, though. The man who was handed the centre forward berth was Henry Morris of East Fife. Henry did not let his country down as he scored a hat-trick. Yet the press were lukewarm about his performance: 'While congratulating Morris on his hat-trick – always a notable achievement in an international debut – his play did little to explain why he was preferred to Bauld. The centre forward position remains open.'

I was doing my best to stake a claim for it. My goal in this game came from a move through the middle and my contribution drew more praise than that of the unfortunate Morris who, amazingly, was never chosen for Scotland again despite his high-scoring introduction to international football.

One headline stated, 'Reilly has the Big Game Flair' and another said, 'Scotland has Six Men of World Cup Class'. I am glad to say they included me as one of those six but I still wasn't the Scotland centre forward.

I was the Hibs number nine, though, and continuing to score

goals. We met Dunfermline in the League Cup semi-final at Tynecastle and lost again at a ground which was fast becoming our least favourite venue. I gave us the lead but the Fifers, who were one division below us, came back with two goals to knock us out of the cup. The match report asked: 'What has gone wrong with the once mighty Hibs?' It was a question we were asking ourselves and we provided a bit of an answer when we returned to league duty to play Celtic at Parkhead.

Despite Gordon Smith and Willie Ormond finishing the game struggling with injuries (there were no substitutes in those days), we outplayed Celtic and were 2–1 up in the last minute of the game. Gordon and I had given us a two-goal lead and although John McPhail had pulled a goal back we thought that we had the game won. Never write off the Celts though. As they had done so many times before and have done so often since, they snatched a last-minute equaliser. My Scotland pal Bobby Evans got the goal so he wasn't my friend that day.

Bobby and I were soon back in international action for the Scottish League against the League of Ireland in Dublin. The game was played at Dalymount Park, which was an intimidating arena when it was full of pumped-up Irish fans, as it was that day. We were expected to win comfortably but only managed a 1–0 victory. I got the goal and it was a good one. In fact the press thought it was better than that as they said, 'Reilly's great goal was brilliantly taken.' It was taken from the outside left position yet again as I still wasn't considered the best centre forward in Scotland by the selectors.

We got our title challenge back on track by beating Rangers 1–0 at Easter Road. I beat three men to lay on the goal for Eddie Turnbull. Our forward line was Smith, Johnstone, Reilly, Turnbull and Ormond and we were starting to get some recognition as a combination. One report said, 'What a contrast between the Hibs forwards and the attacking players representing Rangers.' Outstanding for us was wee Bobby Johnstone, who was now firmly established in the team. These were early days for us as a set of five forwards, but I can honestly say that we were starting to sense that something special was happening between us. I am not sure if we realised just how good a front line we would develop into, but we definitely knew that something out of the ordinary was beginning to come together.

Soon Scotland were back on what we hoped would prove to be 'The Road to Rio'. We met Wales at Hampden in front of 74,000 fans and beat them 2–0. I was again on the left wing and Billy Liddell of Liverpool was on the right.

Billy was only playing there because Willie Waddell was injured. He played on the left for his club yet he had been switched to the other wing to play there in preference to Gordon Smith. Every Hibs fan was furious at Gordon's omission. It was ridiculous and unfair as he was clearly the best right winger in Scotland if not in Britain, but for the selectors it seemed it was 'Anyone but Gordon'. Anyway, we were still on 'The Road to Rio'. Both Scotland and England had won their first two games in the home championship so when we met each other at Hampden in April it would be a World Cup qualification decider. Because we had scored eight goals against Ireland we had a far better goal average so a draw would be good enough to take us to Brazil.

Against Wales, my old Hibs teammate Alec Linwood, who was now with Clyde, had played centre forward and scored. I didn't get my name on the scoresheet although I did make a 'valiant attempt to repeat the memorable Wembley goal with a bullet-paced header'.

At Easter Road, Hibs were fully back to form. We won four successive games and drew praise from the media. Comments like 'Nothing could counteract the speed and courage of the Hibs forwards' summed up how we were playing. Gordon Smith was in prime form and in one game produced a miracle move to lay on a goal for Bobby Johnstone with an overhead kick cross. Gordon scored four against Falkirk, one of which was an 'atomic sizzler' but he still wasn't in the Scotland team. When we beat

East Fife 4–1, I scored one and managed an unusual hat-trick by having three goals disallowed for offside.

It was almost time for the Scottish Cup draw and Hibs were the favourites. One of the preview pieces offered the opinion that we should lift the cup because 'Easter Road houses the best all-round team in Scotland, if not in Britain.'

We kept winning, I kept scoring and the forwards kept getting the plaudits. We needed a goal from someone else to beat Clyde at Shawfield though. We struggled to make the breakthrough and the man who eventually broke the deadlock was my old mate Archie Buchanan. Archie had turned into an outstanding right half and he gained us two vital points with a twenty-yard swerving shot.

Our run of victories had put us right back in contention to win the league but now we had a really testing fixture coming up in the Ne'erday derby match against Hearts at Easter Road. A record crowd of 65,000 filled our ground. I don't know how they got them all in but they did and what an atmosphere they created. Amazingly Hibs and Hearts fans stood side by side, without any trouble between them. There was no segregation in those days. I am not sure if such an arrangement would work now.

The crowds were amazing back then. The war was over but times were still far from easy, so working people wanted to take their enjoyment where they could. On a normal Saturday, if we were at home, our supporters would be at work in the morning. As soon as they finished their shift at lunch time, men in their overalls or working clothes would head for the pubs around Easter Road. They would have a quick drink and then go down to the ground. There would often be huge queues at the turnstiles but everyone seemed to get inside for the kick-off. We would run out to a packed crowd which always gave us a tremendous lift.

During the match, especially when we were playing well and winning, the roars would be deafening. I don't remember individual songs or chants like they have nowadays but I do know that the atmosphere was amazing. Something else which always amazed me was how no one got injured as the fans spilled out after the match. A huge crowd used to jam together to cross the bridge in Bothwell Street. It was an accident waiting to happen but, thankfully, as far as I know, nobody ever got hurt.

We should have won the 1950 Ne'erday derby hands down. We were brilliant in the first half and went ahead through a Gordon Smith header. In truth, we could and should have been four goals up at half-time but it was only 1–0 when we went in for the break. We went off the boil in the second half and our bogey team from across the city came back to snatch a 2–1 win, which really hurt us.

We then took three points from two away games although Eddie Turnbull missed penalties in both games. Then came more heartbreak. Scottish Cup favourites we may have been, but it didn't stop us losing in the third round to Partick Thistle at home. The post-match headline said it all when it declared 'An Inspired Goalkeeper KOs Hibs'. Their goalkeeper Bobby Henderson was unbeatable and defied us no matter what we threw at him. Believe you me, we threw plenty at him but he had the game of his life and we just could not get the ball past him. We did get the ball in the net on one occasion, but what we considered a perfectly good goal was chalked off ten minutes from the end of the match. A strong penalty claim was also turned down. Thistle spent most of the second half kicking the ball out of the park to waste time. We did everything but score but we were out of the Scottish Cup again. That made it forty-eight years since Hibs had won the Scottish Cup. Little did we know as we smarted after our defeat that this particular sorry record wasn't going to change in a hurry.

We had no option now but to turn our attention back to the league. We still believed that we could win it and our next game was going to be massive. Celtic were the visitors to Easter Road and if ever there was a must-win game then this was it. Forty-one thousand of our supporters turned up to show that our cup defeat hadn't dented their faith in their team and we repaid them in style with one of our most famous wins.

Jimmy Kerr had been a fine goalkeeper for Hibs in the post-war years but by this time Jimmy had been replaced by a brilliant young last line of defence in Tommy Younger. It would have taken a top keeper to displace Jimmy and Tommy was exactly that. Tall, blond, brash and agile, he had forced his way into our side as a youngster and made himself a key team member. He also took it upon himself to teach me to drive but that's a story for later in the book.

When we ran out to face Celtic, we felt secure that we had big Tommy behind us. That all changed after half an hour. We were locked at 1–1 and both goals had been penalties. Eddie Turnbull had put us ahead and Bobby Collins had equalised. Eddie had missed penalties in two successive games and most folk in that position would have been looking to take a step back and pass the spot-kick-taking duties to someone else. Not Ned. He never took a backward step in his life. When the first penalty was awarded, Ned stepped forward and lashed the ball past Johnny Bonnar in the Celtic goal.

Just after Collins had scored for Celtic, Tommy Younger went up for a cross with a crowd of both our defenders and Celtic attackers. When the ball was cleared, Tommy was still lying on the ground. He had injured his back, wasn't able to carry on and went off on a stretcher. That left us facing the prospect of playing the rest of the game with ten men and a makeshift goalie.

Our full back Willie Clark went in goal. Willie was one of many unsung heroes in our squad at that time and his goal-keeping for the rest of the match may have been unorthodox but it was also effective. Mind you, the rest of us made sure that Willie didn't have too much to do. As the match report records, 'The Hibs defence was now composed of all the regulars plus Gordon Smith, Turnbull, Johnstone and, at times, even Reilly.' That must have been the only defending I ever did in my life. About the only thing I could tackle was a good breakfast.

It might have been all hands to the pump at the back, but it didn't stop us taking every chance to attack as well. Amazingly we scored three more times without reply. Eddie Turnbull got them all and incredibly two more of them were from the penalty spot. The man who had missed two successive penalties had now scored three in the one match. Eddie was not a man for placing the ball. He hit it with all his considerable power and when he got it on target it was always destined for the corner of the net. Eddie's fourth goal was a trademark twenty-yard screamer that nearly separated the goal net from the stanchions holding it in place.

Jack Harkness in the *Sunday Post* described this match as 'The saga of the season'. I am not sure if there's been a Hibs–Celtic game at Easter Road to match it since. The referee who had the courage to award four penalties that day was Jack Mowat from Rutherglen. Alongside Peter Craigmyle of Aberdeen, he was Scotland's top referee of the time. Mowat was still top man eight years later as he was the official in charge when Hibs met Clyde in the Scottish Cup Final in 1958. Mowat was a self-styled martinet who prided himself on being ultra-strict. I liked Craigmyle, who would chat with the players and praise them for a good piece of play. I often wonder if any referee has ever awarded three penalties against Celtic in one match since that day to remember sixty years ago.

We followed up our win over Celtic by demolishing Motherwell 6–1. I got a goal, but pride of place went to Turnbull and Smith. Gordon got a hat-trick and Eddie was at it again with his cannonball shooting. This time the rocket which gave him his goal hit the stanchion inside the net so hard that it rebounded to the halfway line. All of our front line came in for praise, though, as the papers talked about 'the bewildering running of the Hibs forwards'.

Next came a setback. We lost 1–0 at home to Third Lanark and the man who broke our hearts was one of our own. Lou Goram had been released by Hibs and moved to Thirds and this day he had the game of his life. His goalkeeping was so good that it was described as 'touching heights of splendour'. Like his more famous son Andy, Lou was a character. He used to come up to Easter Road from his home in England to watch Andy playing for Hibs. One day against Celtic a fan threw a canister of CS gas into the Hibs section of the terracing. Play was held up as spectators received treatment for smoke inhalation.

Sitting in the main stand at the other side of the ground, Lou feigned distress. He was taken to the boardroom and provided with a number of restorative whiskies. As soon as play restarted, Lou made a miraculous recovery and took his seat in the stand again to watch the rest of the match.

Goram's heroics dealt our title hopes a serious blow but we had no option other than to soldier on. We managed to beat Falkirk on a mudheap at Brockville and I grabbed a late (but not last-minute) winning goal.

The pitch that day was a total bog and a game would never have been played on it these days. Even though I say it myself, I had one of my best ever games that day. How about this for praise: 'Lawrence Reilly stood out as the most accomplished player afield. He was positively brilliant in abominable conditions.' My performance must have been something special for me to be called by my Sunday name. Mind you, they got the spelling wrong as my dad christened me 'Lawrance' with an 'a' rather than 'Lawrence' with an 'e'.

We then went on a goal spree, scoring sixteen goals as we won three matches in a row and I was on target in all of them. The stars of the show though were Gordon Smith and Willie Ormond. Gordon scored six goals in these games and Willie wasn't far behind with five. We were still clinging on to our hopes of winning the league but we slipped up again when we lost 3–2 at Parkhead. Eddie Turnbull was out injured and when we got yet another penalty against the Celts, Willie Ormond stepped up to take it. Despite his rich vein of scoring form,

Willie's kick was saved by Johnny Bonnar and Rangers could only throw away the championship now.

Attention now turned to the Scottish international team's biggest game of the season. We had to draw with England at Hampden – or even better beat them – to qualify for the World Cup finals in Brazil. To be strictly accurate, there was no actual necessity for either of these results, as even if we lost we were guaranteed to finish second in the British Championship, which would have entitled us to take 'The Road to Rio', as the press insisted on calling it. However, the SFA was adamant that Scotland would only go as champions and that stance was to prove as costly as it was illogical.

The selectors stirred up further controversy when they announced their team for the match. Both Gordon Smith and I were in the form of our lives but we were both omitted. This provoked an outburst of letters to the press from Hibs fans complaining about West Coast bias in Scotland team selections. One correspondent even went as far as describing the team which would play for the right to take the Road to Rio as 'an insult to Edinburgh'.

One capital player who was in the team was Hearts centre forward Willie Bauld. We lost the game 1–0 and Willie missed a great chance. His shot hit the underside of the bar but stayed out and with it went our World Cup qualification hopes.

You can be sure that the outcry which followed was even greater than the storm of complaints which had been provoked by the original announcement of the team. The papers were full of angry missives from East Coast supporters. Since no one from the west side of the country challenged their views, it can be safely assumed that they were in agreement with their counterparts in the capital. If radio phone-ins had existed then, the switchboards would have been jammed for a week.

I was recalled for the match against Switzerland which followed but Willie kept his place and I was on the left wing. We won 3–1 in 'Scotland's best display of the season' and I hit the underside of the bar in almost identical fashion to Bauld's near miss against England. Again the ball refused to cross the line. I wasn't on target in this game but Willie, no doubt to his great relief, was.

I was pleased to be recalled and even more pleased to read that 'Reilly was the best of a clever and incisive attack'. Inexplicably, there was still no place for Gordon Smith. Campbell of Chelsea, who was hardly known on this side of the border, was given the right-wing berth. I don't know what it was that the selectors had against Gordon but whatever it was, they certainly weren't keen to pick him.

We returned to league football with a make-or-break game against Rangers at Ibrox. We had to beat them to have any chance of overtaking them in the league, but we couldn't do it. Their game in those days was based on their formidable defence and, on this occasion, it was clear that they were intent on closing the back door and giving absolutely nothing away. They succeeded and despite our best efforts, we just couldn't put the ball in the net.

A 0–0 stalemate suited Rangers and sealed the league title for them. Jimmy Cairns, our left back, was injured early on and played a full seventy-five minutes with a broken leg. That was just Jimmy. He was the bravest and hardest man I ever played with. If any opponent tried to get rough with me, Jimmy would step in immediately and sort him out. He was my personal enforcer throughout my career and I had an awful lot of time for him.

We finished the season by playing Tottenham in London and then going off on another of our summer tours. We beat Spurs 1–0 and outplayed them in front of 33,000 of their supporters. The *Daily Mail* reporter was so impressed that he wrote, 'Clearly it is my duty to lavish praise on Hibs for a magnificent exhibition which placed Hugh Shaw's players on a pedestal.'

We moved on to Austria and a game with Rapid Vienna, who were acknowledged as one of Europe's best at that time. There was conflict before the game. Rapid wanted each side to field three substitutes but the fielding of substitutes was still a long way away in Scotland so Harry Swan refused. The Austrians appealed that it was only a friendly, after all. Our chairman replied in high dudgeon, 'The Hibs don't play friendlies!' He eventually relented and compromised on one substitute per side.

It was a great game, played in front of 35,000 fans. We went 2–0 up but a very good Vienna side fought back to win 3–2. We put that right with a 3–1 win over Linzer. We were 1–0 down but Gordon Smith and I switched positions and Gordon, Eddie and Willie Ormond scored three quick goals to give us the victory our play deserved. There was another good crowd – 17,000 this time – and one of the Austrian players in particular caught our eye. Their inside left played in a hairnet and at full time I didn't know whether to shake his hand or kiss it.

When we were in Vienna, we stayed in the same hotel as the film star John Mills. Mills' daughter Hayley is also well known these days but back then he was a major name. When we were there, there was a sudden burst of thunder and lightning. As soon as the storm subsided, Mills walked through the lobby and out of the hotel. Bobby Combe brought the house down by quipping, 'He's away to see who's stolen his thunder.'

A hit film at that time was *The Third Man* which was based on a novel by Graham Greene and starred Orson Welles as the main character Harry Lime. It had been filmed in Vienna and we visited the tunnels where the main chase scene had taken place. In fact we recreated the scene with Hugh Howie in the Harry Lime role. The Vienna police agreed to take part in our attempt at acting. They even used real revolvers! I really enjoyed this experience as I was a great film fan in those days and went to the cinema regularly.

We moved on to Germany and beat Augsburg 4–2. I scored the goal of the game after dribbling round three defenders and at full time the 20,000 German fans applauded us off the pitch, which was quite something considering it was only five years since the end of the war. We finished off our tour by beating Muhlburg 3–1 and Bayern Munich 6–1 – yes, 6–1 – before moving to Switzerland to beat Berne 1–0.

I had left the tour by then as I had to join Scotland for their matches in Portugal and France. I could have gone straight to Lisbon but chose to make a quick trip back to Edinburgh, to see my fiancée Kitty and my mum and dad, before catching up with my international teammates. Back home, I had time to read in the local paper that there had been insurrection in the Hibs ranks. The players had got fed up travelling on German trains with hard wooden seats and had refused to make any more journeys until they were put in upgraded compartments with upholstered seats. I am pleased to say that their request was met.

In Portugal we were staying in what was called in the media 'The Millionaires' Hotel'. Looking back at the press cuttings now, two items catch my eye. Billy Steel had gone to play golf on the hotel's course but had returned saying that the price was astronomical and that he wouldn't bother. What was that price? In fact it was no more than £1 per round. The hotel had a luxurious swimming pool and according to the report of the time, 'As the Scots settled down to a display of aquabatics, the pool attendant phoned the press and a battery of photographers was soon on the scene. The pictures should be good because the players had taken the plunge in their underpants as the attendant in charge of hiring swimsuits had gone home.' Imagine what the tabloids would have made of that nowadays.

The boys used to spend time visiting the local Portuguese shops. They discovered a shop where the lady behind the counter was, as they put it, 'a real cracker'. They went on about her so much that I decided that I would have to go and see her for myself. When I walked into the shop I was bowled over by her striking good looks. When I approached the counter, I was almost knocked flat on my back by the smell of garlic on her breath. She may have been top class in the looks department but she was sadly lacking in the personal hygiene stakes.

I'm not sure why, but I wasn't picked for the game against Portugal, which ended 2–2. Willie Bauld was at centre forward and scored, yet for the next game, against France, Willie was left out and I was chosen for the very first time at centre forward for Scotland. We won 1–0 and from now on I would play for my country in the centre of the attack.

The French were so impressed with us that they said that we were good enough to win the World Cup. They couldn't understand why the SFA had declined the opportunity to take part in the finals and to be honest neither could we. I have to say that during my career I had little cause for complaint where the SFA was concerned. Like all officials, they were inclined towards bureaucracy but, in the main, they treated the Scotland players well. The national body's decision, though, to turn down the chance to take part in the 1950 World Cup finals in South America was totally wrong.

Unlike in later years, when we did qualify for the finals with teams which could often only be described as workmanlike, we had a really top-notch side in 1950. We could have gone to Brazil and been really competitive. I honestly wouldn't have ruled out the possibility of us winning it.

England went and flopped badly. They even lost 1–0 to the USA in one of the all-time tournament shocks. The main reason for their disappointing display was over-confidence and I am pretty sure that this had a lot to do with the SFA's stance on qualification. It was that old Scots 'Wha's like us?' attitude and it did us no good at all. We had finished a creditable second in the Home International Championship and been unlucky not to win it. We deserved to play in the finals and we should have gone. It's as simple as that.

I returned home tired but happy. I was still just twenty-one years old but was leading a Hibs forward line which was destined for greatness. I was at last the man in the middle for Scotland as well.

7

DERBY DIFFICULTIES

Everyone at Easter Road knew that we should have won at least one trophy in the season which had just ended. We had a great team and, in particular, an exceptional forward line, and only our own inconsistencies had prevented us lifting silverware. When we returned for training prior to the 1950-51 campaign, we were determined to put that right.

A pre-season photograph showing us setting out on a road run is headed 'Hibernian on the Road to . . .?' We were confident that we were on the road to glory. Before the season started, we had a bit of fun. It was a tradition back then for Hibs to play the local cricket team Leith Franklin on their home pitch at Leith Links just before the football got underway again. These matches were tremendously popular and drew large crowds. The first encounter of the 1950s was one of the best. We won in a close finish by the narrow margin of three runs. Our star was that mighty man Jimmy Cairns. To try to stop Jimmy hitting the winning runs, Franklin deployed six fielders on the boundary. Undeterred, the 'Hibs Smiter', as he was described in the next day's reports, opened his shoulders and smashed two successive sixes. Led by Gordon Smith, we carried Jimmy off in triumph. My contribution was one wicket and six runs but I was intending to score a lot more freely when I got my football boots back on again.

We started as always with the six League Cup qualifying games. We were in magnificent form, scoring twenty-four goals and cruising through our section. The headlines said it all. 'Six

Goal Riot Stamps Hibs as Team of the Year' and 'A Green Clad Tidal Wave' were just a couple of examples. Falkirk were in our section and we beat them 4–0 and 5–4. They couldn't have been too happy when they found out that they had to come back to Easter Road for their first league game of the season and they were right to be apprehensive. This time we beat them 6–0. I had already notched an early-season hat-trick but went one better in this match by scoring four. I was described as 'nippy, elusive and dead on target'.

I was dead on my feet after our next series of matches. We met Aberdeen in the two-legged League Cup quarter-final and this was sure to be our sternest test to date. What we got was a classic cup tie. We travelled to Aberdeen on the Saturday without Gordon Smith, who was injured, and lost 4–1. We were a goal up at half-time and seemed in control but everything the Dons hit in the second half went in and we found ourselves looking down and out.

Such was our self-belief, though, that we still felt we could overturn this deficit and go through to the semis. Forty-two thousand of our fans shared our conviction because they turned out on a Wednesday night to roar us on. Leading up to the game, the press had confirmed that Smith would again be missing and Hugh Shaw had done nothing to disabuse them of that notion. The announcer read out the teams before the match, and the roof nearly came off the old main stand when it was announced that Gordon was playing. It was a psychological masterstroke by our manager, in the days before the phrase 'mind games' had even been invented, and it worked wonders. The crowd started roaring when they heard the team and never stopped throughout the game. Gordon was unplayable and we were unstoppable.

We took the second leg into extra time by being 3–0 up after ninety minutes. Away goals didn't count double in those days so we were set for an additional half hour. Within two minutes I had put us in front from yet another great Smith cross and we seemed destined for victory but, being Hibs, we couldn't do things the easy way. With only one minute left on the clock and in semi-darkness, because there were no floodlights then either, we allowed Harry Yorston to equalise for the Dons.

So the tie had ended locked at 4–4 and a replay was arranged for the neutral venue of Ibrox. Before then we had the little matter of a derby match against Hearts. They beat us again, 1–0 this time, but the game was unique for another reason. For the only time in his life, Gordon Smith was booed at Easter Road. Those doing the booing of course were the Hearts fans and there was no shortage of them in the 50,000 crowd.

Gordon went up for a ball with the Hearts left back Tom McKenzie and they ended up on the ground in a tangle of arms and legs. I don't know to this day what the Hearts fans thought Gordon had done, but they booed him every time he took possession of the ball after that. McKenzie was a big rugged full back who always gave Gordon problems. Our fans often thought he used illegal means to do this but on this occasion the boot was well and truly on the other foot as the Hearts supporters clearly believed Gordon to be the villain of the piece. Their disapproval obviously upset him as the match report records: 'After this incident we saw a lifeless edition of the usually brilliant Gordon.' I didn't have a great day either as I missed an easy chance to equalise, getting the ball caught between my feet when I had an open goal in front of me. It was the kind of chance I would normally have taken in my sleep but derby matches at this time used to bring the best out in Hearts and the worst out in Hibs. For whatever reason, we just could not beat Hearts at that time but we had no option except to put our disappointment behind us and prepare for the upcoming League Cup replay at Ibrox.

By a quirk of the fixtures, we had to travel to Pittodrie to play Aberdeen in the league two days before that. They beat us 2–1, which was not a good omen for the cup match to come. No one was fed up with watching Hibs and Aberdeen play each other, though, because 52,000 of our fans made the trip to Ibrox. Incredibly, after two hours we were still unable to be separated, with the score locked at 1–1. We had now been at each other's throats for five and a half hours of cup football without producing an outright winner.

In their wisdom, the Scottish League decided that a second replay should take place at Hampden the very next day! Can you imagine today's highly paid and pampered players agreeing to play three matches in four days? I can't see it somehow. We never gave it a thought and just got on with it. At last we managed to finish off the Dons and we did it in style, beating them 5–1. I was delighted to get the fifth goal. I outpaced their centre half Alec Young who was a bit 'leg weary'. After this marathon cup encounter, we all were, but what had taken us through was a combination of superior skill and fitness.

The press were really starting to acclaim our forwards now. In the last Aberdeen game, they reckoned that we had provided 'a display of forward play which will be difficult for any team to surpass'. One paper went further. The Scotland team to play Wales at Cardiff was about to be announced and under photographs of Gordon, Bobby, Eddie, Willie and me, their correspondent had written, 'The attack they COULD pick but WON'T'. He must have known someone on the SFA Selection Committee!

He wasn't the only journalist dishing out praise. One of his colleagues coined a phrase which still lives on fully sixty years later, when he wrote: 'If there is one single thing about which every Scottish football fan is in perfect agreement it is that the five best forwards in club football are Gordon Smith, Bobby Johnstone, Lawrie Reilly, Eddie Turnbull and Willie Ormond. The **Famous Five** are the pride and joy of the Easter Road.' It was the first time this term had been used to describe us and it was perfect. That is how we were always known after that and we are still recognised by that name today. Unfortunately, the article did not carry a by-line so the writer who came up with the title for

Hibs' (and probably Scotland's) greatest ever forward line can't be given credit for his words of wisdom.

When the Scotland team was eventually announced, only Eddie and I were selected. I cannot explain this, as we were all on the top of our game – as even the West Coast media were acknowledging – and we were clearly the best around. However, Hibs were getting the benefit of all our talents even if Scotland wasn't.

After the titanic quarter-final struggle against Aberdeen, we had much less trouble when the League Cup semi-final came round. We beat Queen of the South 3–1 at Tynecastle with E. T. getting a hat-trick. He also earned himself a new nickname as 'Edward the Thunderer'. Rex Kingsley, the *Sunday Mail*'s main man, had some advice for goalkeepers when Eddie was around. He told them to 'forget the bonus and duck' when Turnbull was lining up a shot.

This was a rare occasion when Tynecastle proved to be a happy hunting ground for us. It had early memories for me though. As a boy living in Gorgie, if my dad couldn't take me on the train to see Hibs playing away, I would wait outside the gates when Hearts were at home. Fifteen minutes from the end, they would open the gates to let the early leavers out and along with a lot of other youngsters who were there for the same purpose I would race in to watch the end of the game. On another occasion, I had got in free to watch the whole match as I was accompanying the Grassmarket Mission Band who were providing pre-match and half-time entertainment. My job, which could hardly be described as onerous, was to carry the lead trumpeter's instrument until he was ready to start playing it. The soloist in question was called Freddie Clayton and he was really good. He was so good, in fact, that he became a key member of the orchestra of a leading bandleader of the time known as Geraldo. Hibs were pretty good at Tynecastle that day as well and we had convincingly won our way to Hampden for the League Cup Final.

We then went to Fir Park in the league and put six goals past what was at that time a very powerful Motherwell team. This was encouraging for us as we would meet Motherwell again shortly in the League Cup Final. Four of the Famous Five, myself included, were on target. The only one of us who didn't score was Gordon, who picked up an early injury and played on for the rest of the match with his left leg heavily bandaged. We were really brilliant that day. Another of the top journalists was Andy Cunningham. He stated that our forward play was 'all switching, criss-crossing and passing which added up to devastation for the defence'. There was even the rare phenomenon of Willie Ormond scoring a goal with his right foot. Come to think of it, for Willie to score with the foot that he usually only used for standing on was more like a miracle. Andy Cunningham's custom at the end of his match report was to name the man of the match under the heading 'The Cunningham bowler is raised to . . .' On this occasion, I was his nominee. He noted that I had already scored fourteen goals in this still early part of the season and tipped me to be as good as Hughie Gallagher, which was praise indeed.

When Scotland went to Cardiff to play Wales, the Hibs contingent was reduced to one as Eddie Turnbull had picked up an injury. I was delighted to be chosen at centre forward and even more pleased to score two goals. Cardiff City, a big and wealthy club at the time, were so impressed with me that they offered Hibs £27,000 for my services. This was massive money in those days and would probably have been a record fee. I was delighted when Hugh Shaw and Harry Swan told their Cardiff counterparts that they weren't interested because I felt exactly the same. I couldn't have been happier at Easter Road and had no desire to go anywhere.

Next up was our eagerly awaited trip to Hampden to play Motherwell. This was a tremendous chance for us to lift silverware. We had just taken six goals off the 'Well on their own turf and we were in top form. Our form had been so good that the bookmakers, who don't usually get it wrong, had us as 2–5 favourites for the match. Motherwell were available at the much more generous odds of 7–2.

I started to feel a wee bit uneasy the week before the match. We had been kitted out with really smart new training tops with green and white quarters, but there was concern in our camp about the fitness of Gordon Smith, Eddie Turnbull and myself. In the event, Gordon and I played but Eddie missed out. Neither of us should have taken the field. As the match report said, 'Smith, playing with an injury, lay deep in no-man's land' and 'Reilly was a shadow of the boy who dazzled Cardiff last week and maybe his knee twist had something to do with it.'

Motherwell raised their game, ours was below par and we lost 3–0. Our supporters, who made up the vast majority of the 64,000 crowd, were in the depths of despair. We players felt exactly the same. I can still remember big Tommy Younger crying his eyes out at full time. Our name had been on the cup but we had failed to make it stick. Just what is it about Hibs and finals?

On this occasion we didn't have to look far to find the reason for our defeat. We had really missed Eddie Turnbull. He was not the most spectacular member of our forward line but, boy, was he effective. Like a lot of players who put reliability before flamboyance, Eddie's importance to our team only became clear when we had to make do without him. The other factor which contributed to our latest cup final anti-climax was that Gordon Smith and I had taken the field less than fully fit. We both wanted to do our best for Hibs so we convinced ourselves that we could play through our injuries and that everything would be all right on the day. Well, we couldn't and it wasn't! We struggled, as you always do when you are carrying a knock, and we were nowhere near our best. This meant that we only had the benefit of a proper contribution from two members of our forward line and in the end that proved crucial.

We were sick and well aware that, just like the season before, we had lost a cup that should have been ours. I can remember us sitting in the dressing room at Easter Road the next week and vowing that under no circumstances would we let the League Championship slip through our grasp this time. Our determination was soon to be put to the test because our next match was at Ibrox against our biggest rivals. Eighty thousand turned up to roar Rangers on.

We were ready for them but we got off to the worst possible start. A mix-up between John Paterson and Tommy Younger saw John put the ball into his own net after only eight minutes. John was a top centre half and one of my best pals at the club. He was born in Colchester to Scottish parents which in those days meant he couldn't be picked for Scotland. If this hadn't been the case, he would definitely have won his fair share of caps. John's son Craig was also an excellent centre half for Hibs three decades later. John and Tommy didn't let their error get them down. Indeed, Tommy recovered to make 'the save of a lifetime' from a Willie Waddell free kick.

Despite the intimidating atmosphere, we fought our way back into the game and I headed us level just after half-time.

George Young was six feet two and I was only five feet eight but I outjumped big 'Corky' to nod in the equaliser. For somebody who wasn't the tallest, I was always good in the air and got my fair share of headed goals. Young's nickname came from a lucky cork which he carried. When Rangers had won the Scottish Cup, a fan had given him a champagne cork which he kept with him on match days after that. The one time he had forgotten to put the cork in his pocket, Scotland lost to Belfast Celtic. He always made sure he had it after that.

He must have had it this day because we did everything but score in the time which remained. As Rex Kingsley put it: 'No team in Scotland can match Hibs for team play but as long as others can match them in snatching chances, Easter Road will have its problems.' The *Sunday Mail* used to bill Rex as 'straight-hitting' and he certainly was on this occasion. He considered the referee to be whistle-happy and accused him of providing an 'unmusical solo'. In those less politically correct times, he also reminded him that 'football's not a lassies' game'.

We now went on a great run, winning seven league games in a row. Most of them were comfortable but we left it late in a couple of them. In both these matches, I came up with late winners. They weren't quite in the last minute, so at this point it was more 'Late On Reilly' than 'Last Minute Reilly'. In one of the games against Third Lanark, Eddie Turnbull got sent off. It was very rare for a player to be given his marching orders at that time and it was considered to be fairly shocking. Eddie was back in the dressing room when I got the winning goal with four minutes left. He was apparently 'huddled in misery in a cloak of bitter bewilderment and disillusionment'. He just looked cheesed off to me. Eddie claimed to be wondering why he had been dismissed but he was cautioned to 'wonder also what Hibs will do without him if he comes before the Rough Play Committee before Christmas'!

Scotland met Austria in December and the ever-idiosyncratic Selection Committee decided that they could do without the whole Hibs forward line including me. This despite the fact that I had scored two goals in my last international. Playing for my country meant everything to me and I was bitterly hurt to be left out. I just couldn't make any sense of it. Neither could the Austrian goalkeeper. After the Austrians had won, he told the press that he had played against Hibs for Rapid Vienna in the summer. 'Their forwards gave me the shivers,' he said. 'They were much better than the Scotland forwards.' They say goalkeepers are crazy but this one certainly knew what he was talking about.

As 1950 gave way to 1951, everyone at Easter Road believed that we were the top team in the country and that we were good enough to win the league. This belief was about to come under severe scrutiny, as we were heading to Tynecastle to first foot the team which gave us more trouble than anyone else. Surely this time we could lay our derby bogey to rest and take care of the Hearts. Sadly not. With the help of three goal-line clearances they beat us 2–1 and completed the league double over us for the second successive season. We just could not overcome the team that we and all our supporters wanted to beat more than any other. There was no logical explanation for it. It was just one of those things which happen at certain times and drive you mad in the process. They seemed to raise their game every time they played us and get every lucky break going.

The more we played them, the more frustrated we got. They were good but we were better. We knew that and they did too. Yet still we couldn't overcome them. When Alex Miller managed Hibs in the 1990s, Hibs went twenty-two derby games without a win over Hearts. On the other hand, when Hugh Shaw played for Hibs in the 1920s, we beat them all the time.

Maybe that's just the way these matches between city rivals go, with each taking it in turn to have a period of dominance. You can understand that happening when one team is clearly superior to the other but it makes no sense when the team dominating is markedly inferior to the one which keeps losing. That was what was happening to Hibs at this time and it wasn't pleasant. We couldn't let it get us down, though, because we had a league title to win.

8

CHAMPIONS AGAIN

We knew that we couldn't afford to dwell on our latest Tyne-castle tragedy and we didn't. We thrashed Aberdeen (who were every bit as good a team as Hearts, incidentally) on a frosty Easter Road pitch. Because of the icy conditions we wore baseball boots which helped us to keep our feet well enough to score six goals. Gordon Smith was back to his best and 'made Hibs a super scoring machine'. The rest of us served up 'an artistic combination and devastating punch that bewildered and pulverised Aberdeen'. Thirty-two thousand of our fans had retained the faith sufficiently to cheer us on at Easter Road against the Dons. Like us, they must have gone home with mixed feelings. Yes, we were delighted to have won so convincingly but we were still wondering why we couldn't do to Hearts what we did so regularly to other teams.

My two goals against Aberdeen were followed by two even better efforts by Gordon when Motherwell came to Easter Road. The same Motherwell who had beaten us in the League Cup Final were played off the park as we won 3–1. Gordon's contribution was an overhead kick and a scorching shot after wrong-footing a Motherwell defender with a double shuffle. Our right winger's play at this time was truly world-class and I do not exaggerate when I say this – but yet again he was ignored by the Scottish selectors.

When the team to play against the League of Ireland was announced, Bobby Johnstone and I were in the side but Bobby Collins of Celtic was preferred to Gordon on the right wing.

Collins was a good wee player who was really more of a midfield player but he wasn't remotely in the same class as Gordon Smith. The whole thing was totally mystifying.

The back-to-back wins we had achieved over Aberdeen and Motherwell were significant. They helped us to put our Ne'erday derby defeat behind us and more importantly kept us on track to regain the league title. The championship was in our own hands. If we kept winning, neither Rangers nor anyone else would be able to overhaul us. Keeping winning was exactly what we intended to do.

The forthcoming league international at Parkhead was important for players who wanted to catch the selectors' eye for the upcoming match of the season against England at Wembley. I was certainly in that category and I did my chances no harm with two goals and a good all-round performance in a 7–0 canter. I mentioned earlier that I got plenty of goals with my head and I managed another in this game. I bulleted a cross from Bobby Johnstone with my forehead but the ball hit the bar and came back out. I then threw myself at the rebound and headed it in. I suppose you could call it a double header.

If London was the extent of my horizons at that time, our chairman Harry Swan was looking much further afield. Hibs' great play had attracted attention all over the world and countries were queuing up to invite us for a summer tour. Mexico, Brazil, Canada, South Africa and Turkey all wanted 'to entertain Scotland's team of the year'.

We may have been shaping up to be the team of the year but we dropped a league point to Partick Thistle and drew with St Mirren in the Scottish Cup. We were back in business though when the Saints came to Easter Road for the replay. We crushed them 5–0 and inspired Tom Nicholson in the *Daily Record* to claim that the selectors should pick the Famous Five en bloc as Scotland's attack for Wembley. He finished by saying, 'Scotland must have great riches or blind selectors if these players don't get chosen for Wembley.'

We were on a roll now and recorded two famous back-to-back victories over the Old Firm. First we beat Celtic 1–0 in front of 60,000 fans at Parkhead thanks to an Eddie Turnbull special. This was a huge step towards lifting the league title again. Then we moved on to Ibrox to meet Rangers in the Scottish Cup. This was the ultimate test but our attitude was quite simple. We were more than ready and the call in our dressing room was 'Bring them on!'

The game had really caught the public imagination and a barely credible crowd for a Scottish club match of 102,342 had Ibrox bursting at the seams. Nobody was disappointed except maybe the Rangers fans. Twice Rangers took the lead and each time we fought back. Gordon got the first equaliser and then Eddie pulled us level a second time with a twenty-yard swerving volley which was described as 'a goal in a million'. There was even better to come though.

With nine minutes to go, we got a free kick just outside the penalty area. Eddie Turnbull lined up as if he was planning one of his thunderbolts. He approached the ball at speed but instead of shooting slipped the ball to Bobby Johnstone on the left of the box. Bobby flicked the ball over a Rangers defender as he moved back infield then sent a curling twenty-yard shot past the Rangers goalkeeper Bobby Brown into the top of the net to win the game. Brown would later manage Scotland to their famous 3–2 victory over England at Wembley in 1967. I am sure he saw some great football that day but none of it would have compared with what he witnessed at Ibrox in 1951 when the Hibs came to town.

If you think that I am getting a bit carried away with myself then don't just take my word for it. Have a look at what Jack Harkness wrote in the *Sunday Post* on the day after the game. He had this to say: 'Hibernian Football Club was formed in 1875. During their long history they have had some great teams. They've figured in some great games. They've had some great results. But, for the official record, this must go down as Hibs' greatest ever performance.' There's no arguing with that and we were now starting to believe not only that we could win the league – which had been our main target all season – but that lifting that elusive Scottish Cup which meant so much to us was also in our grasp. Even the Rangers players thought so. As we came off at full time, Ian McColl, their international right half, said to me: 'If you don't win the Scottish Cup after this, you'll never win it.'

As I mentioned earlier, over 100,000 fans packed into Ibrox for that match. A Hibs-supporting friend of mine was at the game and he told me that at least 20,000 of those in the ground were Hibs supporters. There was no segregation of the crowd in those days, of course, and followers of both teams stood side by side. My friend also said that to begin with the atmosphere was reasonably friendly. When Bobby Johnstone scored his winning goal, though, the Hibs fans were aware of a definite change in the mood of those wearing Rangers colours. The Hibees began to wonder if they would get out alive at full time. They did, though, and could reflect on one of Hibs' greatest ever displays as they made their way back to Edinburgh.

We now polished off Morton and East Fife in the league and our belief continued to grow. The media shared our confidence. Peter Black in the *Weekly News* wrote: 'Hibs have put themselves on a pinnacle. They are the new standard by which Scottish football must be judged. Hibs of Edinburgh – the number one team in the land.'

The Scottish Cup draw had paired us with Airdrie at their tight ground of Broomfield. It was our third tough away draw in a row. By the kind of coincidence that the fixture list quite often throws up, we also had to go there on league business the week before the cup tie. Our double-winning dream received a bit of a setback as they beat us 2–1. Twenty thousand packed the ground and Airdrie played like men possessed. In fact, after the game Harry Swan made a point of counting their players as they left the field. 'I thought that they had at least fourteen men on the pitch,' he said. They didn't, though. They had the same eleven as us and on the day they were too good for us.

That defeat hurt, but it also made sure that we were fully focused when we went back to Lanarkshire a week later. We now knew exactly what to expect and Airdrie did not disappoint us. They were again inspired and committed in equal measure but this time we were ready for them. The ground was again filled to a capacity that would never be allowed in these safety-conscious days.

Despite the previous week's defeat, our fans were there in number and in tremendous voice. We certainly gave them something to shout about and I had the game of my life. We won 3–0, but had to do a lot of defending. For once our forwards did not dominate and chances were at a premium. In the whole match, I had four chances. I had a header saved and put away the other three. The match report sums it up perfectly when it says: 'The possibility of another shock was heavy in the air when Reilly came riding to the rescue.' It then adds, 'His performance had the hallmark of genius. The ability of the great to make much out of little.' Well, that was quite a compliment, but our fans obviously thought that I deserved it as they invaded the pitch at full time and lifted me onto their shoulders. It was heady stuff and an incredible feeling.

The dressing rooms at Broomfield were in the bottom corner of the ground and I was carried aloft from where I had been standing in the Airdrie penalty area at the end of the match right down to the other end of the ground. There were masses around me and they were slapping my back and ruffling my hair. One supporter kept shouting, 'Lawrie, you're the greatest,' so maybe that accolade came my way before Muhammad Ali laid claim to it a few years later! Eventually, a policeman rescued me and I made my way to the sanctuary of the dressing room. Our spirits were soaring and we were becoming convinced that the possibility of achieving a league and cup double could definitely become a reality.

I was on a personal high. I was developing as a player all the time and my confidence was growing with every successful game. As I sat in the Broomfield changing room that day, I felt that if I took on the world, I would win.

We continued on our merry way with wins over Third Lanark and St Mirren. The last time we had played Thirds, Eddie Turnbull had been sent off. This time he scored what was described as 'an atomic explosive'. Our league form was terrific and we could see nothing to stop us winning the championship if we maintained our performance levels.

Everything was now set up for the Scottish Cup semi-final. We had been paired with Motherwell so we had a chance to avenge our League Cup Final defeat. Tynecastle was chosen as the venue and this did cause us a bit of concern as it hadn't been our happiest ground in recent times. So many fans wanted to see the game that a crowd limit of 48,000 was imposed and the match was made all-ticket, which was rare back then.

Sadly, our forebodings were to prove justified. We couldn't believe the state of the pitch when we arrived at the ground. The next day's papers were correct when they said, 'It was an insult to ask players to play a Scottish Cup semi-final on such a mess.' We thought that the surface would suit Motherwell's style of play more than ours and we were right.

They went ahead after only twenty seconds when the muddy ground caused John Paterson to miss a ball he would normally have cleared with ease. That was bad enough but we were then hit by a real disaster. John Ogilvie, our left back, went into a tackle and emerged from it with his right leg broken in two places. Down to ten men, we had to reshuffle the pack. Bobby Combe went back to left back and Eddie Turnbull took up Bobby's position at left half. This reduced the forward line to the 'Famous Four'. We were determined not to let the fates conspire against us in the Scottish Cup again and drove ourselves relentlessly. I was a man on a mission.

Kitty and I had now been engaged for almost three years. Long engagements were the norm back then, as young couples took time to save for a house and the furniture to fill it. I was due to get married on the Monday after this match and wanted to go to my wedding knowing that Hibs had booked a place in the Scottish Cup Final.

First I crashed a ball goalwards but it hit the Motherwell goalkeeper Johnston's head and flew wide. The match report the following day summed it up when it said, 'How Johnston's head didn't land over the wall in Gorgie Road is one of football's little mysteries.' If I had struck that shot with force, I hit my next even harder and this time I scored. 'Reilly was there to smash an unsaveable eighteen-yarder high into the net from an angle.' That was more like it and I began to believe that we might still achieve the impossible.

My hopes were dashed, though, when Motherwell scored either side of half-time to go 3–1 up. With twenty-seven minutes to go, we had ten men and were two goals down. Most teams would have given up at this point but not the Hibs. I always played with passion but that day I felt like I had a fire inside me. We just wouldn't lie down. Gordon Smith beat four Motherwell defenders in a fantastic run and laid the ball in front of me. I obliged by bulleting it into the net off the near post. We really went for it now. The press report of the time describes it perfectly. 'Tynecastle was a hysterical, howling mob as the wee Hibs men twisted and slid through the mud, straining every ounce to save the day.' I thought that I had done exactly that when I bulleted a header for goal. I caught the ball perfectly but unfortunately it hit the underside of the bar and, yes, you've guessed it, landed on the line before bouncing to safety.

Still we wouldn't accept defeat. We came again and Archie Buchanan tried to make a pass to Gordon Smith. The ball ricocheted off two Motherwell defenders and found its way to Gordon, who crashed it home. Our celebrations were cut short when the linesman raised his flag. Gordon had clearly been played onside so the goal surely had to stand. Remember, though, this was Hibs in the Scottish Cup and the referee inexplicably and, in our opinion, wrongly chalked the goal off.

That was it. We were out and our dream of a historic double was in tatters. Again the next morning's papers said it all when they recorded that, 'Misfortune more than Motherwell put Hibs out of the cup. Maybe they had to try to beat two hoodoos yesterday – Motherwell and the ominous atmosphere of Tynecastle Park.' They could have added a third. The fates which conspire against Hibs winning the Scottish Cup had struck again and they retain their hold over the Hibs to this day.

The following Monday was a much happier day for me. At the age of twenty-two I married Kitty Cruickshank. Kitty and I tied the knot at West St Giles Church just 100 yards from the house where Hugh Shaw, the Hibs manager, lived. It was quite an occasion. People were generally more restrained in the early 1950s, but not on this day. When Kitty and I came out of the church, there was a huge crowd waiting to meet us. When we got into the wedding car, a crowd of women ran after it and tried to mob us. If there had been such a thing as a pop star back then, I would have felt like one. I am not sure what Kitty thought but I wasn't complaining. I was shouting, 'Stop the car!' When we got to the hotel for the reception, we had to struggle through another large crowd. Scoring goals for Hibs and Scotland obviously made you popular and famous. If I'd had any doubts about it before, they were certainly laid to rest that day.

There was another reason to celebrate on this happy Monday, as the Scotland team to meet England at Wembley was announced and, along with wee Bobby Johnstone, I was in the line-up. After reading my story to this point, it won't come as a surprise to you to discover that there was again no place for Gordon Smith.

Kitty and I moved into our newly purchased home in Moredun Park Drive in the Edinburgh suburbs. The Moredun Park area was quite rural in those days and we were very happy there. Not long after our wedding, one of the newspapers printed a photograph of Kitty using her brand shining new carpet-sweeper with me on my knees beside her brushing out the hearth. To come clean, if you'll pardon the pun, that photo didn't tell the whole truth. Housework didn't usually feature in my normal daily routine. I would train with Hibs in the morning, have a game of golf in the afternoon and come home in time for my tea. That was the way it was with most couples then. The man was the breadwinner and the woman took care of domestic duties. Feminists reading this will probably raise their hands in horror but that's just the way things were at that time.

After tea we would put our feet up and listen to the wireless, as the radio was known in those days. Most folk didn't think about getting a television until the Queen's coronation in 1953 so, at the beginning of the 1950s, the wireless was the main source of entertainment in the majority of households. Kitty and I were no different and we used to enjoy comedy programmes like *Round the Horne* with Kenneth Horne, *It's That Man Again* with Tommy Handley and *The Goon Show* with Spike Milligan, Peter Sellers and Harry Secombe. Another popular programme at the time was *The McFlannels*, which was about the life of a Scottish family.

Life was good on and off the field. Hibs were closing in on the league title and I had the prospect of facing England at Wembley for the second time in two years. When we had won the championship in season 1947-48, we had still been a developing team and the title race had gone down to the wire. We were now the finished article and had, in truth, dominated the league for most of the season.

When Hibs played Clyde in Glasgow, a win would bring the championship back to Easter Road. Ironically we had to go into the game with a team full of reserves. In those days, club football was played on the same day as internationals. When Hibs ran out at Shawfield, Bobby Johnstone and I were in London preparing to take on the Auld Enemy. Gordon Smith and Willie Ormond were out injured so Eddie Turnbull was the only member of the Famous Five available for this crucial game. Two of the reserves,

Jimmy Mulkerrin and Jim Souness, were fine players and they scored three goals between them. The ever-reliable Archie Buchanan added a fourth and the game was convincingly won 4–0. This officially made the Hibees Scotland's top team once again.

It also made Bobby and me very happy when we heard the result. If anything, we were now even more determined to beat England to achieve a double of a different kind from the one which we had dreamed about earlier in the season. Hibs were a magnificent side in that season of 1950-51 and the report on the title-clinching victory over Clyde summed up our superiority when it said, 'Champions come and champions go, but surely League winners Hibs will remain at the top for a very long time. They fielded five reserves at Shawfield last night against a Clyde team ravenous for points and won with the nonchalant air of those who are fully aware of being very good.'

Bobby and I now turned our attention to the upcoming business at Wembley Stadium. The new Wembley may have problems with its pitch but the old one certainly didn't. I have been on a few bowling greens but none of them came close to comparing with the immaculate striped sward which the English national stadium was in my playing days. Then there was the crowd. One hundred thousand filled the ground, waving rattles and bawling their heads off.

It may have been a home game for England, but the Scots fans were usually in the majority. They saved for two years, got tickets through supporters' clubs or from relatives south of the border and descended on London. I don't think that the locals knew what had hit them when the tartan hordes flooded the capital but it was fantastic for us Scots players to take the long walk from the tunnel behind the goal to the centre circle as we came on to the field before the game. Wherever we looked we could see and hear our own supporters. It was inspiring and really lifted you. Not that we needed much lifting as we were always well up for the game already.

The SFA had tried to keep us from getting too hyped up for the game by taking us to the BBC studios the day before the game to see the famous English comedian Ted Ray recording his show. Ted's programme was called *Ray's a Laugh*. We were more intent on raising a few Scottish cheers the next day.

We did exactly that by again beating the English in their own backyard. We won 3–2 and once more I showed my liking for Wembley. I made two of our goals and scored the other. I laid on our first for Bobby Johnstone, so it was a real Hibs effort, and I set up the third for Billy Liddell. The second was all my own work as I feinted to go one way but went the other to wrong-foot Jack Froggatt, the England centre half. While he was off-balance, I flicked the ball over him and ran through on goal. I made myself stay composed and calmly placed the ball in the corner of the English net. Jack Froggatt had just had a great season for his club Portsmouth. He didn't have a good day at Wembley, though, even if I say so myself.

There was a lot of praise for my performance. 'Reilly served up a courageous and clever display and a brilliant goal' was good, but it was bettered by 'Reilly was a non-stop, two-footed, hard-headed battering ram who never gave the English defence time to draw breath.' To top it all off, leading media pundit Andy Cunningham again raised his bowler hat in my honour and made me man of the match. After Easter Road, Wembley was my favourite ground. I loved playing there and it definitely brought the best out of me too, as I always seemed to manage to score there.

It's only fair to point out that England did play a lot of the match with ten men as they lost their brilliant inside forward Wilf Mannion through injury in the first half. They gave everything to make up for the fact that they were short-handed. One of the headlines summed it up when it said, 'Scots Defy Ten Heroes'. Mind you, the report beneath the headline recorded, 'Don't let England fool you with their ten-men excuse, we were just as much their superiors when there were eleven of them.' So there! Mind you, even I would have to admit that that doesn't read like the most objective piece of reporting which I have ever read.

Playing right back for England that day was Alf Ramsey. Alf of course went on to manage his country to their 1966 World Cup win and became a knight of the realm, no less. On that day though, he was just a tough and skilful opponent. Alf was an interesting character. He was brought up in the Cockney heartland of Dagenham but tried to distance himself from his roots. He was reported to have taken elocution lessons and when he was interviewed as England manager, he came out with a classic answer. The journalists at a press conference were grilling Alf about his humble beginnings. One reporter asked if it was true that he came from Dagenham and that his parents still lived there. Clearly uncomfortable, Ramsey paused for thought, then replied, 'That is apparently the case.' Maybe Alf was just socially ambitious. There again, maybe he had delusions and was a bit of a snob.

Alf didn't like journalists when he became England manager. He got particularly angry if any reporter had the nerve to question his tactics in print. Hugh McIlvanney, that truly great Scottish sports journalist, tells a good story to illustrate this. At an England press conference, Alf took a particular scribe to task for daring to question his judgement in an article he had written. 'How dare you doubt my knowledge of football?' he said. 'As manager of England I have travelled all over the world.' Quick as a flash, the newspaperman replied, 'Yes, but if a turnip travelled all round the world, it would still be a turnip when it came back.'

Ramsey played for Tottenham, who were easily winning the English League Championship and someone (more than likely Harry Swan) came up with the idea that Hibs should play them to see who was the best team in the United Kingdom.

So shortly after returning from Wembley, I found myself up against Alf again in what the press was billing as 'The Battle of Britain'. In the event, the game ended in a goalless stalemate but it shouldn't have done. When Spurs won the double of league and FA Cup in season 1960-61, their manager was Bill Nicholson. When we played them in 1951, Bill was still a player and a hard one at that.

As I closed in on goal with five minutes to go, he lunged in on me but I was too fast for him and he brought me down. It seemed to be a clear penalty in the eyes of everyone except the person who mattered most. As the post-match report put it: 'Referee Mitchell of Falkirk knows why he didn't give Hibs a penalty five minutes from the end when Nicholson desperately upended Reilly in the box but no one else does.'

The writer added: 'Had Turnbull been given the chance to score from the spot Hibs would have won deservedly. The Scottish champions were a better team than the English king-pins.' Somebody who came in for praise in this game was John Paterson. When the Tottenham officials heard after the game that he had been born in Colchester, they said that it was time that the England selectors came and took a look at him. It never happened, though, which was a shame. John was a top player and it would have been interesting to say the least to have faced my pal in a Scotland v England match. After the game, the Hibs and Spurs players swopped gifts. They gave us silver loving cups and we presented them with tartan rugs. I couldn't really imagine Ian Murray and Jermaine Defoe exchanging those kind of presents these days, could you?

It was a measure of our dominance of Scottish football at this time that we had won the league well before the end of the season. We still had two league games to play, however, and what a prospect they were. We had to face both members of the Old Firm at Easter Road and it goes without saying that as champions we wanted to end the season in real style. We succeeded in doing just that.

Rangers came first and we totally outplayed them to win 4–1. Gordon Smith, the man who wasn't considered good enough for Scotland, got 'two bobby dazzler goals' and Bobby Johnstone and I got one each. We were irresistible, as the press reports show. 'Never can Rangers have been so outplayed or humiliated. Hibs scored four dazzling goals. They might have scored double. They might also have had three penalties.' Nothing changes there then, but on this occasion it didn't matter. We players demonstrated our superiority and loved doing so. Forty thousand of our fans lapped it all up.

Next came Celtic and it was more of the same. We won 3–1, with all our goals coming from the Edinburgh Thistle finishing school. Archie Buchanan got the first and I got the other two. Harry Reading, our old manager who was still the groundsman at Easter Road, would have looked on with pride and pleasure as his former charges put Celtic to the sword.

My first goal was the best of our three as I first timed a pass from Eddie Turnbull past Hunter in the Celtic goal. I caught the ball so sweetly that I doubt if the goalkeeper even saw the ball as it flew past him. It was great to finish the season not only as champions but playing like champions. We had won all four of our games against the Old Firm and had finished ten points ahead of Rangers in second place, at a time when you only got two points for a win. If the current three points for a victory had been in existence then we would have been fifteen points in front of them. We had proved that we were certainly the best team in Scotland and possibly the best team in Britain.

After the Celtic game, we only had time for a quick shower before dressing and racing to catch the coach which was waiting outside the ground to take us to Waverley Station. From there it was on to London and from there across to Paris. Harry Swan had weighed up all his tour invitations and settled on France and we were heading straight there without even time to go home and say cheerio to our wives or families.

It may have been hectic but it was also exciting. We were lucky lads to be able to see so many different parts of the world at someone else's expense. There is no doubt that post-war Paris was slightly more sophisticated than 1951 Leith. Our first match was against Racing Club of Paris and we drew 1–1. The game finished at 11.30pm and was watched by 'beautiful women in expensive furs and sleek-looking men with chewing gum and cigarettes'.

We even had two supporters of our own in the crowd. Kenny McQueen, an Edinburgh bookmaker and former boxing promoter and a huge Hibs fan, who got on well with all the players, had joined us for the trip. The report of the game took time out to say that 'McQueen is such a staunch Hibs supporter that he even wears a green tie!' Things were definitely different back then. Our former teammate Simon Waldie had flown across with Kenny. Simon had left Hibs to join Queen of the South who had just won promotion. Being the real Hibee that he still was, Simon had used part of his promotion bonus to follow his favourite team. We were delighted to see him. We were less delighted with Paris – not because of how it looked but due to the astronomical cost of everything. As Jock Govan put it in his usual direct way, 'Let's get down to Nice as soon as possible. We've had enough of this dump.' A bit harsh, I'm sure you'll agree. The newspaper correspondent travelling with us was more tactful when he said, 'The prices of everything in the shops have staggered Hibs even more than Hearts did on New Year's Day.'

When we gave Jock his wish and travelled on to Nice, we were in for a surprise. Nice AFC were on their way to winning the French championship and we expected a football contest. What we got was a rough-house which the papers called 'The Battle of Nice'. We won 1–0 and I got our goal, 'cracking the ball home from fifteen yards as the keeper came out'. During the game their right winger rugby-tackled John Paterson and the fun continued after the game when the crowd pelted us as we came off the field. Jimmy Cairns got hit by a number of coins but there was no falling to the ground holding his head for Jimmy. I'll let the match report tell you what happened next: 'Big Jimmy Cairns clapped his hand to his forehead in pain as some coins hit him. He tried to dive into the crowd to get at the throwers but the gendarmes ushered him into the dressing room.' If the police hadn't intervened Jimmy might have 'done an Eric Cantona' forty years before the Manchester United rebel leapt into the crowd at Crystal Palace.

However, there was a happy ending to the evening as, 'About 1,000 fans lined the exit from the dressing room as the Scots boys came out in their civvies. Trouble was expected but instead the crowd started to clap their hands in tribute to Hibs' great skill.' It wasn't all sweetness and light though as, 'The efforts of a few at the back of the crowd to start a raspberry died in their throats due to lack of encouragement from those around them.' There you have it. It might be 'see Naples and die' but it was also 'see Nice and get a raspberry blown at you'!

When we were in the south of France, we visited the beach at Bandol. When we were there, I obviously caught the eye of a beautiful French lady. I sat beside her and she drew herself close to me. At that point Hugh Shaw arrived and asked what was going on. 'She's just helping me to learn French, boss,' I said.

'Never mind that,' replied Shaw. 'If you want tae learn French, you can go to night school when you get home!'

Bobby Johnstone and I had to leave the Hibs party in France to join up with Scotland, who were playing four games to finish the season. The first two were at Hampden. We beat Denmark 3–1 and France 1–0. I scored headers in both games and was starting to make a name for myself for my ability in the air. Rising to meet a ball and heading it with power came naturally and easily to me. 'Lawrie's nod with his top piece must be acquiring a reputation among goalkeepers' was how one newspaper put it.

So strong was enthusiasm for the Scottish team after the win at Wembley that 75,000 people turned out to watch us play Denmark. It wasn't only journalists who were paying me compliments, as Jimmy Cairns was quoted on Hibs' return from their tour as saying, 'See that wee fella Reilly. I can't understand how he manages to get his jersey on. His heart sticks out that far.' It meant a lot to have a big, hard man like Jimmy saying that about me.

We then travelled to Brussels to beat Belgium 5–0 in front of another big crowd – 65,000 this time. Our tour and our season were to end with one final game against Austria in Vienna. The Austrians had an outstanding team at that time and we expected nothing less than a really hard contest. The press built the match up as a battle for the 'Championship of Europe' but in the event we got a bit more than we bargained for and a battle of a different kind. As 'Waverley' in the *Daily Record* put it, 'In thirty years of reporting football I have never witnessed such disgraceful scenes as in this international here today. Everything foul in soccer was on view. The players descended to tactics that would have been abhorred on any football field.' He went on to say that, 'the Austrians started the fouling but some of the Scots, goaded beyond endurance, went on to join in.'

There was a pitch invasion by spectators which had to be cleared by the police and eight minutes from the end Billy Steel got sent off for retaliation. As he left the field, a woman attacked him with her handbag. We also lost 4–0, which was our heaviest ever international defeat at that time – outside wartime football – so a great season in both club and international football ended on a sour note.

Waverley ended his piece with, 'I do not deny that Austria commenced the unfair tactics but the Scots went on to join the rough house. They lost the place completely. The spectators included many distinguished people who must have been shocked by the whole affair.' That was us told. He was only half right though. Yes, we did retaliate in the end, but only after the most severe provocation. We wouldn't have been human if we hadn't snapped eventually. The referee from Switzerland let the Austrians get away with murder and all the Scottish players thought that he had a lot to answer for.

It was good to get home and, as I told the press, 'All I want to do is forget football for a while until it's time to go back to Easter Road for training. I feel as if I could do with a rest.'

I enjoyed the next few weeks as I took it easy and reflected on a great season for Hibs. We had won the league and could, with a bit more luck, have pulled off a treble as we had lost in the final and semi-final respectively of the League Cup and Scottish Cup.

It was nice to read what the newspapers were saying in their end-of-season reviews. Jack Harkness in the *Sunday Post* said 'Hibs – best I have ever seen. What an attack. A shot in every locker and a bright idea in every head. Brilliant individualism which still preserves team cohesion.' The *Reynolds News*, a Sunday paper no longer in print, summed things up when it declared, 'Not for many years has the Scottish League been won by so outstanding a club.'

The close season break didn't last long, though, and soon it was time to head back to Easter Road to prepare for another season. We had every intention of completing season 1951-52 in exactly the same way we would start it, as the proud football champions of Scotland.

9

A TRIO OF TITLES

Everyone at Easter Road entered the new season full of confidence. We were well aware that every other team in the country would be trying to knock us off our perch at the top of the Scottish football tree, but we were sure that we could hold on to our title. What gave us this belief was the strength of our team. We had been together now for a number of years and knew each other inside out. We could all play and we all trusted each other to do the right things on the park. We also realised that we had players in our team who could produce a flash of genius when it was needed most.

We weren't just a team, we were a group of pals. We all got on really well together. We ate out together, went to the theatre and the cinema as a team, played golf as a group and enjoyed each other's company in training and matches as well. The boys who liked a drink would also have regular evenings out but they knew when to stop and they never drank to excess. Playing for Hibs and winning matches was much too important for that. The lads who enjoyed going out for a couple of pints were the only social group which I didn't join as I was a teetotaller then as I am today and have been all my life.

In goal we had big Tommy Younger. Tommy was the best goalie I played with or against. When people ask me what his main strength was, I tell them that it was the fact that he didn't have a weakness. Every aspect of his game was high class. Tommy was a cheery big lad who was always full of life and laughter. His nature was another of his assets. He went into every game in a positive frame of mind and when he made a rare mistake – which, being human, he did on occasion – he would never let it bother him. He would bounce straight back full of infectious self-confidence and sheer natural goalkeeping talent. Tommy was also a good driving instructor. He had an old Wolseley which was falling to bits. It would never have passed an MOT these days. The doors had to be secured with string. He gave me driving lessons in this jalopy and he must have done well because I passed my test first time. I treated myself to a nice Ford Anglia which was in a whole lot better condition than Tommy's car.

Our right back was Jock Govan. Jock was a comedian in a team of comedians. He had plenty to say and a lot of the time what he said made you laugh. Jock could play too. He tackled well and was quick to recover if ever a winger got past him. He was years ahead of his time because he also liked to get forward. He was the first of the attacking full backs and would gallop up the wing for a shot or a cross. Hugh Shaw didn't like it when Jock went forward but he always got back and never shirked the defensive side of the game. The Scotland selectors recognised Jock's talent and they picked him for his country on several occasions.

Jock was usually partnered at full back by either Jimmy Cairns or Hugh Howie. Jimmy was a no-frills, rock-solid defender, while Hugh had a bit more football in him and could also play successfully in other positions. Hugh was another who won Scotland caps.

Our centre half John Paterson had the lot. He was good in the air, sure in the tackle, read the game well and had a lot of pace. The only thing which stopped John winning full Scotland caps was his birthplace.

His dad was in the army and stationed in Colchester, so John was born down there. Even though both his parents were Scottish through and through, being born in England was enough in those days to stop a player being chosen for Scotland.

The same thing happened a few years later to Joe Baker, of course. Joe was born in Liverpool but was a Scot in every other way. Due to the regulations of the time, though, he had to play his international football for England rather than Scotland.

John Paterson was one of my best friends at Easter Road. John was my best man and I was his. We also played a lot of golf together. John's course was Glencorse in Penicuik and he was a fair player. John's son Craig followed in his footsteps as a Hibs centre half in the 1980s. Craig was a very similar player to his dad, which tells you that he must have been pretty good.

Our half backs were Bobby Combe and Archie Buchanan. Bobby was a forward at heart but because of the Famous Five he had to play his football further back in our great team. Mind you, when any of the forwards got injured Bobby stepped in and did an excellent job. He was short and stocky and always busy. He could tackle hard and pass well and got his share of goals. He was somebody else who got caps for Scotland. Bobby was very friendly with Gordon Smith.

As I have already mentioned, Archie Buchanan and I went back a long way. We had known each other from childhood and got on really well on and off the park. Archie was a quiet man but a top footballer. He was underrated by the media and perhaps by some of the fans as well. Every single player at Easter Road, though, knew how important Archie was to the success of our team. Although he played right half, he was left-footed. He specialised in cutting infield from the right and sending a reverse pass with his left foot inside the full back to Gordon Smith. This move brought us a lot of goals.

Then there was the Famous Five. We were all very different people but we gelled naturally on the field. We didn't mix as a separate group off the field and we didn't do anything special as a forward line in the way of training. We were just five attackers who came together and combined perfectly.

Gordon Smith on the right wing was indescribably good. I can't find words to tell you just how special a player he was. He had pace and skill, was a great crosser with either foot and could score goals. He got around 400 goals for Hibs, which is some record for a winger.

Gordon even scored a few with his head although heading wasn't his strength. I used to kid him on that he shut his eyes when he headed the ball. He was also a brave player. He didn't have a physical side to his game (he didn't need to) but he was never intimidated by full backs who tried to give him the treatment. One such player was the Hearts full back Tom McKenzie. McKenzie was a rugged individual who caused Gordon more trouble than most. In truth if Gordon had been content to put the ball past McKenzie and run, his pace would have left him for dead. However, because people said that McKenzie could handle him, Gordon felt that he had a point to prove when he came up against him. He would try to beat him in elaborate ways rather than just keeping it simple.

This allowed 'big Tam' to stick close to Gordon and get the better of him. Mind you, it wasn't all one way, as Gordon had plenty of good days against McKenzie as well. The Hearts full back was definitely not Gordon's favourite opponent, though, and he certainly made his physical presence felt in his tussles with our superstar skipper. Gordon was once involved in a car crash in East Lothian. He was covered in bruises and a bit dazed when the police arrived. He asked the police officers where he was and they told him that he was in Cockenzie. 'God,' said Gordon. 'If it's not McKenzie, it's Cockenzie!'

Opposition fans used to give Gordon a hard time, but that only goes to show how much they respected and feared him. Stanley Matthews was the top man in England in our time and was renowned all over the world. Dribbling and crossing were Stan's specialities. Gordon could match him in those departments and he scored a lot more goals.

Gordon won eighteen caps for Scotland but it should have been 118. Because he was a reserved man, it took time for Gordon to settle into an environment. He was never given that time with

Scotland. Gordon's caps were spread over thirteen years, which shows how long his ability was recognised for. It also shows that he was rarely given a proper run of games to prove his worth. In truth, he had nothing to prove. His talent and his record spoke for themselves. His treatment at international level was nothing short of scandalous. Gordon Smith was a quiet, modest genius and the best player I ever played with.

Alan Gilzean, the outstanding Dundee, Tottenham and Scotland centre forward, recently picked his all-time great Scotland team for a national newspaper. Gilzean included Gordon in his side and commented, 'When I played with Gordon Smith at Dundee, he was thirty-eight years old but still exuded class. What he must have been like at his peak I can only begin to imagine.' Well, I'll help your imagination along Alan. He was special, very special indeed.

Gordon's inside partner was Bobby Johnstone. Nicker was another truly great player. He was small and not given to too much chasing back, but on the ball he was magnificent. Bobby drifted past opponents with ease and sprayed superb passes around which helped to make goals for the rest of us. At a time when Scottish football was full of silky, scheming inside forwards, Bobby Johnstone stood above all the rest. He played regularly for Scotland and scored goals for both club and country. Bobby's goals usually came from close range, but he was an assured finisher.

Eddie Turnbull was the perfect complement to Bobby. Eddie supplied the industry which Bobby lacked. He was tireless and was up and down the park non-stop throughout every game. Eddie made his tackles and passes and, of course, scored a lot of goals with that rocket shot of his. He had plenty to say and drove the rest of us on with his advice, which was usually colourfully expressed. Eddie had served in the navy during the war and his turn of phrase was as salty as the seas he had sailed on. Eddie also won international honours. In my opinion he should have had more caps than he got, but the selectors had their own ideas and their knowledge of football wasn't as foolproof as they seemed to think it was.

Willie Ormond on our left wing was another great player. Willie was a bundle of fun and one of those who made our dressing room the happy place it was. Willie was always up to something. I remember one time when we were staying in the Marine Hotel in North Berwick. A crowd of us were in Willie's room when he said, 'You cannae come to North Berwick without diving in.' He then climbed to the top of his wardrobe and did a swallow dive onto his bed which promptly collapsed. The rest of us collapsed as well – with laughter – but then the door opened and Hugh Shaw came in. Willie was lying flat on his face on top of the broken bed and we were struggling to keep a straight face. Hugh demanded an explanation but I can't remember what Willie came up with.

He came up with plenty on the park, though. His main weapon was pace and he would race past full backs and deliver a telling cross. He was a regular scorer too and he achieved all this by using only one foot – his left, of course.

Willie was yet another in our team who won Scotland caps and, again, we thought he should have got many more than he did. Willie had terrible luck with injuries. He broke his leg twice and had a lot of other injury problems as well. He always came back, though, and never shirked a challenge.

Eddie and Willie came from the Falkirk area as did Jimmy Cairns. They travelled to and from training together and were great friends. Bobby Johnstone was a Borderer, of course, but when he joined up at Easter Road, he was adopted by the 'Falkirk Squad' and became part of their group. They trained hard and gave their all on the park but it's fair to say that they enjoyed a wee refreshment or two when they were off it. Bobby was particularly partial to a few drinks. Jock Govan told me that Bobby would even go out on a Friday night before a game sometimes. Jock would go with him and make sure that he got home in one piece. It never affected Bobby the next day, though.

He obviously had a strong constitution and whether he had spent Friday night socialising or not, he was usually brilliant on a Saturday afternoon.

Then there was me. I could be falsely modest but I won't be. I think that I was a natural. I could run, I could dribble past players, I had a hard shot but could also place the ball in the net and I was exceptional in the air for a player of just about five feet eight inches tall. I also had a big heart and never gave defenders a minute's peace. I scored an awful lot of goals but I laid on a fair few for my teammates as well. In many ways, I got more satisfaction from creating a goal for another member of 'The Five', as this showed that I had an all-round game.

I was a terrier on the park but I always played it clean. There's a big difference between being hard and being dirty. That was true of a lot of the players I came up against as well. Willie Woodburn of Rangers was my toughest opponent. He was one hard man but, in my opinion, he was always scrupulously fair. We had some great tussles and I came out on top on plenty of occasions but I never had cause for complaint after a match. Apart from his playing attributes, Willie wasn't averse to a little gamesmanship. He would try to distract me from my game by asking after my dad or enquiring how Kitty was. It never worked, though. I was always focused on the park and I was especially focused in the big games.

Willie and the rest of the Rangers boys used to call me 'Niggles', as they thought that I was always snapping at their heels and that I had plenty to say for myself. I think they meant it as a compliment. I certainly took it as one! I loved winding the Rangers lads up. I would ask them during breaks in play what bonus they were on to beat us. When they told me that they would get £20 for a win, I would reply, 'Is that all? We're on £100 per man.' It wasn't true but they believed me and I honestly think it put them off their game.

It is well documented, of course, that Willie was the first Scottish player to be suspended *sine die* by the SFA. This came after he headbutted an opponent, which was an uncharacteristic aberration. It appeared to be an overreaction on the SFA's part and they later lifted the ban. Willie never returned to playing, though. I think that, as a man of principle, he was making a point to the game's governing body.

Another opponent to reckon with was Davie Mackay of Hearts. Davie went on to have a great career with Tottenham, of course, and is remembered for the iconic photograph of him grabbing Billy Bremner of Leeds by the front of his jersey and lifting him off the ground. Most people didn't mess with Davie, but Ned Turnbull did once. Davie was on the brutal side of hard, although again his tackling was fair most of the time. In one derby match, though, he angered Eddie, who squared up to him and complained about one of Mackay's tackles. Davie's response was straight to the point. He said, 'If you think that was bad, wait till you feel the next one.' It was not often that Eddie Turnbull was lost for words, on or off a football pitch, but Mackay's riposte that day momentarily left Ned speechless.

I was the most capped member of the great Hibs team I played in and I loved playing for Scotland. The bigger the occasion, the better I played – and maybe that is why I took to international football so quickly and so successfully. My temperament was a big part of my armoury. Nothing fazed me. Wembley or Ochilview came the same to me. I wanted to play well and come out on top in every game I played and I approached all matches and all opponents in the same way – with a total will to win and complete self-belief. I was also brave and never afraid to put my head in where it hurt. Courage definitely gives your game an extra edge when you are a centre forward.

That then was the Hibs team which went into season 1951-52, looking to defend its league title. Although the Famous Five got most of the attention, we were a team in every way. I remember a press photographer coming into the dressing room and asking the five forwards to sit together and pose for a picture. Jock

Govan wasn't best pleased and said sarcastically, 'Oh look lads, the *team* is getting its photo taken again.'

I think the attention the five of us got did occasionally annoy the rest of our colleagues and I could understand that. The press may have underestimated the contribution which the rest of our team made, but we in the Famous Five never did. We knew that we had great players behind us and we knew too that we couldn't possibly have enjoyed the success we did without the tremendous support they gave us.

In 1951 the government decided that it was time to cheer the nation up after the austere post-war years that everyone in the country had endured. They came up with the Festival of Britain, which was a series of events and exhibitions across the country, intended to provide entertainment and excitement for everyone. Part of all this was a Festival Football Cup. It was played in summer in very, very hot weather and Hibs didn't win it. In fact, one newspaper said that our best passing move of the competition was when 'Trainer McColl passed a cold sponge to Smith, who passed it on to Reilly and so it went on until it had gone round the whole team'. That was a bit harsh but we certainly weren't at our best in this competition.

We didn't play well in our League Cup section, either, when that competition got under way. We only won two of our six qualifying games and didn't make the quarter-finals. I am not sure what the problem was, but we all realised that we had to get down to business fast when the league campaign got going or the season was in danger of running away from us.

We did just that by beating Raith Rovers at Stark's Park in our opener. Aberdeen were the first league visitors to Easter Road and it was a gala occasion as we unfurled our league flag before the kick-off. We were in top form and were 4–1 up with eighteen minutes to go. Not only that but Aberdeen were down to ten men. I had scored two goals and was on top of the world, but not for long. In true Hibs fashion, we eased off and somehow allowed the Dons to score three goals including a last-minute equaliser. Once again shades of Hibs v Motherwell at Fir Park in 2010!

It was on to Tynecastle next for the first derby of the season and again we should have beaten Hearts but couldn't. The game ended 1–1 and I scored one of my trademark headers. The press made us the better team but once more Hearts denied us the win we wanted. I had a personal victory though. The Scotland selectors were about to meet to pick the team to play Ireland in Belfast and there were two contenders for the centre-forward position. It was between Willie Bauld and me so the game at Tynecastle was billed as the 'Battle of the Spearheads'. I definitely came out on top. One match report said: 'Reilly was back to his best – tenacious and clever. His distribution was well nigh perfect and his headed goal would have done credit to Jimmy McGrory in his prime.' The same reporter also recorded that, 'Smith did everything with the leisurely ease and effective grace of a master.' When the Scotland team was announced, Bobby Johnstone and I were in but again there was no place for Gordon.

Scotland beat Ireland 3–0. Wee Bobby got two goals and the man of the match was Tommy Orr of Morton. I didn't score but played well and was given four stars in the post-match evaluation. My rating was bettered only by Tommy, who got the full five stars. Our goalie was Jimmy Cowan of Morton, who was one of the very best.

When we returned to league duty, we faced Jimmy and his Cappielow colleagues at Easter Road. Jimmy was in amazing form as he did his utmost to keep a clean sheet. His performance was described as 'miraculous' with 'lightning reflexes and flashes of goalkeeping genius'. It took something special on Hibs' part to finally beat him. Gordon Smith passed to me, I back-heeled the ball in the air across goal and Willie Ormond headed it in. Not even Jimmy Cowan could keep that one out.

We then hammered Partick 5–0. I got two but Gordon was the top man. His performance inspired this eulogy in the press: 'The genius of Gordon Smith stood out. When he finally stops playing, they should returf the pitch because Easter Road will never see his like again.'

The Scottish selectors then announced our team to play the English League. Again Gordon was left out. I was moved to the left wing and Tommy Orr was rewarded for his outstanding performance against Ireland by being dropped. What can you say?

We next moved on to Parkhead and drew 1–1 with Celtic. We were still unbeaten in the league and so good were we at that time that a draw with Celtic on their own ground was described as 'an off day for Hibs'.

I was involved in something different around that time. I was invited to join Dr W. G. Clark, Edinburgh's City Medical Officer of Health, at the State Cinema in Leith to introduce a series of health films which the doctor had produced. John Paterson came with me and 1,300 turned out to listen to us and watch the film. I gave a talk on our training routine, which consisted back then of exercises, sprints, lapping the track for stamina and some ball work. We then answered questions from the audience. One report quotes me as saying: 'If you neglect your health, you will become a burden on the community.' I am sure this was good advice but it sounds a bit serious for a twenty-three-year-old footballer to be coming out with.

The Scottish League lost 2–1 to the English League at Sheffield. Willie Waddell missed a penalty and I came up against him again the following weekend when Rangers came to Easter Road. Even this early in the season, this was a major match and we did everything but win it. According to Jack Harkness in the *Sunday Post*, 'If this game had sizzled any longer, we would have had to have called the Fire Brigade.' Hibs had 'pummelled, thrashed and hammered Rangers' famous defence as never before'. Yet with six minutes to go we were a goal down. Thankfully at that point Gordon Smith popped up with an equaliser and that's how the game finished. Harkness concluded that the 50,000 crowd inside Easter Road had been treated to 'the fastest, slickest, heart-throbbing, non-stop game of the season'. They knew how to write in those days!

We then lost in the league for the first time to Morton at Cappielow. I scored and had a goal chalked off and Eddie Turnbull missed a penalty. Jimmy Cowan again broke our hearts as we lost 2–1. This time Jimmy was *super*-miraculous'. He apparently had 'magnetic hands' and was an 'electric diving figure'.

I was restored to centre forward in the Scotland team to play Wales at Hampden. This made me Hibs' most capped player. Including League internationals I had now been chosen for my country twenty-one times, beating one of our great goalkeepers, Harry Rennie, who had gained twenty caps. I had scored twelve goals in these games. In the event, it wasn't a happy occasion for me as we lost to an Ivor Allchurch goal in front of the usual massive Hampden crowd, to spark a press inquest. Here's what one journalist had to say: 'If Waddell goes, then Gordon Smith must come in. Despite his temperament, he is one of the greatest thoroughbreds the game has ever known and has a football repertoire no other forward in the country can match.' I am not so sure about the 'temperament' bit, but I fully agree with the rest.

Another writer, the highly regarded Andy Cunningham, declared that it was time for Scotland to appoint a manager to take charge of the team. He was dead right. He was actually ahead of his time because he advocated that the selectors should choose a 'national pool' of players at the start of each season to avoid the non-stop chopping and changing which went on at that time. That wasn't a bad call either.

Scotland fans may have been discontented but Hibs fans weren't. Forty-two thousand turned up to watch us take on East Fife, who were a top team at that time. We staged a late rally to win 4–2 and Eddie Turnbull got his first goal of the season – which was surprising, as Eddie was usually a regular scorer. We had no floodlights at that time and it was dusk before this game ended. I did my best to solve the visibility problem as 'Firefly Reilly lit up the half-darkness'. The match report concluded, 'Hibs are not yet the sweet moving machine of last season.'

We showed resilience when we won 2–0 at Airdrie, though. The press reckoned that, 'if you want to see a team of fighters, you come to Broomfield'. That was one way of looking at it. We saw it a little differently. Let's just say that Tommy Younger, Eddie Turnbull, Willie Ormond and I all finished the game hirpling with injuries that were not self-inflicted, which made victory all the sweeter! Sadly, Willie broke his leg in this game. The only consolation was that it was his right leg and not his all-important left one.

We were on a roll now and beat Dundee 4–1 at Dens Park. Tommy Younger was in top form, 'diving all over the place'. I switched to goal-maker for the day but was infuriated by Dundee's offside trap. Time and again, I would judge my run perfectly and run through onto a pass. Every time the linesman's flag went up. He either wasn't very good at his job or he had a soft spot for Dundee. I could have scored a barrowload that day if the man with the flag had used his eyes. I got really annoyed and the papers accused me of petulance. I beg to differ. I was just pointing out to the linesman what I considered to be the error of his ways! I was back among the goals when we thrashed Queen of the South 5–0. Bobby Johnstone and I got two each and we were told: 'On this form Hibs are pukka champions. No one did better than Reilly and Johnstone – an irrepressible pair.'

This was again championship-winning form. As a team, we were at our absolute peak. We were the best team in Scotland and we knew it. The only thing which could stop us lifting a second successive league title was our own over-confidence and we were all determined that would not be the case.

I then took a break from playing and joined Jimmy Brown, the Hearts goalkeeper, for a Sports Forum at Central Hall in Tollcross. At that time forwards were allowed to shoulder-charge goalies. I was asked if I thought this practice should be outlawed.

I replied 'definitely not' and reinforced my point by shoulder-barging Jimmy out of his chair.

Our excellent form in the league carried over into Christmas with two more victories. We took four off St Mirren and five off Raith and we and everyone else knew that it was going to take a very special effort from Rangers or anyone else to wrest our championship from us. I brought my tally of goals for the season to double figures but wee Johnstone was again the man of the moment.

I know that the papers went over the top a bit back then, in terms of the flowery language they used, but this piece of seasonal writing takes a bit of beating: 'Bobby Johnstone was hanging around like a sprig of holly one minute and popping up in front of goal like a cracker the next.'

We were feeling unbeatable and I was in such a good mood that I even went along to the Christmas party of the Tynecastle Branch of the Hibs Supporters' Club. Not only did we have a supporters' branch in the heart of enemy territory; they held their festive bash in the Keir Hardie Hall in Bryson Road, the street where I had been brought up and where my mum and dad still lived.

I enjoyed my night, which was just as well because I wasn't going to take much pleasure from the next two matches. First we lost to Motherwell at Fir Park. We used to either hammer 'Well or catch them on the top of their form and lose to them. There never seemed to be any in-between.

This was one of Motherwell's good days and one of our bad ones. They got a penalty for a handball which 'nobody could see and even Motherwell were embarrassed by' and we had a goal chalked off and what looked like a cast-iron penalty claim waved aside. We were clearly feeling a sense of injustice and we let it get to us, as the hard-hitting Rex Kingsley in the *Sunday Mail* reported: 'Hibs played as if there was no justice in the world. A team feeling sorry for itself usually ends up with the right to be.' He was correct. We felt as if the whole world was against us and let our heads go down. That wasn't like us and it cost us dear.

We had no time to continue feeling hard done-by as Hearts were coming to Easter Road on New Year's Day. We had now gone five league matches without beating them and we were desperate to end that run with a resounding win of our own. Again it was not be. We lost 3–2 and again didn't get a bit of luck. If you think that's just me saying that, read what Waverley wrote in the next day's *Daily Record*: 'Hearts were the luckiest fellows in the world to win.' Even their manager Tommy Walker thought so, because he admitted after the match, 'We got so many breaks that I don't think Hibs deserved to lose.'

Lose we did, though, and it was hard to take. The game was played on a pitch covered with slushy snow, but it was a classic. Willie Bauld and I had another of our personal duels. This one ended even as we both scored twice. Jimmy Wardhaugh had got another for Hearts so they led as the game went into its last few minutes and we threw everything at them. Our big chance came with five minutes to go, when Bobby Johnstone went down in the box.

The referee this time was Jack Mowat, who was never afraid to point to the spot in Hibs' favour. He was the man, remember, who had awarded us three penalties in one game against Celtic. Eddie Turnbull had knocked in all three of them and now he had a chance to save us from losing undeservedly against Hearts yet again. Eddie scored an awful lot of penalties for Hibs, but he missed a few as well. This turned out to be one of his worst. He drove the ball straight at Jimmy Brown in the Hearts goal. It hit Brown's legs without him having to move and bounced to safety. There was still time for me to hit the bar with a header before Mr Mowat's whistle confirmed another lucky derby win for the men in maroon.

There was another controversial moment in the game. Alfie Conn tackled Gordon Smith on the touchline and sent him flying into the boundary wall. Gordon hit the wall so hard that he was knocked unconscious. Waverley reported that, 'Half the Hibs team was busy holding back the other half who seemed determined to get to close quarters with Conn.' Mr Mowat wagged his finger at Conn but he neither sent him off nor even booked him.

We weren't pleased about that when we got to the dressing room after the game. I was raging at Eddie Turnbull for his penalty miss. How could a man normally so good at taking spot kicks miss one that meant so much? I just couldn't understand it. We used to all hate to lose to Hearts but I honestly think that it hurt me more than the rest of the team. They had become Hibees but I had been born one. That was the difference.

Two successive defeats meant that our progress towards regaining the league flag was going to be less straightforward than we had anticipated. We were disappointed and furious with ourselves and took out our anger on our next two opponents. We thrashed Third Lanark 5–0 on their own ground and returned to Easter Road to massacre Stirling Albion 8–0. I scored hat-tricks in both games. The papers sang my praises with comments like: 'Lawrie Reilly is one of the most opportunistic forwards in Britain and the man who put Hibs back on the victory path with a hat-trick which was a fitting reward for a player who seldom lets a scoring chance pass.' I was just burning with frustration after our loss to Hearts and I took my feelings onto the park with me. I channelled all my pent-up disappointment into my game and was on fire. I was so charged up that no centre half had a hope of coping with me.

Before the game with Thirds, Hugh Shaw sold them Jimmy Cairns. Jimmy had dropped out of the first-team picture but we were sorry to see him go. One reporter wrote, 'Cairns had a happy-go-lucky nature combined with a bulldog spirit. He was a buoyant player on the field and a popular one off it.' He got it dead right. We were all disappointed to lose him.

In the game against Stirling Bobby Combe, who was standing in for Willie Ormond after his leg break, also notched up three goals. Bobby was again proving his versatility and his quality.

The crowd for the Stirling match was 17,000 fewer than had turned out for the New Year derby game, so our supporters were clearly still hurting after our latest defeat to Hearts. One last thing about the goal feast against Albion was that we got another penalty. Eddie Turnbull took it and blasted it home with ease. When the rest of the lads were slapping Eddie on the back, I was thinking, 'Why couldn't you have done that against the Hearts?'

We were right back in the groove now and played so well to beat Aberdeen at Pittodrie that the next day's match report declared that, 'Aberdeen will regard it as an honour only to be beaten 2–1 by a team which touched such heights.' That was more like it and we were able to celebrate our return to form at our annual dance. The club used to arrange this for the players, management, directors and their wives at the Balmoral Hotel (or the North British as it was in those days) and it was always a great night. It was extra special this year as James Miller, the Lord Provost of Edinburgh, came along and presented us with our league winners' medals from the previous season. Our chairman Harry Swan liked to make a speech and he had plenty to say on this occasion. First he thanked the Lord Provost and said, 'Your presence here tonight will inspire the team to retain our league title.' He then rightly praised our manager Hugh Shaw by telling him, 'Your unstinting devotion to our club inspires us all.' He finished by informing us players that, 'Ownership of a league medal is a very rare thing and something of which to be proud.'

We were proud but we didn't want league medals to be too rare. In fact we wanted another one very soon. The Lord Provost had praised us to the heights. He was of the opinion that, 'All citizens of Edinburgh want me to congratulate you on your achievements.' I am not sure what the Hearts fans thought of that, but we liked it and it made us even more determined to buckle down and hold on to our title. A little run in the Scottish Cup wouldn't be bad either.

We set about taking the necessary steps to keep the league flag at Easter Road by beating Partick Thistle 2–1 at a very foggy Firhill. Archie Buchanan got our winner with only five minutes to go. The fog was so bad that Harry Swan was sure that the goal had been scored by Gordon Smith – but no, it was Archie, one of our unsung heroes, who had come to the rescue. We played well in this game. One report singled out Gordon as 'the quintessence of soccer artistry' and said that the rest of us were 'brilliant individualists who seek only team glory'.

Whoever this anonymous scribe was, he knew his stuff. Our side was full of great individual players, but we were all prepared to put the good of the team before our own glory. By doing that, we enhanced our own performances and got credit anyway. We had inspiration but we also had perspiration. They, and we, were an irresistible combination.

Next, it was up for the cup. We had drawn Raith Rovers at Kirkcaldy. We had just beaten them 5–0 in the league but the cup tie turned out differently. The first game at Stark's Park was played on an iron-hard, icy pitch. There is still newsreel footage of that game available and it would never have been played nowadays. We drew 0–0 and had big Tommy Younger to thank for still being in the cup. Tommy kept us in it again in the replay at Easter Road, which again finished goalless. The second replay would be at a neutral ground and our hearts sank when the SFA chose Tynecastle as the venue.

Before then, we met Celtic in the league in front of 40,000 at Easter Road. Big Younger made his first mistake in months to gift Walsh a goal, but that didn't stop us winning 3–1. I headed our second after Eddie had fired in a thunderbolt free kick from the edge of the box and wee Bobby Johnstone got our third after a move featuring Gordon and me that the papers said should have been filmed and used 'for future generations to enjoy and learn from'. Things were going well in the league again, but could we be equally successful in the Scottish Cup?

It was time to head for Tynecastle for the cup replay. You won't need me to tell you what happened. The pitch was a mud heap and Raith played above themselves. They beat us 4–1. This was a team, don't forget, whom we had totally outclassed just a few weeks earlier. One report described our defenders as being like 'drunks on a skating rink'. I used to get furious when our defenders had a bad day – which didn't happen that often I have to say. Apparently I would stand with my hands on my hips, glowering at the men at the back while shaking my head and muttering about their incompetence. Jock Govan used to laugh and say, 'There he goes again.' No doubt my head-shaking routine was in full flow that day.

One report summed up this match by saying, 'Once again in the Scottish Cup, Hibs find themselves in the wilderness of the ousted.' That was one way of putting it. You could describe it but you just couldn't explain it. It was as mystifying as it was disappointing.

We had no option but to focus all our energies on winning the league and we had no time to feel sorry for ourselves either, as our next port of call was Ibrox. As usual, the light blues were our main challengers for the title and we were determined after our cup disaster that there would be no more slip-ups. It ended 2–2 and I had an eventful afternoon.

I scored one of my best ever goals when I out-jumped Willie Woodburn and headed the ball past him before running on to it and chipping it past Bobby Brown in the Rangers goal as he came out to meet me. I then got booked after an 'extraordinary incident'. John Prentice brought me down well inside the box but the referee gave a free kick outside the area. I was so annoyed that I chased after Prentice in anger. Fortunately my teammates caught me before I did him any damage. Come to think of it, I probably should have gone after the ref.

Eddie Turnbull had scored another penalty (why couldn't he have done that against Hearts?) to give us the lead and we may not have won the game but I did win a bet. Sammy Cox, the Rangers left back, was a good pal of mine from playing for Scotland. Sammy had told me before the game that his wife was about to give birth. I told him that it would be a boy but he insisted that it would be a girl. We struck a bet and at full time a steward came on the field to tell Sammy that he had a son. I was quick to give him the old 'I told you so' routine and he had to pay me the princely sum of two shillings and sixpence which is 12.5 pence in current money. Today, Sammy probably wouldn't have been playing as he would have been at his wife's side for the birth. That wasn't how it was in the early 1950s, though.

As I left Ibrox, I could reflect on a day which had been anything but dull. I had scored a goal 'for memory corner', had my name taken and won a bet. On balance, I had probably come out on the positive side.

Now came two home league games in a row, both of which we won as we closed in on our third league flag in five years. We scored nine goals in the process. I was in top form, getting four goals in these matches to take my total for the season to twenty-five. Bobby Johnstone wasn't far behind with twenty-three. One report was headed simply 'The Genius of Reilly'. That was nice to read, I can tell you. Was I a genius? Well, that is really for others to say. All I know is that newspapers were understated in those days and didn't throw praise around lightly, so I must have had something going for me.

We used to play a lot of prestige friendlies against English teams in those days and these games were taken very seriously. We now embarked on a programme of three such matches as league fixtures were on hold due to the next round of the Scottish Cup – which, I don't need to remind you, didn't feature Hibs.

We began by travelling to Doncaster to play the first match under their newly installed floodlights. We won 3–0 in front of 18,000 fans and their manager Peter Docherty, who had been an outstanding inside forward for Ireland in his playing days, told us after the match that he had seriously considered sending his players out wearing eyeshades to combat the glare of the lights. This was our fourth experience of floodlit football. The previous three games had been in Paris, Berne and, wait for it, Stenhousemuir!

We then moved on to Manchester and easily beat Manchester City 4–1 at Maine Road. Jim Souness, who was deputising for the injured Gordon Smith, got all four goals to show how good some of our fringe players were. The *Manchester Evening News* were so impressed with us that they wrote 'Manchester fans did a Sinatra swoon in front of the green jerseys.' Incidentally, City's consolation goal was scored by Don Revie, who went on to manage Leeds United with so much success.

Manchester United completed the trio of top English teams that we had tested ourselves against. The headline says it all: 'Shock then Hibs make it a Classic'. The shock referred to was an early goal for United by Roger Byrne. Byrne, of course, became United captain and an England regular before tragically losing his life in the Munich air crash of 1958.

His goal that day simply galvanised us and Eddie Turnbull crashed in an equaliser with a terrific shot. We had obviously impressed the Manchester public again because lots of them wrote letters to Hugh Shaw saying things like 'Thanks Hibs, you've done Scotland proud' and 'I have seldom seen such attractive football as Hibs displayed.' The best was, 'I was amazed by the wonderful football Hibs served up.' Hugh Shaw was so pleased that he had the letters printed in the local press.

Maybe all that praise went to our heads because we managed to lose our next game to Queen of the South by no less than 5–2. My hands would certainly have been on my hips that day and my head would have been shaking good style. Gordon Smith was back on the right wing but not even that could stop us being embarrassed. In fact one Hibs fan in the crowd, with his tongue firmly in his cheek, shouted, 'Send for Jim Souness.' If we had thought that the league was in the bag then this was a wake-up call for us. We had succumbed to exactly the type of over-confidence that we had promised ourselves we would avoid.

We got back on the rails with a 4–1 win over St Mirren. Willie Ormond had now recovered from his latest leg-break and created three of our goals with 'picture perfection crosses'. I got one of those goals and Willie crowned his display with the fourth goal.

Then came some big news. Scotland's team to play England at Hampden was announced and it included no less than three of the Famous Five in the forward line. To the great rejoicing of the Hibs faithful, Bobby Johnstone and I were joined in the team by Gordon Smith.

The England game was the main event of every season and was eagerly awaited. Sadly, this one turned into a bit of an anti-climax as we lost 2–1. It was a good day for Gordon and me, though. I scored Scotland's goal and 'Reilly's leadership was perfect and his tenacity was tireless.'

Gordon Smith had impressed the men in the press box too because they considered that 'Smith had his best international ever. His crosses were perfect. He is here to stay'.

Playing against England inspired me. They had some great players in those days – players who were miles better than today's so-called 'Golden Generation'. Yet we Scots were never in awe of them. We just wanted to beat them more than any other country and quite often we did. One of England's greatest ever players was Tom Finney. We were fierce rivals on the park but got on really well off it. I would go as far as saying that Tom was the best player that I ever played against. He just shaded it over Stanley Matthews for me. Tom and Stan could both create goals but Tom could score them as well. He could also play in a number of positions whereas Stan was purely and simply a right winger. Tom and I are still in touch. When a gala dinner was held in Preston to mark Tom's great career, I was privileged to be the only player from a Scottish club who was invited to attend. Tom and his colleagues may have got the better of us at Hampden this time but that certainly wasn't always the case.

Stanley Matthews told me a story of another time when Scotland played England at Hampden back in the 1930s and the final outcome was rather different. England were 1–0 up at half-time and well in command. They came out first for the second half and the Scots made them wait on the park. While England tried to keep warm, the Scottish team sat in the dressing room and the pipe band marched up and down the centre of the pitch whipping the crowd into a patriotic frenzy. When the Scots eventually appeared, the roar was thunderous. Stan said that he now knew what the Hampden Roar sounded like and he had never heard a sound like it in his career. When Scotland equalised, the noise levels went up a few more decibels. By this time, Matthews was convinced that no set of football supporters could be any louder than this. When the Scots scored the winning goal, he discovered that actually they could, as the crescendo of noise increased even further.

Back at Easter Road, we were closing in on the second successive league title which had been in our sights since August. Each team played thirty league matches in a season then and we had completed twenty-eight. We were two points ahead of Rangers, with a superior goal average, so two more points at home to Dundee in our second last game would secure the championship for us.

We had no intention of slipping up but didn't underestimate our opponents. Dundee had reached the Scottish Cup Final and had no intention of coming to Easter Road just to make up the numbers. They emphasised that by taking the lead in only four minutes. Only a great save by Tommy Younger to keep out a vicious shot by Billy Steel prevented us falling even further behind.

We rallied though and Willie Ormond's purple patch continued. Willie was clearly intent on making up for the time he had lost to injury. He scored two goals, one a bullet header and the other a shot, to give us the lead. The ever-reliable Bobby Combe added another just after half-time and it was now mainly a matter of how many more goals we could add before full time. In the event, we didn't get any other goals due to 'Dundee's defenders expertly employing the offside trap to the discomfort of Reilly and Co. and the ire of the crowd'. Yes, the Dens Park defence was at it again and their negative tactics stopped me from scoring on a night when I definitely would have liked to have notched up a goal.

I didn't let it worry me, though, because we had proved what we knew to be the case. We considered ourselves the best team in Scotland and it was official once again. We could be inconsistent and we would occasionally lose to inferior teams but at our best we were unstoppable. These days when a team wins the league the celebrations are high-profile. The trophy is presented on the pitch, music is blasted over the public address system, the champions make a lap of honour and the fans go wild. Television and radio reporters come on to the field and interview the players and all in all, there's a tremendous fuss. Quite right too. When a team become champions, they deserve the acclaim of the crowd and they have every right to show emotion.

It was a lot more low-key in 1952. When we won the league we congratulated each other, waved to the crowd and left the field. We got changed into our street clothes, went up to the boardroom and listened to a speech from Harry Swan. Gordon Smith and Hugh Shaw shook hands for the cameras, a drink or two was consumed and then we all went home!

We had one game left against Motherwell at home. They had caused us problems in the past, but we were determined that they wouldn't do so this time. Thirty-five thousand turned up at Easter Road on a Wednesday night and they witnessed the new champions in full flow. We won 3–1 but it should have been five because both Eddie Turnbull and Willie Ormond missed penalties. This time the spot-kick failures didn't cause us any problems because Willie, Bobby Combe and I got the goals which enabled us to win comfortably and finish a triumphant season in style. We had won twenty games out of thirty and lost only five. Once again we had failed to beat Hearts and we had underperformed in the cups. These blemishes apart, it had been another magnificent season. The newspapers all paid tribute to us and their general conclusion was that we were not only the best team in Scotland but also the best in Britain.

Tottenham Hotspur might have challenged that claim, except that we went down to London after winning the league and totally outplayed them. We won 2–1 and Gordon Smith got both our goals. I created the second by dribbling round the Spurs goalkeeper Ted Ditchburn and sliding the ball across goal for Gordon to tap it in. He was so pleased with my 'assist' that he extended his hand to congratulate me while he was in the act of knocking the ball into the net. Our two main men at White Hart Lane, though, were Jock Govan and Archie Buchanan, who showed the English public that there was a lot more to Hibs than the Famous Five. Thirty-three thousand turned up to watch us win in the capital. On the other side of the city, Hearts were losing 2–1 to Chelsea at Stamford Bridge. Only 7,000 bothered to make the journey for that one.

We had time for one more friendly before Gordon and I went off to play for Scotland again. This time it was Bolton Wanderers at Easter Road.

Nat Lofthouse, their centre forward, was also the leader of the England attack, which gave the game a bit of added spice. As it turned out both Nat and I scored twice in a 2–2 draw so it was very much honours even.

Scotland beat the USA 6–0 at Hampden in front of an amazing crowd of 107,765. It was a great night for me as I got my first hat-trick for my country, including two goals in a minute. Gordon Smith didn't have his best game and in the press next day one scribe declared, 'Gordon Smith is definitely not the best outside right in Scotland.' He was probably the same man who had hailed Gordon's performance against England only a few weeks earlier.

An end-of-season feature in Edinburgh back in the 1950s was the East of Scotland Shield Final between Hibs and Hearts. It was taken really seriously. Both sides fielded full-strength teams and there was always a big crowd. We finished our domestic season the way we wanted to by going to Tynecastle and winning 3–0. That was with ten men as well, for we played without Gordon Smith for eighty-five minutes. I got my usual Tynecastle goal and Bobby Combe, who was in for the injured Bobby Johnstone, again showed his class, with two of his own.

The headline of 'Hibs Ten Give Hearts a Soccer Lesson' said it all. In truth we had outplayed them in most recent games without being able to finish them off. This time, to our great satisfaction, we did exactly that.

We might have finished off Hearts but we hadn't finished our season. As always with Hibs, we had a close season tour to look forward to. This time we were off to Holland and Germany. We beat a Dutch Select 4–2 before moving on to Germany to face Borussia Dortmund. Borussia had just beaten the current German League champions 9–0, so they were clearly a force to reckon with.

We had a great support as thousands of Scottish soldiers came across from their base in Wupperthal to cheer us on. Tommy Younger – who was still doing his national service in that same camp – was especially popular with the lads in uniform. We beat Dortmund 2–1 and I got both goals. My German isn't fantastic but I knew enough to be able to understand the next day's headline in the local paper which translated as 'Reilly's Masterly Display'. It was nice to have my talents recognised in a country other than my own and I knew that I was becoming a better centre forward with every game I played. I was still only twenty-three years old but I also knew that I still hadn't reached my peak. I believed that I was good but I was certain that my best was still to come.

We had two more games against Werder Bremen and St Pauli. I could only describe the refereeing in both games as laughable. I certainly thought it was less than neutral. We won the first and drew the second. Poor Willie Ormond got sent off against Bremen. It was a ridiculous decision and Willie was astounded. He pleaded with the referee to stay on, saying, 'Please give me another chance.' The boys thought this was hilarious and wound Willie up about it for months afterwards. Every time any of us passed him in the corridor at Easter Road, we would put an impassioned look on our face and say in a wheedling voice, 'Please, don't send me off. I beg you, please give me another chance.' It was childish, I know, but at the time we thought it was hilarious. I am sure Willie didn't think that it was quite so amusing.

Rex Kingsley of the *Sunday Mail* accompanied us on tour and was full of praise for us. In his end-of-tour report, he wrote in his usual straight-shooting way: 'Hibs have reached unbelievable heights in Germany, sometimes against fourteen opponents including the referee and linesmen.'

Believe it or not, we were supposed to move on from Germany to start another tour in Argentina. Thankfully common sense prevailed. Quite a few of the lads were carrying injuries and we were all exhausted. Harry Swan wouldn't have liked declining the money on offer for touring South America (it was £12,500, which was a fortune at that time) but he made the right decision in calling the tour off.

There was no respite for me, as I had to travel to Denmark to join Scotland for their summer tour of Scandinavia. After my best ever season at centre forward the Scotland selectors picked me at outside right, which wasn't entirely logical. Mind you, it did allow me to complete a unique hat-trick. I had now represented Scotland at outside right, outside left and centre forward. I don't think anyone else has managed that before or since.

Although there were 40,000 Danes in the ground, the game felt more like a home match. The Royal Scots Fusiliers pipe band played before the game and Highland dancers entertained the crowd at half-time. The Hibs party had stopped off on their way home from Germany to watch the game, which was a great boost. I got the winning goal too, with a diving header from a Billy Liddell corner – so for me it was definitely 'Wonderful, wonderful Copenhagen'.

Things weren't quite so wonderful when we moved on to Sweden and lost 2–1. That ended a highly successful season for me on both a personal and team level. I was really tired and pleased to be going home. There were still nearly three months to go until the new season kicked off in August, so I would have plenty of time to recharge my batteries.

On the flight back to Edinburgh, I sat back, closed my eyes and reflected on just how good it was to be part of a Hibs team which had won the Scottish League three times in five years.

10

IN THE FORM OF MY LIFE

The weeks leading up to season 1952-53 provided the relaxation I needed after a long, hard campaign with Hibs and Scotland. I was kept busy with a whole variety of activities. I teamed up with colleagues to play in a charity golf tournament, played cricket for Hibs against Leith Franklin and didn't do at all badly ('Reilly was a more than competent wicketkeeper') and presented the winner's cup to Miss Portobello 1952, which was no hardship. Kitty and I were getting used to married life and were thoroughly enjoying it. All in all, it had been a very pleasant summer break.

Down at Easter Road, we had our eyes on winning a cup or two as well. The pre-season previews in the newspapers were all asking if Hibs could keep up their successful run. We were sure that we could. Mind you, we lost one of our stalwarts just before the season proper got underway as Jimmy Kerr moved to Queen of the South. Jimmy had been a great goalkeeper for Hibs but had lost his first-team place to Tommy Younger and wanted to get back to playing regular top-team football. The Hibs Supporters' Association held a presentation evening for Jimmy to mark his fifteen years with the club. What did they give him in those less health-conscious days – an inscribed cigarette case and lighter! Not really what you would think was an appropriate gift for a professional sportsman.

Having missed out on League Cup qualification the previous season, we were determined to win our section this time. It wouldn't be easy, though, because we had been drawn in the

A very young Prince Philip wishes me well before Scotland play England at Wembley in 1949. His comments brought me luck as I scored in our 3-1 win.

Bobby Johnstone and I leave the field after giving our all in one of the many floodlit friendly matches which Hibs played in the 1950s.

Reilly at the charge in the days when centre forwards got away with using their shoulders on goalkeepers.

Five-a-side time. Rangers and Hibs line up at Tynecastle before the final of one of the five-a-side tournaments that were so popular in post-war football.

"The Evening Dispatch"

The Duff with the smooth. Challenging Willie Duff, the Hearts goalkeeper in an Easter Road derby.

Back from the brink. I return to football as captain of Hibs reserves at Tynecastle after a nine month lay-off which had threatened my career.

On the road to recovery.
Regaining my strength
on the SS Gothland
after being laid low with
pleurisy and pneumonia.

A beauty from Bobby. I look on as
Bobby Combe, a much underrated
member of Hibs Championship
winning team, hits the target
against Raith Rovers.

Rising to the occasion. I was
always good in the air. Here I
wince with effort as I challenge
the Dundee goalkeeper. Look
how much higher off the
ground my feet are.

The Boys for Brazil. The Hibs team (in their specially designed summer strips) wave to the crowd during one of the matches in our groundbreaking tour of Brazil in 1953.

In the swing. Hugh Howie and Bobby Johnstone look on as I demonstrate my prowess with a golf club.

The Raith Rovers' defence looks on helplessly as I hit the target with the old Easter Road terracing in the background.

Pick that one out! I power a header past Hearts' Willie Duff at Tynecastle.

Five of the Very Best. The Famous Five line up for the cameras prior to a match in the early 1950s.

A Cowan Clutch. The great Morton and Scotland goalkeeper stops me from scoring.

You've either got or you haven't got style. Striking a pose in training. Note my initials on the side of what passed for trainers in the early 1950s. A touch of class or what?

They don't make them like that anymore. I take delivery of my new Ford Anglia car.

What a feeling! Scoring against England at Hampden.

My favourite distance. Gil Merrick and Alf Ramsey can't stop me scoring my first goal for Scotland against England in 1953. My second goal in this match earned me the nickname 'Last Minute Reilly'.

The Beginning of the End. I am helped off Windsor Park, Belfast, with the knee injury which was to bring my career to a premature conclusion.

Penalty Ref! Brought down at Hampden by England goalie Gil Merrick as Alf Ramsey and Billy Wright look on.

I've waited a long time for this! Former England goalie Gil Merrick gets his own back for all those goals I put past him at Hampden and Wembley at a recent footballing function.

The friendliest of rivals. Sir Tom Finney and I meet up again before a recent gala dinner to celebrate his illustrious career. Even after all these years, we still both play to win!

Farewell to the licensed trade. With Iris and friends on my last day as mine host of The Bowlers' Rest. Behind us from left to right are Willie Clark, Eddie Turnbull, Jimmy Kane, Gordon Smith, Tommy Preston, Willie Woodburn and John Paterson.

same group as Celtic. We started by beating Partick Thistle 5–1 and I got what was called a 'perfect hat-trick'. I managed to score with my right foot, my left foot and my head, which wasn't a bad way to start the season.

Next we played Celtic at Parkhead. We had much the better of them at that time, so they had obviously decided that it was time for a new approach. The papers used restrained language when they called Celtic's play 'tousy'. We were less tactful. We considered that we had been kicked off the park. One Celtic player even spoke to the press anonymously and congratulated Hibs on showing restraint.

When Celtic came to Easter Road for the return match, we had to win to qualify for the quarter-finals. We did just that in front of a crowd of 60,000. We won 3–0 and I got two of them, including one with 'the famous Reilly head'.

Our good start to the season had earned Eddie Turnbull, Willie Ormond and me places in the Scottish League team to face the Irish League in Belfast. Just as well, because the Irish gave us a real fright before Willie and I stepped in with two goals each to seal a 5–1 win. The match report concluded that 'six minutes of Hibernian fire turned potential Scottish defeat into victory.'

We didn't make the best of starts to our league campaign as we lost 3–1 at home to Queen of the South. It was Gordon Smith's 500th appearance and he got our goal but it wasn't the happy occasion he and we had hoped for. It was a very sad day indeed for Bobby Johnstone. Bobby's dad died a few hours before the game. He bravely turned out but not surprisingly was a shadow of his normal self.

When we returned to cup duty, things went much better. We beat Morton 6–0 at Cappielow in the first leg of the League Cup quarter-final. I didn't score but was judged 'the best forward afield'. Gordon Smith got on the scoresheet and was considered to be at his 'gayest'. Smith's nickname, of course, was 'The Gay Gordon' at a time when the word simply meant 'full of joy'.

Another teammate received recognition at this point. My pal

John Paterson was chosen to play for the Scottish League against the Welsh League. The selectors could pick any player who represented a Scottish club, but usually restricted themselves to Scots-born players. They broke with tradition this time, though, and selected John even though he had been born in Colchester. Everyone at Easter Road was delighted for the big man. The press reported John's inclusion as follows: 'His heart lies in Scotland. What's more, he even served in the Black Watch during the war.' There was no doubt then that John was very much a true Scotsman.

Harry Swan had rewarded Gordon Smith for his great service to the club with a testimonial match against Manchester United at Easter Road. Thirty thousand turned out on a September Monday evening for a marvellous match, which we won by the resounding margin of 7–3. To everyone's delight, Gordon scored a goal, I got a couple and so did Eddie Turnbull. Both Eddie's goals came from the penalty spot and were awarded by a certain Jack Mowat. You might be thinking that Mr Mowat gave Hibs rather a lot of penalties. Well, he did, but they were justified. We were often in the opposition box and frequently fouled. Some refs chose to turn a blind eye. Mr Mowat, as Scotland's best, always had the courage to point to the spot. Incidentally, he also awarded United a penalty in this classic game.

The press went to town on our display. They also had some advice for the Scotland selectors. One reporter wrote, 'Hibs' second-half display was one of the most colourful and incisive. The team dovetailed superbly and the forwards excelled themselves. If SFA officials were present, I am sure that they will be inclined to nominate the whole Hibs attack for the coming international against Wales.' As past experience had shown, this forecast, although perfectly justified, was unlikely to come to pass.

When I look back on that famous victory over Manchester United fifty-eight years after it happened, I have to think that it was one of our best ever team performances. It was also one of my greatest individual displays.

Gordon generously bought crystal gift sets for the Manchester United players and presented his own teammates with gift tokens, which was a nice gesture. The evening ended on a light-hearted note. The wife of one of our directors, Bob Powrie, returned to her car after the match to discover another car parked so close to her that she couldn't get into the space between the cars to open her door. I managed to open the window of Mrs Powrie's car and my wife Kitty showed great agility to climb over the other car and into Mrs Powrie's car through the now open window. Kitty was then able to move the car forward and let Mrs Powrie in. She received a round of applause and was able to claim that she was possibly the most agile member of the Reilly household. Her husband did not agree with that assessment of course.

We then met Morton in the League Cup quarter-final second leg and took another six goals off them. I got two more and the team had now scored nineteen goals in three games. What's more, twelve of these goals had been put past Jimmy Cowan, still rightly regarded as one of Scotland's greatest ever goalkeepers.

There was even better to come as we returned to league duty to face Hearts at Easter Road. We hadn't managed to beat the Jam Tarts in a league match for over three seasons and were desperate to show them who was boss.

We did that and more as we beat them 3–1. It was a day to remember and a personal triumph for me as I got all three of our goals. I got quite a few hat-tricks in my time but this one was, without doubt, the sweetest of the lot. One newspaper claimed next day, 'Hibs scored three goals against Hearts but it could easily have been seven.' Well, that score would come to pass twenty-one years later!

I got lots of praise. 'Reilly was magnificent. He is a forward line in himself.' The team was complimented too: 'Hibs have taken care of one of the two most unaccountably elusive things in their life. They have laid the Hearts bogey. Will they lift a cup next?' We all certainly hoped that we would.

Incidentally, Hearts' consolation goal in this game came from a Bobby Parker penalty awarded by Jack Mowat, which goes to show that Mr Mowat's fairness was not in question. He even turned down two strong Hibs claims for spot kicks. He was simply a top referee who called it as he saw it. This victory gave us great satisfaction. It had definitely been coming and now that it had arrived we enjoyed it to the full. Our supporters had obviously sensed that something special was in the offing as 55,000 of them had turned up for this match. They went home delirious and, like us players, probably thinking, 'Who can stop us now?' I was certainly thinking along those lines. At last we had sorted Hearts out properly and I had scored a hat-trick in the process. What could be better? I had a real warm glow inside me as I made my way home that night.

Scoring a hat-trick against Hearts is a rare achievement for a Hibs player. Since I performed that feat fifty-eight years ago, only three other Hibs players have managed to follow in my footsteps. Joe Baker got four in a cup tie at Tynecastle in 1958, Pat Quinn notched a treble on the same ground a decade later and Mixu Paatelainen managed three of the best in the famous 6–2 derby win at Easter Road in 2000. I still remember my three from 1952 with great pride. At the time it confirmed to me what I had felt during our summer tour: I was definitely reaching my peak as a centre forward and defences had better beware!

Motherwell's defenders certainly needed to be on their guard. We met them next at Fir Park and demolished them 7–3. I was at my very zenith as a centre forward now and banged in four goals in this match. One of my goals was the best I ever scored and the press got it exactly right when they called it 'the goal of goals'. I beat three players then dribbled round the goalkeeper before placing the ball in the net. That renowned scribe Andy Cunningham raised his bowler to me after the match and wrote, 'Lawrie Reilly is the greatest centre forward I have seen since Hughie Gallacher.' Even the normally restrained Hugh Shaw came out with, 'They should have made this game into a film starring

Lawrie Reilly.' You know, older Hibs fans still mention that goal to me even now.

My rich vein of form continued when I joined the Scottish League for their game against the League of Ireland. Four of the Famous Five were chosen for this game, with Eddie Turnbull missing out. A well-known journalist, Tommy Muirhead, took the selectors to task when he declared that, 'The Hibernian forwards are probably the best club attack in the world. Only the SFA Committee would consider that it could be improved by replacing Turnbull with Dundee's Billy Steel.' Muirhead was right. Steel was a fine wee player, but it would have made far more sense to have chosen the Hibs forward line en bloc. Anyway we won the game 5–1 and I got another four-goal haul. Three of them were headers so it was another hat-trick and another special one. I was on top of the world and also on top of the scoring charts.

When the Scotland team to play Wales in the first full international of the season was announced, I wasn't surprised to be selected but was taken aback and delighted to see that Gordon Smith had been restored to favour. Gordon had played against England and the USA, been dropped for the tour to Scandinavia and now restored for the Home Championship. Whatever you could call this selectorial approach, you certainly couldn't describe it as consistent.

Before travelling to Cardiff, though, I had some important Hibs business to attend to. We had our League Cup semi-final against Dundee coming up. The Scottish League had scheduled the game for Tynecastle, which wasn't the best for us but we had outclassed Dundee at the end of the previous season, so surely we would make it to Hampden for the final this time. Yet again it wasn't to be. We lost 2–1, with me getting our goal. I always seemed to manage to score at Tynecastle even if we rarely did ourselves justice there. Bobby Johnstone had what looked like a good goal contentiously chalked off and Gordon Smith missed a sitter ten minutes from the end. Gordon's failure to score was described as 'a miss in a million' and the newspaperman who wrote, 'Hibs again fell victim to their relentless Tynecastle hoodoo' was totally on the ball. We hadn't been, though, and another great opportunity to lift silverware had been depressingly thrown away. We would normally have beaten Dundee nine times out of ten. It always seemed as if the tenth time occurred in a cup tie and it had happened again. We were frustrated beyond words and our supporters must have been in the depths of despair.

However, as always, there was league business to attend to and we were only too aware that we had a golden opportunity to win the title three times in a row, which would be an unbelievable achievement for a team outwith the Old Firm. Our next game was against the team which was the premier member of that duo in the 1950s – Rangers. We travelled to Ibrox for what was always a crucial game, totally determined to make up for the slip-up in the League Cup. We did too. We silenced 65,000 Rangers fans with a great 2–1 win. Even though I say so myself, and at the risk of repetition, I was at the height of my powers at this time and playing really well. The *Pink News* agreed, because they called me 'a great leader' and said that I had scored 'a magnificent goal'. I felt great as I shook hands with my Scotland teammates in the Rangers side at full time. I was proud of my personal performance and equally happy about the way the team had played. My joy wasn't complete though. Our win was really satisfying but it just made the loss to Dundee at Tynecastle all the more annoying.

My form was attracting attention. Newcastle United offered £30,000 for me. Harry Swan told them that they had more chance of signing 'The Man in the Moon'. That was exactly what I wanted to hear. There was also speculation that the Geordies were about to make a £25,000 bid for Ned Turnbull. Rumour was also rife that Hibs were giving that offer serious consideration. That was not good news.

I had a bit of a superstition going at that time. Before we had played Partick at the start of the season, Mike Gallacher, one of my teammates, had given me a new pair of bootlaces. As I had gone out and scored a hat-trick against Thistle, Mike continued to supply me with new laces before every game. It was obviously having a positive effect because I was scoring goals galore. I was profiled in one of the Sunday papers before I set off for Cardiff with Scotland and the writer concluded that, 'Reilly has moved from the very good to the genuinely great class. He is not quite twenty-four yet, but he has won twenty-three caps, received a benefit payment and acquired a black Ford saloon.' He finished his article by urging Gallacher to make sure he gave me more laces before I left for Wales.

Most working men couldn't have dreamed of having a new car, being in a nice house and having a little money in the bank at the age of twenty-three, so I was a lucky lad. I knew this, but I was also aware that it wasn't all down to luck. I lived a healthy life off the field, trained hard all week and gave it everything I had on match day. Whatever good fortune I had (and footballers certainly weren't rich in those days) had been earned through a combination of hard work and talent.

We beat Wales 2–1 and I didn't score. Gordon Smith had to miss the game through injury but I was apparently 'forever darting here and there'. I must have darted to good effect because I was awarded a maximum five stars in the post-match ratings.

Hibs then announced that 'no further transfer offers would be considered for Eddie Turnbull'. That was a relief to all of us, although we couldn't quite work out why we had been prepared to listen to offers in the first place. We got a bit of a clue when Hibs' annual accounts were published. Despite winning the league for the second successive year, the club had only made a profit of £318 which was well down on the £18,000 surplus made the previous season. We found this surprising as we were still playing to good crowds and none of us players were on big wages.

Our next match was huge. We were travelling to London to

face the mighty Arsenal in a special challenge match under the Highbury floodlights and the game was going to be shown live on BBC television across Britain. The game was billed as a friendly but both teams knew that there was a great deal of national pride at stake and this fixture was bound to be anything but friendly. We really fancied our chances. After all, we had beaten every other big English club and Arsenal, at that time, were no better than either Manchester United or Spurs, both of whom we had proved too good for.

Everyone wanted to see this match. The Duke of Edinburgh met the teams before the game. Fifty-five thousand crowded into the ground, which included a large number of Hibs fans who had journeyed to London on the Flying Scotsman train and many more packed into bars with televisions. In the event we had a shocker and lost 7–1. To this day I cannot explain what went wrong. Everything they hit went in and we missed a lot of chances but frankly we were embarrassed.

The newspapers were full of theories. They reckoned that Hibs were 'just too cocky' or 'unsettled by the Turnbull transfer business'. The English press had a field day. One paper commented that, 'Hibs will go down in history as the first team on television that was never seen.' Even my dad, who had travelled to the game, was dumbfounded. He said, 'I just don't know what went wrong with the Hibs that night.'

I scored our goal and I felt that I more than matched anyone in an Arsenal strip. In fact I told my teammates in the dressing room after the game that if they had all played as well as me, we would have won 11–7. I was only half joking as well. I am sure that if we had played the Gunners again the next night, we would have won.

Unfortunately there was no second chance and we were on the receiving end of a freak result which haunts me to this day.

Again things improved when we got back to league business that autumn. We won 3–2 at Clyde and my continuing high level of performance sparked even more speculation. I was now linked with a £40,000 move to England which would be like a £10 million deal now. The *Daily Mirror* paid my parents a call to see what they thought of all of this. My mum embarrassed me by telling them that I was 'a good boy with a sweet little wife'. She added: 'All this paper talk of £40,000 hasn't gone to his head. He is the same modest, home-loving boy he was when he was nine years old.' Thanks, Mum. My dad told them of how he used to pay me sixpence a goal when I played for Edinburgh Thistle. He had to stop that custom when I scored seven goals one day and he had to fork out three shillings and sixpence.

We then lost a game we should have won when Third Lanark beat us 2–0. Their goalie Jocky Robertson was small for a keeper but capable of brilliance on his day. We caught Jocky at his best and just couldn't get the ball past him.

The press interest in my background continued and the *Pink News* arranged a photo call for myself, Kitty and my parents. The piece they published acknowledged the important role which my dad had played in my development as a footballer. It also noted that 'Reilly's attractive wife Kitty arranges all his personal appearances'. That sounds rather grand but in fact my visits were to youth clubs, supporters' clubs, sports quizzes and the like. It was my way of putting something back. I never dreamt of asking for anything for attending these functions.

I was selected again for Scotland against Ireland when the next Home International match came round. I was the only Hibs player in the team as Gordon Smith was still injured and I managed to hit the target again. There were 23,000 Irish fans in the 65,000 crowd. Some of them had crossed the Irish Sea but most of them were Scottish-based. They were there to support Celtic's Charlie Tully and cheer on their team. They had plenty to cheer as Ireland held the lead until the last minute of the game. As the seconds ticked away, big George Young lobbed the ball forward and I got on the end of it to head us level. This was the beginning of my habit of scoring important last-minute goals for club and country.

The Scottish media considered this a poor result for our national team. The call went up again for Scotland to have a manager. Looking back now, it seems incredible that we didn't have one. The name in the frame was Matt Busby and that would have been a great selection. Matt did eventually become Scotland boss but not until 1958. Sadly, I had retired from the game by then, so I never got a chance to work with a man who had done a magnificent job at Manchester United and who had never hidden his admiration for me as a player.

The general consensus was that I had been starved of the ball during the game against Ireland. The *Pink News* had a humorous slant on this when it printed a cartoon of a lady Hibs fan carrying a pie and a bottle of beer into Easter Road and telling the stewards, 'They're no gaun tae starve Reilly the day.' I would have welcomed the pie but I wouldn't have thanked her for the beer.

Anyway, it was time to move back to domestic football again. As autumn began to turn to winter, we knew that we faced an almighty challenge to retain our league title and achieve the feat of being champions of Scotland for three years in a row – but we were determined to do exactly that.

11

MAKING A NAME AS
LAST MINUTE REILLY

I certainly wasn't short of service in our next league game. We comfortably beat our League Cup conquerors Dundee 3–0, despite missing many chances. Thirty thousand of our supporters were there and they were obviously still feeling aggrieved about recent events at both Tynecastle and Highbury. The *Sunday Post* reported that 'Reilly and Johnstone roused the ire of the home support when they smashed the ball wide from dead in front of goal to put the tally of lost chances well into double figures.' Both Bobby and I did manage to score eventually and my goal raised my total for the season to eighteen.

After the game, I had to drive to Glasgow to appear on a live programme at the Metropole Theatre. This was Scotland's first televised variety show and the stars included Gracie Fields and Tessie O'Shea. Those who were less than kind referred to O'Shea as 'Two-Ton Tessie.' John Lennon of the Beatles famously called her his 'favourite group'. She was a big girl, but a great performer and she and Gracie put on a tremendous show. George Young and I walked on at the end to be interviewed about Scottish football. We got asked a couple of straightforward questions, gave our answers and walked off to a round of applause, feeling like stars. Big George and I didn't get to meet any of the real stars as we had to sit in a small dressing room backstage until it was our turn to go on, while the top showbiz names on the bill all had their own separate dressing rooms in another part of the theatre.

Hibs next hammered one of our main challengers East Fife 5–3 and I managed to bag yet another hat-trick. The *Daily Record* claimed, 'Rapier Reilly is Britain's best.' The newspaper's 'special correspondent' also stated we would be champions again and headed his report, 'Reilly paints sign to the League Flag' – which was a reference of course to my former occupation as a painter and decorator.

That bold prediction took a bit of a knock when St Mirren beat us 2–0 in our next match. The Easter Road pitch was totally frozen. Indeed, I wore newly designed knee pads to protect myself against injury. That was one innovation which never caught on. It was a disappointing and potentially costly defeat but we had now played ten league games and were six goals and two points better off than we had been at the same stage the previous season, so everything wasn't doom and gloom.

Celtic were our next visitors and they drew a crowd of 35,000, with thousands still queuing outside when the game kicked off. We were held to a 1–1 draw although we would have won if their centre half Jock Stein (who of course went on to be a legendary Parkhead manager) hadn't cleared off the line from Bobby Johnstone in the last minute. I again got our goal and it was definitely one of my better efforts. The *Daily Express* thought that it was 'one of the goals of the season and a fitting reward for Reilly's brilliant leadership'. Bobby Johnstone tricked two Celtic defenders and crossed the ball and I made a run across the box and glided the ball into the corner of the net with my head. As can be seen from the newspaper quotes, I was at the very top of my game. I had just turned twenty-four and was still full of pace, energy and enthusiasm. I also had the experience of eight years of first-team football to combine with these qualities. It was nice to be called the best centre forward in Britain and at that time I think I may well have been.

John Paterson and I had received letters from Celtic supporters before the game. To quote the press report: 'These letters threatened Paterson and Reilly in crude and obscene language that they would be "done up" if Celtic didn't win the match.'

John and I handed the letters to Hugh Shaw who passed them on to the CID and we never gave them another thought. Although John and I were two of Hibs' best players on the day, we didn't come to any harm after the game and I can only assume that the threats in the letters were of the empty variety.

Prior to the match, Hibs made the headlines for another unusual reason. We signed the nineteen-year-old Musselburgh Athletic centre half Vince Halpin, who was six feet five inches tall. The newspapers claimed that young Vince was Britain's tallest footballer. He may well have been, but sadly he never managed to become a first-team regular at Easter Road.

It was all happening for me as I won the King's Cup Golf Tournament at Kingsknowe and appeared on the front cover of *The Boys' Book of Soccer*, which was expected to sell well that Christmas at the price of ten shillings and sixpence (52.5 pence in today's money). Like all my colleagues I also received a really nice festive gift box full of goodies from Hibs.

We had another poor result, though, when we lost 5–4 to Partick Thistle at Firhill due to a last-minute deflected goal from their left winger Jimmy Walker. I got two goals but Walker doubled my tally with four. He also stole my reputation for late goals. The *Sunday Post* claimed that Walker's winner was 'The perfect end to a perfect game'. Not for us it wasn't.

We had to start winning again and we did. We beat Queen of the South 7–2 and I again notched up a double, which took my season's tally to twenty-seven. We then beat Aberdeen 3–0 and Gordon Smith scored his 300th Hibs goal in this game. Given that Gordon had played 518 games and was a right winger, this was a phenomenal achievement.

The year 1952 ended happily for me when the *Pink News* made me their Sportsman of the Year. Mind you, I couldn't wait for 1953 to start. As usual our opponents were Hearts and we were travelling to Tynecastle to first foot our deadly rivals.

Tynecastle may have been our hoodoo ground and Hearts may have been our bogey team but we travelled there with confidence. We had beaten them at Easter Road in September and we knew that we could do it again. We had to if we wanted to retain our title, because so close was the race between Rangers, East Fife and ourselves that every point was absolutely vital.

There was so much interest in the game that Hearts had to declare a crowd limit of 49,000 and make the fixture all-ticket. Every single ticket was sold out well in advance of the match and what a contest the capacity crowd was to see. As the match report put it: 'If any finer football was played anywhere on this earth yesterday than the Hibs produced at Tynecastle, then the 49,000 supporters who were there will refuse to believe it.'

We won 2–1 and it was tight in the end but we undoubtedly deserved to win. I got my usual Tynecastle goal to give us the lead and then we got a penalty. The ref this time was called Charles Faultless. We certainly didn't find any fault with his spot-kick decision. Up stepped Eddie Turnbull to crash the ball home and banish the memory of exactly one year ago. Our celebrations were unrestrained because we knew how important this goal was. Even Tommy Younger, at the other end of the field, joined in the jubilation. All credit to Ned for having the courage to take such an important kick and bury it convincingly. Hearts did get a late consolation but we held on to give our supporters the perfect start to the New Year. It was ironic really, because Hearts were now definitely stronger as a team than they had been a couple of years earlier when we couldn't beat them for love or money. Yet here we were beating them twice in the one season. As a famous English footballer turned television pundit used to say, 'It's a funny old game.'

We continued in the same vein when Motherwell came to Easter Road. Surprisingly after our derby win, there were fewer than 30,000 there to welcome us for our first home fixture of 1953. Maybe it was the cold weather or a lack of cash because Christmas and New Year were expensive times and working people didn't have a lot of money back then. Two games close together was probably just too much for some of our fans to afford. Those who did come were served up a treat. We put seven goals past the Fir Parkers for the second time in a row. I got my sixth hat-trick of the season and we won 7–2. I had now scored thirty-one club goals and seven international goals in season 1952-53 and I was hungry for more.

If you listened to my wife, mind you, I was hungry for something else. When Kitty was asked by the press what my secret was, she replied, 'Mince, mince, mince. That's all he wants. I offer to make him some of these fancy things which you read about in the paper but all he ever wants is mince.' She was right too. I liked plain food then and that is still what I prefer now.

I had been presented with a shield which all my medals had been mounted on. That included league medals and those which I had won in five-a-side tournaments and reserve competitions. It was an impressive array but there was still a little room left on the shield and I knew what I wanted to fill that remaining space. It was a Scottish Cup winner's badge of course and I was sure this could be the year when we got it.

Then came a setback in the league, when we lost 4–2 at Raith Rovers. Tommy Younger was injured and his young deputy Tommy McQueen took his place. Sadly, McQueen didn't have the best of days and his errors contributed to our defeat. I tried to take my mind off that disappointment by making one of my 'personal appearances'. I went with my mum, dad and Kitty to the Royston and Wardieburn Community Association. According-ing to the coverage in the next day's *Evening News*, I gave a talk, answered questions, signed autographs and was the 'life and soul' of the dance which ended the evening. The 120-strong audience were so impressed by me that they invited me to become the honorary president of their association. I accepted. The association is still going strong today and for all I know, I might still be their honorary president!

The Hibs' support was out in force again for our next game as 59,000 packed Easter Road for the visit of Rangers. We needed to win and should have won but didn't. Rangers goalkeeper George Niven broke our hearts. The *Sunday Post* headline declared that Niven was 'A one-man barricade which held back those hurricane Hibs.' The match was described as, 'stupendous, magnificent, colossal, thrilling and dramatic'. It must have been quite a good game then.

It finished 1–1 with another E. T. penalty providing our goal. This one was a rocket, and not even the inspired Niven could get near it. I was again in form. I was playing so well at this point that I fully expected praise in the press after almost every game. The next day's match report didn't disappoint me when it asserted that, 'Hibs centre was way out on his own – a perfectly magnificent player.' While it was nice to read such complimentary things about myself, it didn't take away the disappointment of dropping another vital league point.

We started our Scottish Cup campaign by demolishing Stenhousemuir 8–1. I only managed one goal and, as was becoming a habit for me, it came in the last minute! The games and the goals were coming thick and fast now. I got two when we beat Falkirk 3–1 in the league and yet another hat-trick when we took care of Queen's Park 4–2 in the next round of the cup. When we demolished Clyde 5–1, I helped myself to another couple to bring my season's total to forty-nine.

My wife nearly caused a riot at the Clyde match. She was in the directors' box and had bought a sweepstake ticket. If the player whose name was on your ticket got the first goal you won twenty-five shillings, which was a fair sum of money then. Kitty had Tommy Ring of Clyde and he obliged by giving his team the lead. She leapt to her feet and cheered and got quite a few long, hard looks. She told everyone not to worry. She assured them that her husband would soon score a couple of goals and that Hibs would win easily. She was right too! She also said that if we won the league, she was going to ask me for my winners' medal to put in a brooch. She added that she wouldn't think of asking me for a Scottish Cup medal if we managed to get one of those, because she knew that I wanted one so badly I would never part with it.

We were heading back to Broomfield for the next round of the cup. The draw seemed to bring ourselves and Airdrie together on a regular basis and they were always tough games. Demand for tickets was high in Lanarkshire – so high that one of the Airdrie directors said that he had stopped going out. He couldn't leave his house without being accosted by fans who were desperate to attend the match.

Twenty-four-and-a-half thousand supporters eventually crowded into the Diamonds' intimidating little ground. This time we came through comfortably. We won 4–0 and it was Gordon Smith's turn to supply a hat-trick. I got our fourth but I also injured my knee. This meant that I was missing when we returned to Airdrie on league business the following week. If the supporters were concerned at the loss of their star striker, they needn't have been. The amazing Bobby Combe stepped into my position and scored four goals in a 7–3 rout. Bobby could play anywhere and star anywhere.

If I couldn't play football, I was still able to do well on the golf course. I finished just behind the professional winner in the East of Scotland Golf Alliance tournament and then I beat Hibs' best golfer Willie Clark when we went on a team trip to Kilspindie.

I was soon back on the football field, but our season took a distinct turn for the worse. We lost at Dundee in the league. The game turned when the referee awarded a goal I had scored and then changed his mind and chalked it off. He then turned down what appeared to be a stonewall Hibs penalty claim for good measure. Things got worse when we lost to Aberdeen in the Scottish Cup quarter-final. Archie Buchanan earned us a replay with a late equaliser at Easter Road but, in front of a record midweek crowd of 42,000 at Pittodrie, they won the replay 2–0. The prize we coveted most had eluded us again. Was it psychological? I honestly don't think so. I think it was simply 'in the stars'. We had played most of the first match with ten men as

Hugh Howie had been injured and Hugh and Gordon Smith both missed the replay. There wasn't much we could do about any of these things. They were sheer bad luck but they certainly didn't help our cause.

So, now, the league was all we had left to play for. With seven games to go, we were just ahead of Rangers and East Fife but the 'Gers had a game in hand. We faltered again in our next match at Paisley when we drew 2–2 with St Mirren. It may sound like I am making excuses when I say that there were some referees who did Hibs no favours, but believe you me I am only stating what I consider to be the truth. This particular official disallowed a goal from me after Bobby Johnstone and I had put us 2–1 up. The match report described his decision as 'very doubtful'. The referee had already awarded St Mirren a penalty and, in the last minute, he gave them another one. Almost the whole Hibs team surrounded him to protest and that was something which very rarely happened in those days. It shows how contentious we considered this penalty to be. Davie Lapsley, St Mirren's captain, stuck the kick away to deprive us of a crucial point. Since Gordon Smith was again out injured and Willie Ormond spent most of the game as a limping passenger, I think it's fair to say that we weren't carrying a great deal of luck at this stage of the season, but we were determined to hold on to our championship. All that reverse at Love Street did was make us even more committed to making it three league titles in a row. When we sat simmering in our dressing room at Paisley after what we considered to be a total travesty of justice, there was a lot of anger and no shortage of resolve in our ranks.

We got a boost when all of the Famous Five were chosen in the Scottish League team to play the English League at Ibrox. Originally four of us had been picked and Eddie Turnbull had been left out. Jimmy Bonthrone of East Fife was chosen ahead of Eddie but had to withdraw because he was getting married on the day of the game!

This meant that Eddie was in and that for the first time, the five of us would line up together in the dark blue of our country. Our joy was short-lived, though, as Gordon, Eddie and Willie all had to pull out with injury.

I cheered myself up by scoring our winner as we beat a very strong English team 1–0, and the press judged me to be 'The outstanding forward of the game who inspired the Scotland attack to glorious heights'. One correspondent was so taken with my performance that he was moved to verse. Commenting on the selection of the Five and then the subsequent withdrawal of three of them he wrote:

> Four little Hibs caps full of punch and drive
> Bonthrone took a wife and then there were five
> Five little Hibs caps full of goals galore
> Gordon felt an ankle twinge and then there were four
> Four little Hibs caps fit as fit could be
> Willie took a knock and then there were three
> Three little Hibs caps feeling rather blue
> Eddie got an injured leg so then there were two
> Two little Hibs caps went out and did their stuff
> The English team decided that two was quite enough!

All of us except Willie were fit when we went to Parkhead for a must-win league game. Win we did, with Bobby Johnstone getting two important goals. I got the third, 'flashing past Stein to score'. This gave us real hope of finishing champions again.

Then came a couple of real setbacks. We drew two games in a row. On a day of torrential rain, Partick held us 1–1 at Easter Road. Our shooting let us down. As the *Pink News* put it, 'Hibs' finishing was deplorably bad, even allowing for the difficult conditions.' It was the same score and the same problem when we returned to Pittodrie. I managed a goal but the match report was of the opinion that 'something has gone wrong with Hibs' front rank'. It wasn't at all like us at that time to throw away points in vital games and it was even less usual for our forward line to misfire. We knew that the loss of these points could hurt us badly. Rangers weren't winning every game either, but they were dropping fewer points than us and their goal average was far superior to ours.

Hibs then had to travel to Brussels to play Rapid Vienna in a match billed as the 'Floodlit Championship of Europe'. The Black Watch Pipe Band travelled all the way from Dusseldorf for the occasion. First they piped us into the local town hall to meet the lord mayor and on the day of the match they piped Hibs on to the field. Five thousand curious Belgians watched our team enter the Town Hall and 40,000 watched the game. Rapid beat us 3–2 but we were under strength as Bobby Johnstone and I had had to join the Scotland team for its final Home International match of the season against England at Wembley.

This match turned out to be one of my finest hours in football. Scotland played part of the game with ten men after Sammy Cox was carried off on a stretcher, but we managed a heroic 2–2 draw. I got both our goals and my second came with the final kick of the game. The legend of 'Last Minute Reilly' was now well and truly established.

Listen to this from the press: 'No centre half could have stopped Reilly' and 'In the dying seconds Lawrie Reilly was able to crown his great goal-scoring career with the most memorable goal of all.' I felt ten feet tall but was brought back to earth that same night. The Scots fans were celebrating the draw as if it had been a victory. They had filled Piccadilly Circus and themselves with strong liquor. The team was driving past and we decided to get out and have a look. The supporters were singing our names but they were so taken up with their revelry that they didn't even notice us standing just a few yards away from them. We looked at each other, smiled wryly and returned to our coach.

Some of our lads celebrated enthusiastically at the team hotel that night but I kept to my lifelong routine and stuck to the fruit juice. I didn't need anything to stimulate me as I was still full of adrenalin. I lay awake that night in the heart of London playing the game over and over in my mind. I had now scored four goals in three games against England at Wembley and had still to lose on that great stadium's hallowed turf. I knew that my last-minute goal had been something special but I had no idea that it would earn me the nickname by which I am still known fifty-seven years later.

A battery of photographers was waiting to greet me when I returned home to Kitty next day. As she opened the front door, the cameras flashed and the reporters' pencils went into overdrive. One of them surpassed himself when he wrote 'Reilly, Rollicking Reilly of Wembley's last minute, came home to his wife with goals and glory in his bags.'

The poets were at it again as well. One composed the following:

Nippy as a ferret and slippery as an eel
Game as a bantam cock with a heart and nerves of steel
He sports a braw green jersey when he isn't wearing blue
Can you guess his name right now or do you need
    another clue?

I would reckon that most folk could supply the answer to his question. I was hoping that I could be poetry in motion when I returned to Easter Road because we were about to face one of our main challengers in East Fife. The Fifers along with the ever-powerful Rangers were locked with us in a battle for the title and we just could not afford another slip-up.

The Hibs support realised the importance of this game and 40,000 of them were in the ground to give us the backing we needed. It helped and so did a diving header from Willie Ormond which sealed a vital 2–1 win for us. We next beat Third Lanark 7–1, yes the same Third Lanark who had taken two priceless points off us earlier in the season. Believe it or not, their goalkeeper Jocky Robertson was again their best player, but we were on fire and not even Jocky could keep us out this time. We may have hit seven but I didn't get one of them. I did get some praise though – 'Reilly had a magnificent game. His ability stamps him out as one of the most gifted all-round forwards in world soccer.'

Unfortunately, Rangers were matching us result for result and they still had their advantage in goal average to boost them. Our last match was against Raith Rovers and we had to beat them while hoping that Rangers would lose or draw. We did all we could by beating the Fifers 4–1. This gave us ninety-three goals for the season, which was a new league record. It wasn't enough, though, as Rangers avoided any last-minute slip-ups and pipped us for the title on goal average. We could look back on turning points like Partick Thistle's late deflected winner at Firhill or the controversial last-minute penalty equaliser for St Mirren at Paisley – but, in truth, we had drawn and lost games which we should have won comfortably. We were still the best team in Scotland but we had let too many careless points slip against inferior opposition. We should have won the league three times in a row but we had failed to do so. It was a great opportunity lost and a massive disappointment for everyone at Easter Road.

The league was over but there was still plenty to play for. First, we beat Hearts 4–2 in the East of Scotland Shield Final. We had now beaten them four times in a row and at last turned our superiority over them into results. I got two and Eddie Turnbull hammered in another derby penalty. The referee was again a certain Mr Jack Mowat! My goal took my total for the season to forty-seven and there was more to come.

Bobby Johnstone and I played for Scotland against Sweden at Hampden. The fans were so pleased with our fighting draw at Wembley that 83,000 of them turned out to cheer us on. Unfortunately we let them down and lost 2–1. I was told that I was 'sharp as a needle'. Bobby, on the other hand, despite scoring our goal, was described as 'ordinary material'.

There was one more domestic competition and it was something special. Princess Elizabeth was about to be crowned Queen and a cup competition featuring the four top teams from both England and Scotland was organised to mark the occasion. The Coronation Cup would be a tournament to savour and winning it would be prestigious beyond words. Having surrendered our league title by such a narrow margin, everyone at Easter Road was determined to make up for it by triumphing in what was sure to be a historic cup competition.

We beat Spurs in the first round after a replay. We won the second game 2–1. I got both our goals and it was 'Last Minute Reilly' once again as my winner came in the dying seconds. We convincingly demolished Newcastle United in the semi-final. There were 48,000 at Ibrox and apparently there were quite a few thousand Old Firm fans in the crowd with our supporters to shout for a Scottish victory. I can't really see that being repeated today. I was on target again and the match reporter reckoned that 'Hibs cut gaps in the Tyneside rearguard so wide that Lawrie Reilly could have driven the Coronation State Coach through them.' I don't know about that, but I do remember thinking to myself that if these were the best defenders the English top league had to offer, I would have no problem being a success if I ever decided to move to England. Not that I ever did have any thoughts of going south. I was more than happy with my beloved Hibs and at that moment I was convinced that we were about to lift a cup at last – and a very special one at that.

Before the final, the press shocked Hibs fans by revealing that Jock Govan, Bobby Johnstone and I still had not signed new contracts with Hibs. This was true. Our wages rarely changed from season to season but that was not the matter in hand. We were deadlocked on other issues which the club were refusing to resolve. None of us had any desire to leave Easter Road but there were certain matters of principle which had to be addressed.

All that was set to one side, though, as we lined up to meet Celtic in the Coronation Cup Final. Interest was so high that a crowd of 117,060 packed the famous Hampden slopes. We were a better team than Celtic. That was not in doubt. Could we prove it in a cup final, though? That was most definitely the key question. We were desperate to do exactly that and we could not have been more motivated than we were going into this game. Sadly we came up short again when it mattered most and lost 2–0.

You're probably reading this thinking that Hibs just couldn't handle the biggest occasions. There may be some truth in that, but it doesn't tell the whole story. We didn't play at all badly in what was a great match –'one of the most enthralling and exciting games ever to be fought out at Hampden Stadium'. Neil Mochan scored a goal in a million and their goalkeeper Johnny Bonnar had the game of his life. At one point, he made such a miraculous save from a Bobby Johnstone header that even Bobby patted him on the back! The newspaper headlines say it all: 'Not a Break for the Fighting Hibs', 'Brilliant Bonnar Defies the Hibees' and 'Hibernian's Trophy Hoodoo Continues to Beset Them' sum it up pretty well. We were devastated but we hadn't choked. The fates just seemed to have it in for us when it came to winning cups. I walked off Hampden that night in a state of despair. As a young player, I had coped with cup disappointments by telling myself that it was only matter of time before we lifted silverware at the national stadium. Now I wasn't so sure. I was starting to wonder if we were ever going to capture a trophy in a knockout competition and it wasn't a nice feeling.

We didn't have too much time to feel sorry for ourselves because we were about to embark on an amazing adventure. Hibs' latest close-season tour was spectacular even by our pioneering standards. We were about to become the first British football team to tour Brazil.

Harry Swan wasn't a man who did things by halves and he had arranged for us to make an epic journey from Edinburgh to Rio. We were travelling via Paris, Lisbon, Dakar and the Azores. We would be in the air for a total of twenty-five hours and cover 12,000 miles at an average speed of 300mph. Tommy Younger, who had covered 112,000 miles flying between his army camp in Germany and Edinburgh during his national service, described our itinerary as 'a tuppenny bus ride'.

Our chairman had also arranged for us to have a special strip to cope with the South American heat and humidity. We normally wore heavy cotton tops with collars and long sleeves, long shorts, thick socks and toe-cap boots. Our Brazilian kit would consist of 'short sleeves, brief pants, light hose and cork-soled boots' and should help us to be comfortable in much higher temperatures than we were used to.

We began our trip on the day of Queen Elizabeth's coronation. Every time we stopped over for refuelling, we checked the television sets in the airport lounges and they were invariably showing the events from London. It was a marathon trip to put it mildly and when we walked down the steps of the plane on arrival in Rio de Janeiro we were met by a battery of television cameramen and interviewers. One of the TV men stuck a microphone in Willie Ormond's face and said, 'How do you feel to be in Brazil?' Willie replied, 'Bloody exhausted.'

We were to play in an eight-club international tournament. We were in a section of four, with three Brazilian teams, and would have to finish in the top two to qualify for the semi-finals. We started with a game against Vasco Da Gama in the Maracana stadium. The Maracana holds 200,000 and, while not at full capacity, was well filled for the match. It was a classic match, with the lead changing hands several times. Every time they scored, the crowd set off firecrackers and rockets. It was quite a sight and quite a sound.

Archie Buchanan and I had both scored but we trailed 3–2 entering the last minute of the game. You don't need me to tell you what happened next. I managed to equalise and the next day's headline was pretty predictable. Sure enough, the subeditors didn't disappoint and came up with 'Last Minute Reilly – even in Rio'. It was my eighth last-minute goal of the season. After the game, Archie and I reflected on how far we'd come in a short time. It was quite a journey from Edinburgh Thistle in a public park to Vasco Da Gama in the Maracana stadium.

Before our next match, we had quite an eventful time. We began by playing a round of golf. When Hugh Howie went to look for his ball in the rough, he stood on a three-foot-long snake. Hugh didn't believe in cruelty to animals but he didn't subscribe to danger for humans either. He used his five iron to kill the snake then hit his approach shot onto the green. I can't remember whether he was in a fit state to hole his putt or not.

We then went to Copacabana beach for a game of volleyball. When we were there we marvelled at the skill of the youngsters playing football in their bare feet. Brazil won the World Cup in Sweden five years later and I wouldn't be surprised if some of the teenage footballers who dazzled us that day were in their team. We also swam at the Copa and that maybe wasn't a good idea. At that time, unknown to us, the beach had sewers discharging directly into the sea. I was one of the swimmers and ended up in hospital with a very upset stomach indeed.

Hugh Shaw had told me to drink plenty of milk as that would be good for my stomach lining. He was sitting with me in the hospital ward when the doctor came to examine me. He asked what I had been taking and when I told him that I had been drinking milk, he almost had a fit. Apparently Brazilian milk then had chemicals in it and consuming it would greatly aggravate an upset tummy. The doctor asked what fool had told me to drink milk. I simply said, 'Somebody at my club.'

'Whoever he was,' said the doc, 'he doesn't know the first thing about medicine.' My manager just sat there, staring at the wall and saying absolutely nothing.

When I was discharged from hospital I returned to the hotel to be told that the ice-cream seller up the road, whose sister was a famous Brazilian film star, was offering free ice cream to the members of the Hibs' party. Sammy Kean said, 'You won't want any, Lawrie, with your stomach bug.'

I replied, 'Too true I do.' I loved ice cream and dicky tummy or not I made sure that I was at the front of the queue when we went to the shop.

I was fit enough to play in our next game against Botafogo. We lost 3–1 although I got our goal which 'capped a splendid move featuring all five Hibs forwards'. We had to win our final match in the section to progress to the next stage, but by that time our long, hard season and the intense Brazilian heat had caught up with us. We went down 3–0 to Fluminense and, to be honest, we were out on our feet at the start of the game, never mind the end of it. It had been the experience of a lifetime but we were exhausted and not sorry to be going home.

We did leave a legacy though. We had clearly impressed our hosts because when an encyclopaedia of Brazilian football was published shortly before the 1970 World Cup, it contained a full chapter on Hibs' visit and the quality of our play. The writer was particularly complimentary about the Famous Five. This publication came out not long before Brazil's most famous team inspired by Pele and including all-time greats like Carlos Alberto, Rivelino, Jairzhino and Tostao thrilled the world with their classic play in Mexico. The fact that football experts in Brazil rated Hibs so highly during such a vintage period in their own football history, shows just how good we were back in 1953.

When I got back to Edinburgh there were three bits of news waiting for me.

Although my contract expired on 31 July, I had been selected to lead the line for the Edinburgh Select in their match against Wolves on 1 August. Bobby Johnstone and Jock Govan had now re-signed, leaving me as Hibs' only contract rebel. A major point of principle was at stake and I told Harry Swan that I wouldn't be putting pen to paper until our differences were resolved.

I also discovered that I had been voted Scotland's Player of the Season for 1952-53. With fifty-five per cent of the vote, I was well ahead of George Young in second place. Big Corky had only managed to gain twenty-five per cent of the poll.

Finally, the press informed me that Botafogo had told Hibs to name their price for Gordon Smith and me. Harry Swan might have loved money but he didn't want to risk inciting a riot among the Easter Road faithful so he declined the offer.

Normally the close season was a relaxing time for me. As well as my usual summer holiday, I would play lots of golf and generally take things easy to recharge my batteries for the season ahead. This time, I had a lot of serious thinking to do. I did not want to leave Hibs but I had no intention of giving ground on a matter which I considered to be of crucial importance to my future wellbeing. The big question was, 'Would Lawrie Reilly still be a Hibs player when season 1953-54 got underway?'

12

SHOWDOWN WITH SHAW

When season 1953-54 came round, I still had not re-signed for Hibs. The reason for this was very simple: I wanted to secure my future without imposing any unfair financial burden on the club. I put to Hugh Shaw and Harry Swan what I considered to be a perfectly reasonable request. They rejected it out of hand. I then refused to put pen to paper on a new contract.

This caused me to be withdrawn from the Edinburgh Select team to play against Wolverhampton Wanderers on 1 August. My contract had expired on 31 July so I wasn't able to train with Hibs and the club was no longer paying me wages. The press went into overdrive speculating what the dispute was all about.

Initially, they didn't really know what was going on. One paper put it like this: 'We believe Reilly has made a request which would involve Hibs in making a promise which they do not feel is justified.' They weren't actually too far out. The difference between my position and that adopted by Hibs was that I considered that my request was completely justified and I made it clear to the club that I wouldn't play again until I received what I was asking for.

My weekly wage with Hibs in the early 1950s was around £14 per week. When you played for a club for five years, you received a benefit of £750. I had already received one such payment. It was taxable, mind you, so you ended up with less than £500. I was more than happy to accept these terms with one proviso. I wanted Hibs to promise me a testimonial match. This was not unreasonable and it wouldn't cost the club anything as the player had to cover all the expenses associated with the game. Gordon Smith had just had a testimonial and had done really well out of it. I had no problem with that. Gordon deserved every penny that he had received. I just couldn't see why what had been awarded to Gordon couldn't also be awarded to me.

I was really taken aback when the club dug its heels in and refused my request. I next asked for the opportunity to train in the mornings and work in the afternoons and make my money up that way. I had been offered a part-time job as a travelling salesman with a car accessories company and the money on offer was good. Hibs said that I could do what I was asking if I agreed to switch from full-time to part-time wages. That made me even more angry so I submitted a written transfer request.

I didn't really want to go anywhere. I wanted only to play for Hibs, the team I loved, but I am a determined character and I was also prepared to stand up for my rights over what I believed to be a point of principle. Some of my teammates had assured me the previous season that they would support me and also refuse to re-sign. When it came down to it, though, they all backed down and signed for exactly what they had been receiving before. I wasn't made that way and no matter how difficult the situation became, I had no intention of capitulating to the club.

Hugh Shaw then fanned the flames by declaring, 'The Smith game was agreed to before I became manager. It was a mistake. If I had been manager, I would not have agreed to it. It can't be done for every player so it shouldn't be done at all.'

That was nonsense. Not every player would want a testimonial nor expect to get one. However, exceptional players like the members of the Famous Five or Bobby Combe had every right to ask the club for something which would have cost it nothing. Players' wages then weren't anything like what they are now and a testimonial match was a fitting reward for faithful long-term service to a club. The fans would be the ones who would have to pay and they would make their own decision as to whether or not to attend a game. Nobody could force them to part with their money if they didn't want to. On the other hand, if the supporters valued a player's contribution to their team, they had every right to support him by going along to his testimonial.

There was no shortage of interest in securing my services. Arsenal, Newcastle, Spurs, Rangers, Dundee, Burnley, Manchester City, Chelsea and Liverpool all made it known that they would be interested in buying me. Tom Whittaker, the Arsenal manager, went as far as to tell the media: 'We have made a big bid for Reilly. I told Hibs that I was prepared to fly up to Edinburgh immediately but they said that the player was not available for discussion.'

That was news to me but, in truth, I didn't want to move to England. I was quite happy living in Edinburgh and I asked Hibs only to consider offers from Scottish clubs. They responded by saying that they valued me at £35,000 and that, in their opinion, no Scottish club could afford to pay that. I then made my position crystal clear to the club when I told them: 'I would rather quit than move to England. I am not a racehorse to be auctioned off.'

This sparked a further war of words in the press which ended with me saying, 'Nothing would please me more than to go on playing for Hibs, but I don't see why I should stay with a club which is willing to do more for one player than for another. I've given my all for Hibs and I've tried to be loyal but I also have to be loyal to myself. I simply want my future assured.'

The press was giving the situation blanket coverage. They were quoting Hibs and me, their reporters were all voicing varying opinions and they were printing lots of letters from fans. One supporter calling himself 'Easter Roader' sent a poem to the *Evening News* which they printed. He wrote:

Come back Lawrie Reilly to old Easter Road
Without you the goals have been few
We've tried hard but failed son so please hurry back
And we'll start where we left off with you
Although we've won matches, the margin's been neat

And we've all wiped the sweat from our brow
The Saints and the Bairns were not easy meat
So come back, Lawrie Reilly right now
Spare a thought for the boys who've watched you for years
Without thee the game's not alive
Please come back Lawrie Reilly and we'll give three cheers
When you make that Hibs 'fore' line a five.

This was actually a play on an old Irish song called 'Come Back Paddy Reilly to Ballyjamesduff' and could have been sung every bit as easily as recited.

It didn't have any impact on Hibs, though. Even when a Supporters' Club spokesman came out and said that the fans backed me to the hilt, the club still stood firm. My dealings were all with Hugh Shaw but I was pretty sure that the manager was simply doing the chairman's bidding. Harry Swan had always been the power broker at Easter Road and I was certain that nothing had changed.

Although I stood firm in my dealings with Hugh Shaw, I have to say that I liked our manager. His style was to praise players rather than to criticise them and I could identify with that. Unlike many team bosses of the 1950s, he was capable of joining in with the players in training. He had been a fine player for Hibs in the 1920s, of course. He wasn't one for fancy team talks. His rallying call to us as we prepared to take the field was, 'Go oot and gie them "The Reels o' Bogie".' As inspirational rhetoric went it wasn't in the Winston Churchill class but it usually had the desired effect. It's only in recent years that I have discovered that 'The Reels o' Bogie' is one of Robert Burns' more bawdy songs. I've never got as far as finding out the words though. However much I admired Mr Shaw, I had no intention of diluting my determination to receive a fair deal from Hibs.

I always thought that the relationship between Hugh Shaw and Harry Swan was an interesting one. They worked together for a very long time but I never heard the manager call Swan by his first name. He always addressed him as Mr Chairman. Harry Swan was the man in charge and he liked people to know that. He may have been diminutive in stature but his lack of inches certainly wasn't matched by any shortage of self-belief.

Then the whole saga took another twist. A Hearts fan tried to start a fund to take me to Tynecastle. He suggested that if 30,000 Hearts fans all put in ten shillings, their club could make up the balance and they could meet Hibs' asking price. Nothing came of that, I am glad to say, but there was never any chance of me signing for Hearts anyway. It just wasn't a possibility. I would have considered any Scottish club but them.

Hibs had started well in their League Cup section but they were doing poorly in the league. Jimmy Mulkerrin and Tommy D'Arcy were filling my position and doing their best. Without being big-headed or disrespectful to Jimmy or Tommy, they were good club players but they were no Lawrie Reillys.

My dad and I were photographed in the stand at Starks Park watching Hibs lose 4–0 to Raith Rovers. It is obvious by the looks on our faces that neither of us was gaining any pleasure from the ongoing situation. The club had it in its hands to resolve the situation, of course, but remained intransigent.

One reporter wondered if I was ready to give in. I wasn't! Another speculated on whether the club would even have me back. I think it's safe to say that they would have welcomed my return with open arms. Jack Harkness in the *Sunday Post* pointed out that the SFA had £100,000 in the bank and suggested that they use some of it to give me what I would have expected to make from a testimonial match to get me back playing again. That was another element of this prolonged affair. Not only was I ineligible to play for Hibs, but I wasn't allowed to represent Scotland either. You won't be surprised to hear that the SFA did not take Harkness up on his suggestion.

By now I was keeping fit by training at Meggetland with a local amateur team, Alexander Sports Club. I was also doing my travelling salesman work and receiving a lot of support for my stance as I visited various businesses. I also kept myself busy by painting the railings around my house. I was changing them from their original black to a deep shade of green, so my allegiances hadn't changed even if I was in dispute with my club.

I was also being asked to write articles for various newspapers. I wrote a series for the *Sunday People* and did match reports for the *Sunday Post*. The income I received from this, combined with what I was getting for my sales work, was in advance of what Hibs normally paid me so I wasn't losing out financially.

My first report for the *Post* was on Hearts v Queen of the South at Tynecastle. Queens won 4–1, which didn't break my heart. I next covered an Old Firm game. The action on the pitch was fast and furious and there was trouble on the terracings at half-time. I wrote, 'Hearts–Hibs derbies are tough but I don't think I'd like to play in an atmosphere like that.'

I wasn't playing in any atmosphere at all at that time, of course, but my determination to gain what I considered myself to be rightfully due hadn't weakened one bit. A lot of our supporters had written to me at Easter Road and Hugh Shaw passed the letters on to me. I think it's fair to say that they were equally divided in their views. I had a lot of support but quite a few others thought that I should get myself back to the club and sign on the dotted line.

That wasn't going to happen and as a sign that I was prepared for the long haul, I sold my car. My sales position provided me with a nice new car as part of the job. When I wasn't selling car accessories or painting, I worked on my golf game. My dad, as you would expect, continued to watch the Hibs. The only difference was that, for the first time in ten years, he was having to pay to get in.

He was there all the same, a Hibs man through and through. It must have been difficult for him to stand in the crowd, watching his team, wanting his boy to be out there on the pitch, but at the same time supporting him all the way in his principled stance against the club which father and son both loved.

There were a couple of bonuses for Kitty and me. An eighty-year-old Scotland fan wrote to me. He had been at Wembley in 1953 and as the game had neared full time, he had been surrounded by Englishmen crowing over their team's expected win. He believed in his country and in his centre forward though. He made a number of bets with them that Scotland would come back and level the score. When I did exactly that in the last minute, he picked up £5 in winning bets. He thought that I might be feeling the pinch now so he had sent me £1 with the letter to tide me over. Kitty had received a massive box of chocolates from a Burnley scout who clearly thought that the way to a man's heart was through his wife.

It was now nearly two months since the start of the season. Hibs had qualified for the League Cup semi-final but were struggling in the league. Still our impasse continued. I was considering consulting a lawyer to see where I stood legally. The press was urging resolution. Waverley wrote in the *Daily Record*, 'If Reilly reveals an attitude to make peace he will win the applause of the whole football world. Come on Lawrie!' I was willing to make peace and in fact I was more than keen to do exactly that but only if a fair solution could be reached.

Then came the first official offer. Stirling Albion made a bid of £16,000. The newspapers were urging Rangers to come in for me as well. The headline revealing Stirling's bid read: 'Stirling Want Reilly, Rangers Need Him'.

Then on 28 September, I took a phone call at home at 8.30pm. It was Hugh Shaw. He said that Hibs had been approached by a 'go-between' and urged to take steps to get me playing again. I wasn't surprised at the manager's call because the self-same intermediary had been in touch with me earlier in the day. Shaw asked if I could come in to Easter Road right away. I was there for 9pm and one hour later, I had re-signed for Hibs in the boardroom.

The club was happy for me to train in the mornings and carry on with my job in the afternoons. This would give me two wages so I wasn't complaining.

I was told in confidence that I would be given a testimonial match when I retired but that I couldn't make that public while I was still playing. I was more than happy to accept that.

The stories in the next day's press described me as 'footballer cum businessman Lawrie Reilly'. I was quoted as saying: 'Both the club and I are extremely delighted that the matter is settled. As for the testimonial game, I can't tell you anything about that.' No one pressed me about the testimonial but I am sure that most journalists were shrewd enough to make a guess as to what the eventual outcome of that situation would be.

Sugar had just come off the post-war rationing list and a grocer's shop near Easter Road put up a poster reading: 'THIS WEEK'S NEWS: SUGAR SIGNS OFF AS REILLY SIGNS ON'. I liked that. I liked being back with Hibs even more. I was desperate to start playing again and I didn't have long to wait.

The day after I re-signed, Hibs were playing Manchester United at Old Trafford. The rest of the lads had already travelled to Manchester. Hugh Shaw asked me to get myself down in time for the game. I left home at 4.30 in the morning and drove to Turnhouse airport and caught the first available flight to Manchester. It was a stormy day and a very turbulent flight. By the time I got to the ground, I was feeling poorly, so choppy had the journey been. I had only just popped into the dressing room to be welcomed back by my teammates when I had to race out again to be seriously travel sick.

I was determined to play in the game, though, and I did. It was a wet and windy night and the ground was heavy. I hadn't played in a match since the end of the previous season four months earlier, but things couldn't have gone better for me.

We drew 2–2 and I scored both our goals. The *Daily Express* headline put it perfectly when it proclaimed: 'Reilly scores twice in fairy tale return and Hibs Old Magic is Back.' After the game, I told the press pack: 'I don't think that I have ever been happier,' and I meant every word.

I was greatly relieved to be back playing with Hibs but I was even happier because I had stood up for what I had believed in and won. I had gained future security and that was a good feeling. It was also good to know that justice had been done. I had served Hibs admirably and I deserved recognition for that. I now had that recognition and couldn't wait to give my all once again for the club I loved. There may have been a queue of top English clubs trying to secure my services but I hadn't been remotely interested in any of their offers. For me, it was Hibs, first, last and always.

In case you are wondering who the mystery go-between was who helped to broker the deal between Hibs and me, I'll let you into that secret right now. It was none other than the SFA secretary, the recently knighted Sir George Graham. Sir George had been concerned about my unavailability for Scotland. He had also always had a soft spot for me and knew that I would be wanting to get back playing for Hibs as soon as possible.

He had contacted Harry Swan and urged him to find a way of meeting my demands without losing face. Our chairman had done exactly that and a difficult and unhappy situation was finally brought to a swift and amicable end. I think that both Hibs and I were equally happy to have sorted things out. I now had peace of mind that my worth to Hibs was being recognised, which was all I had ever wanted, and the club had their star centre forward back in harness.

I genuinely think that if the other players at Easter Road – who had been full of big talk about backing me up – had kept their promises instead of giving in and re-signing, then the whole matter would have been addressed much more quickly. However, none of that was important now. I was back in the fold and raring to go. My only aim was to get fit and to keep scoring goals. That was to prove more difficult than anticipated, as fate had a rather nasty shock in store for me.

13

A PROBLEM WITH PLEURISY

The opportunity to resume my domestic career came at Palmerston Park in Dumfries as I played my first league game of the season against Queen of the South. We had already lost two league matches 4–0 during my absence and we were keen to make up for lost time. Queens had won four games in a row and were on a roll. Well, they made it five through a late goal which enabled them to beat us 3–2. I had managed to get on the scoresheet again but it wasn't enough.

Already, the league championship was looking like an outside bet for us. We were desperate to win a cup and once again had a very good opportunity. Although Hibs' league form had been poor during my stand-off with the club, they had been brilliant in the League Cup. We had won five and drawn one of our sectional matches and then comfortably disposed of Third Lanark 4–0 home and away in the quarter-final.

Our semi-final opponent was East Fife. The Fifers were much more of a top team then than they are now and were certain to give us a tough game. The match would be even more difficult for Hibs because it was being staged at Tynecastle, the graveyard of our hopes on so many occasions.

Thirty-eight thousand were there to help us get to Hampden and we should have done. For all its negative connotations for Hibs as a team, Tynecastle was a good ground for me. I always seemed to score there. This day I had notched up two and we were 2–1 up going into the last quarter of an hour of the game. Then the roof fell in. Hugh Howie, usually so reliable, conceded two needless penalties. The referee was once again Jack Mowat and he once more demonstrated that he was fearless as well as fair by twice pointing to our penalty spot. East Fife's burly full back Don Emery was their penalty king and he crashed home the first award to level the scores. Tommy Younger made a brilliant save from his second but the rebound came out to Don who dispatched the ball into the net and Hibs out of the cup in one fell swoop.

Mind you, we could have equalised but for once Last Minute Reilly failed. I was through on the goalkeeper in the closing seconds of the game. I tried to lob the ball over him but underhit it and succeeded only in chipping it in to his hands. Maybe I was just a little rusty after my lay-off. Gordon Smith had been concussed in the second half and didn't know the score after the game. The rest of us wished that we didn't know it either.

We got back into the groove when we beat Falkirk away 4–2. My good form continued as I got my first hat-trick of the season. I had now scored eight goals in four games since coming back, which was good going by anyone's standards. I combined particularly well with Bobby Johnstone. Andy Cunningham described our combination as follows: 'Reilly and Johnstone are Hibs' terrible twins.' He then added, 'In sheer skill and all the cheek which goes with genius, Reilly was miles ahead of any other player.' Thanks, Andy.

We next beat Clyde 4–0 and this time I didn't score. Jack Mowat gave Hibs a penalty on this occasion, which Eddie Turnbull crashed home. The *Sunday Post* headline was 'Reilly – Real Soccer Champagne' – and me a non-drinker too.

The next step in my return was to reclaim my place in the Scotland team and I was delighted to be chosen for the match against Wales at Hampden. Before that Hibs lost to Partick at Firhill so our patchy league form continued. The *Sunday Express* headline was 'Glorious Goalie Stuns the Hibs'. The keeper in question was Tommy Ledgerwood who was probably Thistle's best ever last line until Alan Rough came along.

Wales were a very strong side in those days. They were packed with great players and none was greater than big John Charles. The Leeds man was equally at home at centre half or centre forward. He played most of his career in attack and was brilliant there, but I always thought he was even better in defence. He was leading the attack this day and got two goals. The game ended 3–3 and Bobby Johnstone and I kept the Hibs' flag flying by getting on the scoresheet.

I had the chance to snatch a winner, in the last minute of course, when I tricked their centre half Ray Daniel and ran through on the Welsh goal unopposed. The Arsenal man had a lot of experience and knowing that he was beaten for pace, he pulled me down just before I got into the penalty area. These days, he would get a straight red card. Back then, no action was taken, the free kick was cleared and Wales salvaged a draw.

John Charles, by the way, moved on to Juventus where he had a marvellous career and established himself as one of the legends of Italian football. Big John was a really nice lad and a complete gentleman. For someone so massively talented, he was really unassuming and modest. His nickname, the 'Gentle Giant', suited him perfectly.

After the game, I told the press: 'It's good to be back in a Scotland jersey. Everything is fine with Hibs now. I've never played for any other senior club and I hope that I never will.'

When we returned to league duty we travelled to Parkhead to face Celtic. Their centre half and captain was the legendary Jock Stein. Jock became an all-time great manager, of course, but he was a pretty good centre half and a successful captain as well. What he wasn't normally was a goal-scorer, but he managed to get an important goal in this match. I had put us 2–1 up with a 'lovely shot' and a 'spanking header' but nine minutes from time, Jock came forward for a corner and his header beat Tommy Younger and denied us victory. I played against Jock many times and would describe him as a steady rather than brilliant centre half. As you can imagine, though, he read the game expertly and, I have to say, he always played me scrupulously fairly.

I can't recall him organising his teammates, though, or show-ing obvious signs of tactical acumen. I never dreamt when I played against him that he would reach the heights that he did as a manager. Maybe he had no time to demonstrate his future managerial skills in Hibs–Celtic games because he was too busy trying to cope with me.

I had a great scoring record at Tynecastle and I never had any problems hitting the target at Parkhead either. As my record at Hampden and Wembley was also pretty special, I was clearly a man for the big grounds and the major occasions.

Another draw with St Mirren followed. This time it was 3–3 and we needed an overhead kick from Bobby Johnstone in the last minute to save a point. I must have played well because I was described next day as 'Britain's best'. Gordon Smith made the headlines for the wrong reasons. He received a rare and uncharacteristic booking. Gordon had taken non-stop punish-ment and eventually made a 'retaliatory gesture'. The referee, who had allowed those responsible for kicking Gordon to escape unscathed, immediately booked him. Even the match reporter 'felt heart sorry for Smith'.

Gordon was mentioned in dispatches for the right reasons when we played East Fife next. He produced an 'inspired swerve and dummy' to lay on the second of my two goals as we won 2–1. However, we followed that by dropping three points from our next two games. Our team was changing and not for the better. Players like Hugh Howie and Jock Govan had dropped out and their replacements Packy McFarlane and Pat Ward, while good club players, weren't in the same class. Tommy Younger had also broken his thumb. His replacement was 'wee' Donald Hamilton who was only five feet eight and not Hibs quality as a goalkeeper.

We were unlucky to lose at Airdrie, where one of our sup-porters shouted: 'Your team's aw kick ba and nae fitba!' – and we weren't getting too many breaks. I got an unwanted break in training though. We were playing five-a-sides and my mate

Archie Buchanan totally wrong-footed me with a feint. I went the wrong way and collided with Archie at pace. I came off worse and rearranged my nose. It was lying at an angle when Hugh Shaw came to take a look at it. 'Are you sure it's not always like that?' said our observant manager. I drove to the Western General and Archie came with me to keep me company. The doctor there decided on an operation to reset my beak and I had to stay in overnight. As we had come to the hospital in my car, this meant that Archie had to get two buses home. I can't even say 'it served him right' because the accident was completely my fault.

I had to miss the next game and so did Gordon. Hibs were definitely a team in transition and lost at home to Stirling without us. Our one win in this pre-Christmas period was in a general knowledge quiz. We took on a team of school teachers at the Stella Maris Church Hall in Leith. The distinguished QC and judge Lord Wheatley was the questionmaster and Tommy Younger, Willie Ormond and I amazed ourselves and the audience by coming out on top.

It was proving to be an unlucky season and we were hoping that things would take a turn for the better. Unfortunately they got much, much worse. We met Raith Rovers at Easter Road and won 5–0. What's wrong with that, you might say. Nothing, but the score doesn't tell the whole story. We finished the game with nine men. Archie Buchanan received a cartilage injury and Gordon Smith broke his leg.

I had opened the scoring, Eddie Turnbull had scored two and missed a penalty and Gordon had also managed a double. He was going through for his hat-trick when their keeper Charlie Drummond dived at his feet. Gordon's leg snapped in the collision.

Archie had to have an operation and spent Christmas in hospital. Gordon was allowed home, but because his leg was encased in plaster up to his thigh he could not fit comfortably into a car.

Gordon had bought a pub, The Right Wing, and a grocer's shop with the proceeds of his testimonial and he had to travel home in the back of one of his grocery vans so that his leg could be fully stretched out. Why the hospital didn't send him home by ambulance I have absolutely no idea.

We then lost to Rangers 3–0 at Ibrox in front of only 20,000. There were contributory factors for the crowd. It was a dreadful day and there was a transport strike on in Glasgow. The fact that Aberdeen were well ahead of both Rangers and Hibs in the league probably had something to do with it as well.

Things didn't improve with the New Year derby at Easter Road. There was a much better crowd, mind you, as 46,000 turned out for the game. I put us ahead but in the second half, big Jock Govan, back in the team and normally so good, cost us a goal. Jock went on one of his forward runs and beat two Hearts defenders. He should have passed at that point but took on another man and lost the ball. Hearts broke swiftly and their counter-attack ended with our former player Jim Souness putting the ball past Donald Hamilton. Donald didn't cover himself with glory for that goal and Tommy Younger might have saved Hearts' winner as well. The goal came about when Willie Bauld cracked the ball home from close range after it had bounced around in front of our keeper without being claimed. Mind you, we had no excuses. Prior to their winning goal, Hearts had had two goals chalked off and they finished the game the stronger team. Our best player on the day was Bobby Combe, who had taken over from Gordon Smith as captain.

We now managed three wins in a row and I was on target on two of these games. Were we back on song? Not really, because we then proceeded to lose to Falkirk. Another former player came back to haunt us as the prolific Angus Plumb scored their winner.

Our only hope for the season now was the Scottish Cup and we started well. We won 2–1 at St Johnstone. One of our young players, Tommy McDonald, had taken over from Gordon Smith.

Tommy was tricky and could score goals. He got one in Perth that day and a St Johnstone own-goal completed our victory. For once we had carried some luck in the cup and Harry Swan was moved to say, 'We've never had many breaks in the cup, so maybe this is an omen.'

We continued on an upward trend and beat Clyde 6–3 at Shawfield. Bobby Johnstone got a 'brilliant hat-trick', Eddie Turnbull missed one penalty and Willie Ormond scored another. Young McDonald came in for some praise when the match reporter stated, 'McDonald is playing so well that he will be a hard man for even a fit Gordon Smith to displace.'

Harry Swan's cup prediction looked reasonable when we again played and hammered Clyde in the next round of that competition. We won by the much-loved Hibs' score of 7–0 and I got my eighteenth goal of the season. I made a few as well and the Sunday newspapers recognised a new dimension to my game. They said: 'Lawrie was terrific. He's fresh and dangerous and no longer tries to do it all himself although we know that he often can. This way he will play a lot longer and Hibs will win a lot easier.' As you are just about to find out, this was not to prove the greatest prediction of all time.

Tommy McDonald was on fire and had scored two more against Clyde. Donald Hamilton in goal had improved too as 'his grip was so sure that it nearly burst the ball at times'. We then beat Partick Thistle 2–0 at Firhill. The compliments were flying in the match reports. 'Hibs are certainly back in Glamour Street' and 'The Big Five which has replaced the Famous Five after Smith's injury is still the best attack in Scotland' are only two examples of what the papers were saying about us.

Everything seemed set fair, then, as we prepared to meet Aberdeen at Easter Road in the third round of the Scottish Cup. Little did we know what lay in store. The Dons were doing well in the league and we had no right to expect anything other than a tough game. We might have looked for a fair share of luck though. However, once again, in the competition we most wanted to win, we didn't get a break. As Jack Harkness put it in the *Sunday Post*: 'Hibs waited in vain for the merest smile from Dame Fortune.' Aberdeen knocked us out 3–1, but an even bigger personal blow was about to come my way.

I played against Aberdeen with a heavy cold, which probably wasn't the wisest thing to do. I felt poorly during the game and much worse after it. I went to bed when I got home and the doctor diagnosed pleurisy and pneumonia. These illnesses are extremely debilitating and cause real problems for your lungs and respiratory system. They were considered very serious back in 1954.

The doctor made it clear that my season was over. The familiar shout of 'Gie the ba to Reilly' hadn't been heard at Easter Road in the early part of season 1953-54 and it wasn't going to be heard in the latter part either. I was told to stay in bed and I received daily penicillin injections. This was a real setback. After missing the first two months of the season through my dispute with the club, I had come back in and played really well. I was a handful for every defence, scoring frequently and feeling on top of the world – and then this!

Kitty issued regular bulletins to the press. She started with: 'When Lawrie is well again, I will take him away for a holiday.' The media had sympathy for both me and Hibs. They described the 'tale of woe which is Hibernian's most unfortunate season of illness and injuries'.

Scotland were due to go to Switzerland for the World Cup Finals in the summer of 1954. This time the SFA had agreed that we would go even if we finished second in the Home International Championship, which we eventually did. There was a lot of speculation about whether I would make it back to fitness in time to travel to the finals. I could have saved everyone the bother of debating whether I would make it or not. I knew I had no chance. The illness had wiped me out and I was as weak as a kitten. The headline 'It will be a World Cup without Reilly' soon confirmed that sad fact. I had missed out in 1950 due to the intransigence of the SFA and now four years later, at my absolute peak, I was again being denied the chance to play my part in the greatest footballing show on Earth. It was absolutely sickening.

Kitty continued to care for me and to keep the public informed on my progress or, more to the point, lack of it. She said, 'Lawrie has to get properly well before he even thinks about football again. His health is much more important than that.' She followed this with, 'I just don't believe anyone realises how ill Lawrie has been. It's only in the last few days that he's been able to receive visitors. Prior to that only the doctor and I were able to go in and see him. Not even Harry Swan and Hugh Shaw were allowed in to see Lawrie.' To be honest, I don't think Harry Swan would have wanted to visit me anyway. Hugh Shaw probably would have done, though.

When I felt a little better, I gave my first interview, telling the reporter, 'I have lost nearly a stone in weight. My legs are like spindles. I couldn't have had a better nurse than Kitty.'

In the meantime, Hibs had sold Tommy McDonald to Wolves. Harry Swan probably thought that he would have Gordon Smith back the following season so, despite Tommy's promise, he could afford to let him go. Tommy did well at Molineux before moving on to Leicester and coming home to finish a successful career with Dunfermline.

At Hampden, Scotland lost 4–2, to England who were inspired by Tom Finney. Willie Ormond was on target for the Scots and my former colleague George Farm, now with Blackpool, was in goal. After the England match, he took time out to visit me before returning down south. I had been George's best man but I wasn't best pleased with my old mate for shipping four goals against the English. Scotland next beat Finland 2–1 with Bobby Johnstone and Willie again getting the goals. Hibs were certainly doing their best to support the national cause.

Scotland then went on to have a disastrous World Cup campaign. They were hammered 7–0 by Uruguay and came home with their tails between their legs. We had a manager by this time, as Andy Beattie, the boss of Huddersfield Town, had taken the job on a part-time basis. Andy wasn't a great success and resigned after a few months in charge. He cited lack of support from the SFA as the reason for his departure. When asked to elaborate, he said that he had requested six complimentary tickets for the match against England but had only been given two. That didn't really seem like a reason for walking out on your country. Anyway, although I was sorry that I couldn't help Scotland out in Switzerland, it certainly seemed like it was a good tournament to miss.

Hibs had managed to rally a bit in the league. Despite being without Tommy Younger, Hugh Howie, Archie Buchanan, Gordon Smith and me, they had taken eighteen points out of a possible twenty to pull themselves up to third place as the season neared a close, which wasn't a bad effort at all.

Kitty's plans to take me away on holiday hit a snag when the doctors said that I would have to go into hospital for three weeks of physiotherapy to build my lungs up again. In the event, three weeks became seven as the pneumonia part of my illness proved particularly stubborn and difficult to shift.

Eventually, I was well enough to leave hospital and Kitty and I went off on a cruise to Denmark aboard the SS *Gothland*. The captain was David Sinclair, a local man from Trinity and a dyed-in-the-wool Hibs supporter. He made me a member of his crew with light duties in the wireless department. I didn't receive any remuneration but we did get a free cruise so I wasn't complaining. The captain looked after me well. He even erected a hammock on deck for me to stretch out on and restore my strength by enjoying the sea air and the healing rays of the sun.

We went ashore in Copenhagen and I bought myself a pair of lightweight cutaway Italian leather football boots in one of the big department stores. They were cutting edge at that time and only cost me £3 so they were a great buy. When I brought them home, my colleagues with both Hibs and Scotland were really impressed by them.

I had been told by my doctor before I left on the cruise that under no circumstances should I undertake any strenuous exercise. When we were in Copenhagen, the crew of the *Gothland* played a friendly match against the local Lifeguard Section. I said I would play in goal and did so. We were losing at half-time and I decided that I would play centre forward in the second half. It wasn't exactly what the doctor had ordered. I took it very easy and did just enough to win us the game. At full time, the Lifeguard captain asked why they hadn't brought me outfield until the second half. 'You know,' he said, 'that wee fella's not a bad player!'

I felt much better but still nowhere near fit enough for professional football when our ship dropped us back in Leith. I thanked Captain Sinclair profusely. He had been really good to me. Incidentally, when I was taking part in a book-signing session with Ted Brack and Pat Stanton recently in the Gyle Shopping Centre in Edinburgh, Captain Sinclair's niece approached me. In her hand, she was holding a photograph of me lying in a hammock on the SS *Gothland* in the summer of 1954.

I had to be patient when I got back and take lots of rest while starting to build up my fitness with a series of initially gentle exercises. This time I followed the medical instructions to the letter. On 24 August, the *Daily Record* gave both me and the Hibs support the news we were looking for when it announced, 'Last Minute Reilly, the man with the golden touch, has been told he can start training again.'

14

FIGHTING BACK TO FITNESS

It was great to be back but I was under no illusions about how far away I was from full match-fitness. I had had a real shake and felt very weak. Being me though, I fully intended to put everything I had into my training and get back playing as soon as possible. Although I had packed a lot into my career so far, I was still only twenty-five years old and I hoped to have many years of top-flight football ahead of me.

At the end of my first week, Hugh Shaw passed his verdict. 'He's looking like a million dollars now. He's so keen that I've got to hold the wee devil back.' I joined the rest of the Hibs lads for the pre-season team photograph. I was the odd one out, though, as they were all in their strips and I was in my street clothes as I wasn't yet ready for action.

One of our promising younger players, Tommy Preston, had been playing centre forward in the early matches and doing well. An *Evening News* cartoon showed two fans watching a game. Their conversation went like this: 'Tommy Preston's looking down in the dumps. He must have heard that Lawrie Reilly's on the way back,' said the first one.

His pal replied: 'He shouldnae get too upset aboot losing his place. A centre like Lawrie only turns up once in a lifetime.'

'Aye,' came back the first supporter, 'but Tommy's wondering why it had to be in his lifetime.'

That was good. It encouraged me to keep working hard towards my return to playing. When would that be, though? That was the big question. The press were not slow to speculate.

Hibs were playing Spartak Prague on the September Monday holiday and a lot of people hoped I would come back in that game. One reporter wrote: 'This is a game which will pack Easter Road for it probably heralds the return of the greatest centre forward of this generation – Lawrie Reilly.' I liked that. I had been on the sidelines for quite some time and I knew that getting back to my best would be a real challenge. Comments like that were really good for my confidence.

In the event, the Spartak game came too soon for me but my return wasn't too long delayed. Hibs were due to play Hearts in a reserve match at Tynecastle in October and Hugh Shaw earmarked that for my comeback game. He and I kept that to ourselves, though. When the game came round there were a few thousand spectators in the ground as reserve derbies always attracted decent crowds in those days. If the word had got out that I was making my long-awaited return, then there might well have been a full house. I was made captain for the night and it was great to be back.

I have to admit that I was a little nervous, but once the game started, I felt like I had never been away. We lost 2–0 but that didn't matter. I was able to feel my way gradually back into playing football again and I came through the ninety minutes unscathed. Naturally, I was asked at full time how I felt. I was able to answer honestly 'I feel great. I have absolutely no ill effects from the game.'

I got another low-key game under my belt when we travelled down to Reading for a friendly match and this inspired the poets in the papers to lift their pens again. This was the best effort:

Hib Hib Hooray

A certain something's in the air
As Hibs supporters everywhere
Smile then joyfully declare
'Lawrie's back'
Each flick, each trick, each snappy shot

Provides the entertaining thought
Of little words that mean a lot
'Lawrie's back'
What then can we do to tell
The world we'd like to wish him well
What better than a rousing yell
'Welcome back'.

Then, nearly ten months after going down with pleurisy and pneumonia, I made my return to competitive football. The Famous Five were reunited as we travelled to Shawfield to meet Clyde on league business. We caught Clyde, then a very fine side, at their absolute best and went down 6–3. The *Sunday Post* report asked, 'Just how good were Clyde?' and answered its own question by stating, 'They were great!' They were certainly too good for us on this day. I did get on the scoresheet, though, and it was nice to know that I hadn't lost my ability to put the ball in the net. It was also nice to be back at work doing what came naturally to me. It was even better to realise that despite my long lay-off and weakening illness, I could still do what was required on the park. I was under no illusions, though. I knew that I still had a fair way to go before I was fully back to my best.

I was desperate to play in front of my own supporters again at Easter Road and I soon got the opportunity. Hibs had installed floodlights and they had spared no expense in erecting one of the best-quality lighting systems in the country. Newcastle United had been invited to be the first team to play under the new lights and Hugh Shaw told me that I would be making my home comeback against them.

The next day's match report simply records, 'Reilly's return pleased the crowd.' That was a bit of an understatement, as I received a marvellous reception which really touched me. The game turned out to be all about goalkeepers. Tommy Younger was left out of our team because he had asked for a transfer. I don't know what Tommy's reason was for doing this. I suspect that he might have asked for a testimonial match!

In goal for Newcastle was a young Scot, Ronnie Simpson, who had a magnificent game. Ronnie, of course, was to join Hibs a few years later. In our goal was Willie Miller, making his debut. Willie started the game well but just when it looked like we were going to win our first match under our new lighting system through a Gordon Smith goal, he let a harmless-looking shot squirm under his body into the net and the match ended in a draw.

We then beat Kilmarnock 3–2 at Easter Road, thanks to two goals in the last five minutes from Willie Ormond and Eddie Turnbull. We had another debutant in this game. Seventeen-year-old Jackie Plenderleith played centre half and 'rolled passes along the carpet to start attacks'. Most centre halves in those days just hoofed the ball up the park, but that was never Jackie's game. He was a footballer from the moment he stepped into the team.

My former clubmate Hugh Howie now went into print with some advice for me. He told me not to worry and assured me that I would soon be back to my best. He then revealed why he was so confident that this would happen: 'Lawrie is the most determined person I know,' said Hugh, 'and that will help him to get back to his old form and fitness.' Anyone who knows me will agree with the Howie assessment. I am a very determined man and that determination, in my opinion, has played a major part in any success I have had in life.

We next beat Motherwell 4–2 and I got two of our goals, which pleased me. Eddie Turnbull was switched to right half for this match and Tommy Preston was brought into Eddie's position of inside left. Slowly but surely, the shape and personnel of our great team were beginning to change. After this match, Bobby Johnstone declared, 'Lawrie is right back to his best now.' It was nice of Bobby to say this, but I knew myself that I still wasn't yet back at the height of my powers.

The next match encouraged me, although the score didn't. We

lost another floodlit prestige friendly to Manchester United. This was a stronger United team than those we had met previously. The Busby Babes team was now becoming established and among those in opposition to us that night were great players like Bill Foulkes, Roger Byrne, Jackie Blanchflower, Johnny Berry, Dennis Viollet, Tommy Taylor and Albert Scanlon. We lost 3–1, but I played much better and scored an excellent goal. James Sanderson of the *Daily Express* described it perfectly: 'Lawrie Reilly got a roar that almost lifted the roof off the stand when he scored his goal in eighteen minutes. What a flash of the real Reilly it was. His salmon-like leap to bullet-head Smith's cross past Wood was as deadly as it was graceful.'

This game was a turning point in my comeback. For the first time I had felt really sharp and I had been relieved to do so, as little doubts had begun to surface in my mind as to whether I would get fully back to my old self again. That goal was important for me. It was the old me at last. I had been starting to think that my career was at stake, but when I jumped to fire that ball past the United keeper with my head, I felt the old spring in my legs and my heading power was back to normal as well. It was reassuring and encouraging in equal measure.

I got two more goals in our next game against Dundee and the headline of 'Razzle Dazzle Reilly' made it clear that my return to form and full fitness was now gathering momentum. This was important not just for Hibs but also for Scotland.

The greatest team in world football at that time was Hungary. Their team was full of great stars like their captain and outstanding goal-scorer Ferenc Puskás, their deep-lying centre forward Nándor Hidegkuti, the classy right half who was also an MP, Josef Bozsik, the elegant striker Sándor Kocsis and their acrobatic last line of defence Gyula Grosics, who pioneered the wearing of an all-black goalkeeper's outfit. Hungary had gone to Wembley in 1953 and demolished England 6–3 to give them their first defeat on home soil. They had then gone to the World Cup in Switzerland and lost a final they should have won to Germany, whom they had beaten 8–2 in the sectional matches earlier in the competition. When England demanded a return match, the Hungarians gave it to them and this time beat them 7–1 in Budapest. Now the Magyars were coming to Hampden to play Scotland and all of the country seemed to want me to be fit to lead the Scottish line in this match.

I was so keen to be fit for the game that I gave up my travelling salesman job and returned to full-time football. Hibs next beat East Fife 5–1, although we played much of the game with ten men after losing Eddie Turnbull to injury. Bobby Johnstone was in great form and got a hat-trick. Bobby and I always had a good understanding and although I didn't score in this match, the journalist who covered it considered that I had played well and remarked on my 'uncanny understanding' with wee Bobby.

The press was full of speculation on whether I would be ready to face Hungary when the game came round in December. Some critics thought that I should. Others disagreed. One scribe was of the opinion that 'Reilly certainly hasn't got back all his old agility in jumping for an airborne ball'. Another felt differently when he wrote, 'As the race to lead Scotland's line grows, Reilly has to be favourite.'

How did I feel? I knew that I was getting there, but in my heart of hearts, I was probably also aware that I still hadn't completely recovered my old energy and sharpness. I was desperate, though, to be out there at Hampden against Puskás and Co. I very much wanted to play and that made me work all the harder in training and redouble my efforts in matches. I didn't realise it at the time but I was trying to do too much too soon and I would suffer for my over-eagerness before the season was out.

My main rival was Willie Bauld, who was now playing consistently brilliantly for Hearts. To help them make their minds up on who should be picked for this match, which was now assuming unparalleled importance, the selectors arranged a trial game. Scotland would face Falkirk at Brockville and my performance in this trial would make or break my international comeback hopes. If I led the Scotland line well, I would almost certainly be in against the Hungarians. If I flopped, then the centre forward spot would go to Bauld.

The game between a Scotland eleven and Falkirk was played in the worst weather conditions that I can remember from my whole career. It was icy cold, there was a strong wind and torrential rain poured from the sky. I managed to score a goal and lay on another for Bobby Johnstone as we once again performed our double act, but the game should never have been played. We were all so chilled at half-time that we stripped to our boots and socks and stood under a hot shower for five minutes before changing into clean, dry kit for the second half. I had once had a cold shower at half-time during a Scotland tour to try to combat the unbearable heat and humidity. Now I was reversing this situation to keep the cold at bay.

I did enough in the match to be chosen by the selectors to face Hungary. My selection was described as 'The most sensational international comeback of all time', which might just have been a little over the top.

Alec Young in the *Daily Mail* wrote: 'I congratulate the Hibernian centre and sincerely hope that he will give the crowd an abundance of flashes of his known genius.' That was kind and a happy day was capped when I took delivery of a brand new fawn Austin A30. Kitty and I had planned to take the car out for a run that evening. Our idea was to drive down to Portobello to visit some friends. We eventually made the journey but we were three hours behind schedule because that is how long I spent on the telephone, taking calls from friends, family and teammates wishing me well at Hampden.

My next game for Hibs was against St Mirren and I scored our winning goal by shoulder-charging the St Mirren keeper Jim Lornie over the line with the ball. In those days, as long as the contact made was shoulder to shoulder, shoulder-charging was allowed. I caught Lornie perfectly and sent him flying into the net. The copywriter who wrote the caption for the picture in the next day's paper was obviously of a literary bent because, beneath the photograph, he had written 'Lornie Doon.'

The build-up to the match with Hungary was massive, so much so that 113,146 members of the Tartan Army paid thirty shillings (£1.50) each to fill the old national stadium with noise and passion. One Hungarian writer claimed that the Hampden Roar was so loud that it shook the wireless sets in Budapest. It certainly inspired Scotland and we put in a creditable performance. We weren't good enough, though, to beat the Magical Magyars, who won 4–2. The Hibs' duo in dark blue had mixed fortunes. Bobby Johnstone scored a 'typically brilliant' goal but I had a quiet game. Sheer determination and pure adrenalin had earned me selection for the match, but it wasn't enough to allow me to excel at the highest level, which is what any match against Hungary undoubtedly was at that time. The Hungarian writer I quoted above was impressed with the Scottish team, because he ended his article by stating, 'Victory was Hungary's but the glory went to Scotland.'

Hibs' next league match was a shocker, as we lost 5–0 at home to Celtic. Frankly, this was an unbelievable score line as we used to very much dominate the Parkhead team in those days. The press let us have it. Comments included, 'The Hibernian forward line made football look like hard labour.' That had definitely never been written before. As for me, they described my performance by declaring, 'Reilly looked ragged and tired.' They were right too. The game at Brockville had been the worst possible experience for a man trying to come back after ten months out of football with pleurisy and pneumonia and now I was paying for it.

A rumour spread around Edinburgh that I had had a recurrence of my illness and that my lung had collapsed. That wasn't true, but after playing ten games in five weeks, I had run out of steam. I had been so keen to get back that I had pushed myself too hard too quickly and I was now suffering from my own impetuosity.

We did restore some pride when we met Partick Thistle at Firhill. We achieved a much-needed 3–0 victory. Gordon Smith was outstanding. As the *Sunday Mail* reported, 'Captain Smith was at the helm, cool and audacious, a true master.' The same report also concluded that 'Reilly's goal was thrillingly taken'. Partick had beaten Celtic 4–2, the Celts had whipped us 5–0 and now we had outplayed Thistle 3–0. It wasn't very logical.

If we thought that we were back on the rails, then we were mistaken. We met Rapid Vienna at Easter Road in another of our floodlit friendlies and lost 2–1. I suffered the indignity of being barracked by my own supporters for the only time in my career. The fans could see that during a transition phase for a once-great team, our playing standards had declined. They were also embarrassed and furious about our thrashing from Celtic. Most of all, they had expected my return to be like the waving of a magic wand. They thought that with me back scoring goals again, everything in the Easter Road garden would be rosy once more.

Well, it hadn't quite worked out like that. I had done well enough but, not surprisingly, I hadn't yet completely recaptured my old form. The barracking really hurt me. The supporters were used to getting the very best from me but I think that at this point in my ongoing recovery, they were expecting just a little too much.

Yet, so topsy-turvy was our form that our next league match saw us beat Rangers 2–1 at Easter Road in front of 43,000 very supportive fans. I played well enough for the match reporter to say that 'Reilly is still a great player'.

I knew that to be the case but I also knew that I needed time. The initial adrenalin rush of my return had abated and a little patience was necessary on the part of everyone. It was even more needed after our next game. We travelled to Tynecastle for the New Year derby knowing that if Hibs weren't the team that they had been, then Hearts were most definitely on the up. They had just won the League Cup and were to go on and lift the Scottish

Cup and two league flags over the next few years. Their Terrible Trio of Conn, Bauld and Wardhaugh had now been augmented by two outstanding wing halves in John Cumming and Davie Mackay. They outplayed us and beat us 5–1. Our former player Jim Souness rubbed salt in our wounds by scoring against us again and, comparing the respective performances of the two centre forwards, Tom Nicholson in the *Daily Record* summed it up when he wrote, 'In the centre, Bauld was the boy.'

We next lost at home to Aberdeen although I was pleased to read, 'Reilly was much more full of running than of late.' My pride had made me force myself on and helped to overcome my tiredness, but tired I most certainly was. Hugh Shaw now decided to give me a two-week rest. He was right to do so. I had tried to achieve too much soon and was suffering from the effects of my own enthusiasm.

The rumour mill got into full swing again. I was apparently about to retire. No chance. I would never be fit enough to play again. Nonsense! I did receive a lot of requests for interviews around this time and, being an obliging sort of chap, I agreed to them all. I also tried to answer every question put to me honestly. That led to a few headlines of the sensational variety and, looking back, I would have done well to have employed a little more circumspection. Straight-talking Rex Kingsley took me to task in the *Sunday Mail* when he wrote, 'Some of the questions thrown at Lawrie were so transparently loaded that even a dumb blonde could have seen them coming.' Mr Kingsley clearly wasn't a feminist.

I may have been a little naïve in responding to some of the enquiries thrown at me by the press with complete honesty but, in truth, there was only one question which was exercising my mind. I simply wanted to know if the rest imposed on me by my manager would prove successful and enable me to return to football as the player I had been before pleurisy and pneumonia had decided to pay me a visit.

15

THE END OF AN ERA

My post-rest comeback was on the stage of the Usher Hall, of all places, where Bobby Johnstone and I took on Willie Bauld and Jimmy Wardhaugh in a head tennis match during the interval of a charity concert. I am afraid to say that Bobby and I lost.

I was on the way back, though, and I was delighted that when I ran out to face Clyde, the fans cheered me onto the park. They also backed me all the way through the game as well. We went two goals up in this match and I scored the second with a typical header, but Clyde came back to score three goals in seven minutes and beat us for the second time in a matter of weeks. This was desperate stuff and our fans did not like it one little bit. This time Eddie Turnbull was singled out for their treatment. The match report makes sad reading when it tells us that, 'Abuse showered down on Turnbull, who was returning from injury to restore the Famous Five once again.' The reporter was of the opinion that, 'Hibs fans have been spoiled by success. Their recent behaviour just shows how short memories some of them have.'

If our supporters were not best pleased with their team, what came next would have made them suicidal and apoplectic at the same time. The Scottish Cup draw sent us back to Tynecastle to meet Hearts, who were on the crest of a wave. At this point, Hugh Shaw decided to get involved. He said that results in derby games always went in cycles. He recalled that during his playing career, Hibs had once beaten Hearts eight times in a row. Our boss said that he had no worries about going to Tynecastle on cup business and that he fully expected to return with a victory.

These were brave words by the man in charge at Easter Road and were no doubt intended to boost the morale of his troops. In fact, they had totally the opposite effect. They further inflamed an already fired-up Hearts team, which proceeded to take another five goals off us, this time without reply. Hearts had played second fiddle to Hibs for some years and they now sensed it was their turn to take centre stage. They had absolutely no intention of letting their opportunity slip. Believe it or not, we started the better team and could easily have been three up in fifteen minutes. Ormond and I missed open goals and I was robbed of what looked like a clear penalty. After that it was all downhill and I was so embarrassed that dark January weekend that I never took a step outside my house. Losing a derby is hard to take. Being slaughtered in one is ten times worse. We were out of the Scottish Cup yet again but this time we had no excuses.

Bad luck hadn't come into it. We had simply been outplayed. When Hearts started scoring in this game, too many of my colleagues let their heads go down and accepted what they considered to be inevitable defeat. That was never my style and I gave everything I had as always. It wasn't enough, though, and we were once more humiliated at Tynecastle. As I left the field that day, I knew exactly how down every Hibs fan in the ground was feeling. I knew it because I was a supporter too and I was feeling every bit as bad as all the Hibees in the stands and on the terraces.

Our spirits lifted the following Saturday, when we won 3–0 at Kilmarnock. I got a hat-trick and my performance was hailed as 'Vintage Reilly'. The rest which my manager had prescribed for me had undoubtedly done me good. I was feeling much more like my old self now and, in this game, I had been able to move with a freedom and energy that had been lacking before my enforced lay-off. The Hibs party was so relieved at playing well and winning at last that we had a sing-song on the train back from Ayrshire. We were celebrating our first away win of 1955, John Paterson's coming wedding and my hat-trick. I can't remember what songs we sang but the same journalist who had called my display 'vintage' finished his piece by saying that I had 'a lot to sing about'. What we didn't realise at the time was that this was the last match in which the Famous Five would take the field together. If we had been aware of this, there would have been a whole lot less singing and a lot more thinking on that train journey home.

I was back on scoring form again and was on target in each of our next three games, but our inconsistency continued as we won one but drew two of these matches. Now came the contest which we had all been waiting for. Harry Swan had arranged a return fixture with Arsenal. This time the match was at Easter Road and we were determined to avenge the 7–1 humiliation which had come our way at Highbury.

Despite our recent reverses, 23,000 came out to shout us on, on a cold night of snowy blizzards, and watch a match which was 'more cup tie than friendly'. I scored with a trademark header and laid another on for Eddie Turnbull, who was also back in the fans' good books. We were 2–0 up and should have won, but Arsenal fought back and due to a mistake by Tommy Younger and a brilliant equaliser from Jimmy Bloomfield two minutes from time, they levelled the scores.

We had restored some of our self-respect as a team and I had done a lot for my personal pride. The *Daily Mail* expressed the view, 'Lawrie Reilly is back to near international form. He led the line with spirit and enterprise and with plenty of nippiness at close quarters.' That pretty much summed up my own feelings. As a player, you know when you are playing well and feeling good, and that is exactly where I was after the Arsenal match.

My timing was good too, as the SFA selectors were just about to announce their team to meet England at Wembley. I had done enough to catch their eye and I would play in this prestigious spring occasion at London's famous old stadium for the fourth time in succession. I had scored on each of my previous three visits and I was hopeful that I could do the same again this time. Once again I would be partnered at Wembley by Bobby Johnstone, but sadly the wee genius from Selkirk was no longer a Hibs player.

Harry Swan had accepted a £22,000 offer from Manchester City and the Famous Five was no more. I don't think that Bobby had asked for a move although I know that he was also keen on a testimonial match and that his requests for this to date had been knocked back by the club.

That is the only reason I can think of for Bobby leaving Hibs, as he was very happy and popular at Easter Road. He was very soon to be high in the popularity stakes in Lancashire as well.

My record at Wembley was pretty good. I had played there three times, been on the winning side twice and scored a last-minute equalising goal to preserve my unbeaten record on the third occasion. I had also scored four goals on my three outings there. I had every reason then to look forward with a bit of confidence to what was, as always, being regarded as the match of the season. Thousands of Scots would again be making their biennial pilgrimage to England's capital and our press was in bullish mood. Under the heading 'Magical Wembley', one writer proclaimed, 'I think Scotland will go to town.'

That forecast was to prove optimistic. England ran riot and beat us 7–2. There were a number of reasons for this. Fred Martin of Aberdeen, our goalkeeper, had a nightmare. Indeed, Jack Harkness, himself a former Scotland goalkeeper, wrote in the *Sunday Post* next day: 'Martin has signed his own death warrant.' It's a bit melodramatic, I know, but since Martin had also been the man between the posts when Uruguay had put seven past us in the World Cup, his future international prospects didn't look good.

Then there was Stanley Matthews. The Wizard of the Dribble was now forty years old but still going strong. He gave our left back Harry Haddock of Clyde a torrid time and was so good that 'even stunned Scots raised themselves from the slough of despair to roar their delight at this latest exhibition from the miracle man of football'. Good though Stan was that day – and he was very good indeed – it says something for the Scottish football fan's love of the finer things of the game that our supporters were able to acclaim him as he tore their team apart. Stan, of course, amazingly was still making full backs' lives a misery in England's top division ten years later before he eventually called it a day at the age of fifty.

Another factor was the eighteen-year-old who was playing left half for England. This was Duncan Edwards, the young Manchester United colossus who combined strength and skill with an irresistible will to win. Edwards was unstoppable this day. Little did he or we know that he would sadly be taken from us just three short years later in the Munich air disaster.

Finally, Denis Wilshaw of Wolves, a very good player but by no means an all-time great, chose this match for the game of his life. Wilshaw notched up four of England's goals and was a thorn in our flesh all afternoon.

I got my usual Wembley goal and in the next day's reports it was stated, 'Reilly was the best of the lot.' This was no consolation, though, and it was a sorry bunch of Scottish players who headed back home for the inevitable inquest in the newspapers. Remember, this was a time when there were a lot of really good players in Scotland. We should have been able to compete with the best and there was tremendous interest in our performances. More than 100,000 fans regularly turned up at Hampden to support us and, if our victories were a cause for national celebration, then our defeats could spark a period of mourning across the country.

We had a tour to Yugoslavia, Austria and Hungary coming up in May and a home game against Portugal before we left. The selectors swung the axe with a vengeance. Seven of the Wembley team were left out of the sixteen players chosen for the touring party. I was among those retained and to my delight I was joined in the squad by Tommy Younger and Gordon Smith.

Before we attended to our international commitments, Tommy, Gordon and I had one more game with Hibs. We drew 1–1 with Queen of the South and I finished my domestic season with a goal which was described as 'one of Lawrie's old-time specials'. It was a high note for me to end a difficult domestic campaign on, but for the team as a whole it was an anti-climactic finish to a season which had been really disappointing. I had missed the first few months of the campaign, Tommy Younger had been omitted from the team for a while after asking for a transfer, Bobby Johnstone had been sold and Archie Buchanan had missed most of the season after breaking his leg in September. We had been poor by our own high standards, and we were going to have to improve significantly in season 1955-56.

We had a very good reason to look forward to the new season because a new competition called the European Cup was about to get underway. Due more to our previous successes than the season just finished, Hibs had been invited to represent Scotland and Harry Swan had accepted with alacrity. This was a bit of a slap in the face to Aberdeen, who were the current Scottish champions, but everyone at Easter Road was determined that we wouldn't let ourselves or our country down.

The impact of Scotland's Wembley humiliation was clear for all to see when we faced Portugal at Hampden. Instead of the Hampden slopes being packed with a six-figure crowd, only 25,000 or so spectators were dotted around the national stadium. We had let our supporters down and they were making a point to us.

We began our rehabilitation process by beating the Portuguese 3–0. I got a 'typical goal' and, yes, it was in the last minute. Tommy and Gordon played too and both played well. Now we were heading for Yugoslavia and the first of what would be three very testing matches against top European national sides.

We were staying in the high-class Majestic Hotel in Belgrade. This establishment was so classy that it had its own resident orchestra, which was billed as 'The Best in the Balkans'. There was only one problem: my room in the hotel was directly above the ballroom and when the orchestra played it was impossible for me to get any sleep. On the night before the match, I knew it was important for me to get my full eight hours of rest so I asked Sir George Graham to have a word with the hotel manager. In his own inimitable way, he ensured that the orchestra stopped playing at nine o'clock, which was three hours earlier than usual. The bandleader was most displeased and the ballroom regulars were seriously put out. Scotland's centre forward, however, was absolutely delighted.

I slept like a baby and was raring to go next day. Scotland played really well to draw 2–2 and our goals were both made in Leith as Gordon Smith and I were the scorers. We now moved on to Austria and the chance to avenge our 4–0 defeat there four years previously.

We knew exactly what to expect. The Austrians would display their footballing skills but would also indulge in rough-house tactics. They would be cheered on as they did this by the usual capacity crowd of 65,000 screaming fans.

George Young had been injured against Yugoslavia and, to everyone's delight, Gordon Smith was appointed captain to replace George. Gordon had been superb against the Yugoslavs and he was even better against Austria. We won 4–1 and, even though I say so myself, played magnificently.

The Austrians were as physical as ever but this time we refused to allow ourselves to be provoked. We kept our heads and our minds on the game and to quote one of the match reports 'humbled the Austrians.' The headline above that particular article read 'Viennese Waltz to Scotland's Tune' and that encapsulated things nicely.

Our captain was outstanding. In his own elegant, graceful way he continually glided past defenders and made crosses or fired in shots. Gordon got our second and I got our fourth with a header in the last minute of the game. Yet again I had put the ball in the net as the referee raised his whistle to his mouth to blow for full time. It wasn't something I planned. It just seemed to happen.

Because of his artistry, Gordon Smith came in for special treatment from the Austrian defenders. Gordon took his punishment stoically all afternoon until one defender hit him with 'one of the most brutal tackles ever seen on a football field'. As he got up, Gordon raised his arms to defend himself from further attacks. You might think that this was a fairly mild gesture but it was apparently sufficiently inflammatory to incite a crowd invasion. An Austrian supporter ran on to the field and made for Gordon with serious intent.

I got myself between the fan and Gordon and pushed the Austrian away. At that point, the police came on to the field and arrested the man. The situation quietened down quickly after that. That should have been the end of the matter but it wasn't. Back home, the newspapers praised me for coming to Gordon's aid but with typical embellishment turned my protective push into a stunning right hook. I didn't know whether to be pleased or angry.

The quality of Scotland's performance was reflected in the post-match quotes which Gordon and I gave. He said, 'I am unbelievably happy. Our team was wonderful.' I offered the opinion: 'This is the best Scottish team that I have ever played in.'

I was pretty pleased with my own display in this match and the press obviously agreed as they thought, 'Lawrie Reilly's performance was a tonic. He is back to his old pre-illness form.' This message was being repeated by quite a few scribes and I can tell you it was music to my ears.

Before we left Austria, we played a bounce match against a local amateur team. Every player in our party got a run out at some stage of the proceedings and you will realise that we didn't take the game too seriously when I tell you that Tommy Younger played centre forward. Tommy fancied himself as an outfield player and he predicted that he would get his name on the scoresheet. Gordon Smith scoffed at this but I wasn't so sure. I knew that Tommy was no slouch in front of goal so I offered Gordon the generous price of 10–1.

If Big Tam didn't score I would pay Gordon ten times his stake. If the big fella hit the target, I collected the money. Now Gordon wasn't usually a gambling man but he obviously thought that he was on to a good thing and accepted my odds. Our goalkeeper turned striker did me proud and banged in a hat-trick and Gordon had to cough up.

Our last match of the tour was the ultimate test. We were travelling to Budapest to face Hungary once more, this time in their own backyard. It was only a year since they had demolished England 7–1 – the England team who had just beaten us 7–2 – so we knew we were in for the most daunting of challenges. We were playing so well, though, that we genuinely believed that we could surprise the best team in the world. Interest in the game was massive back home. Our Wembley indiscretions had been forgiven and our touring heroics had given us back the full support of our fans.

The Hungary match was to be played on a Sunday and the BBC refused to broadcast a commentary 'on the Sabbath Day'. Back then, football was never played on Sundays and it would have been considered almost sacrilegious to have done so. However, this game was exceptional. Every Scots supporter wanted to follow our fortunes against the Magyars and the *Daily Record* decided to mount a campaign to have the match covered on the radio.

Their sports editor thundered, 'I too was brought up in a Presbyterian household, but I consider the BBC's attitude to be a let-down to the listening public.' The BBC dug its heels in, so the *Record* took the unprecedented step of hiring a radio wavelength for the day and organising its own commentary, provided by the Hungarian News and Information Service 'in English'!

Those who tuned in were able to enjoy a classic match. We led at half-time through a goal from our captain. This was Gordon's third international goal in successive games and he was proving to all and sundry that, given a decent chance, he was more than capable of excelling at international level.

The Hungarians came back in the second half like the great team that they were and eventually beat us 3–1. Mind you, if Billy Liddell hadn't missed a penalty ten minutes from the end, who knows how the game might have finished. Liddell was revered on Merseyside. His standing at Anfield was so high that some of the supporters called the team 'Liddellpool'. I could never quite get this as Billy never really impressed me when we played together for Scotland. He certainly didn't please me when he missed that crucial spot kick in Budapest.

Despite our defeat by the great Hungarian side, it had been a hugely successful tour and we had restored the pride of our nation. When our plane touched down at Prestwick at the end of our return journey, we were given a very warm welcome home. The *Daily Mail* headlined their report of our landing with 'Crowd Mobs Scots Team. Biggest Welcome for Years.' Given that we had left the country deep in ignominy, it was good to come back as heroes.

We arrived back in Scotland on 31 May to discover that Hibs were restarting training on 1 June. Hugh Shaw magnanimously told us that we could have a week off and return to Easter Road on 8 June. Tommy and Gordon were happy with this but I wasn't. Kitty and I had booked and pre-paid a holiday and I told our manager that I would return to training when I got back from a break which, in my opinion, I deserved and most certainly needed. This wasn't a case of 'Reilly the Rebel' once again, it was just plain common sense.

Gordon Smith had carried out his captaincy duties impressively both on and off the pitch during our tour. After each match, there was a banquet and Gordon had to get up and make a speech. Waverley in the *Daily Record* clearly didn't have a high opinion of the articulacy levels of professional footballers. He praised Gordon's words after the Hungary match in the following terms: 'I have never before listened to a leather-chaser make such a sound speech.'

What Gordon actually said was: 'The Scottish players on this trip reminded me so much of my own club Hibernian when we were at our best – a team of comrades ready to fight to the last for each other.' We would need to fight to the last when the new season got underway, because we had a lot to prove after an extremely disappointing 1954-55 campaign.

Before we embarked on what was to be an unforgettable European adventure, I had time for one more summer distraction. I often played golf with Jimmy Murray, the golf professional from Baberton. Jimmy had qualified for the Open Championship at St Andrews and he asked me to be his caddy. I was delighted to accept and thoroughly enjoyed carrying his bag and offering him advice as we made our way round the Old Course. Unfortunately Jimmy didn't make the cut to play in the final two rounds but, as I told him afterwards, that had more to do with his playing than my caddying. Jimmy's son Ewan, by the way, was a fine golfer who gave up his playing career to become one of Sky Sports' leading golf commentators.

We hoped to give the Hibs supporters a season to remember in 1955-56 and they were certainly doing the right things at that time. The Hibernian Supporters' Association had just opened 'fashionable new club premises' in Carlton Terrace at a cost of £4,500, which was not insignificant in the 1950s. The press described this move as 'A Red-Letter Day for Hibs Supporters'. Sammy Kean, Jock Govan, Hugh Howie and I went along to the official opening of the new clubrooms. Bobby Johnstone travelled up from Manchester for the occasion as well. We all expressed the hope that there would be much to celebrate in the club's handsome new function suite as the new season unfolded. In the next couple of chapters, you'll find out how close we came to realising these wishes in the most spectacular fashion possible.

16

THE FAMOUS FIVE MARK TWO

Season 1955-56 promised to be a little different. The first ever European Cup competition was due to take place and the Hibees were going to be there. In fact, we would be Britain's sole representative in a tournament which retains its prestige and popularity to this day. Chelsea were English champions but the FA had shown that they were happier looking back than looking forward by banning them from entering. Apparently the powers that be down south thought that English clubs had nothing to learn from playing against foreign opposition.

We, at Easter Road, had played against more Continental teams than most due to our regular summer tours. We were well aware of how skilful players in Europe were and we knew that we would face extremely tough matches when the games got underway. In fairness, we shouldn't even have been involved. Aberdeen were Scottish champions and they should have been the ones taking part. However, because of Hibs' high standing abroad, we received the invitation to compete and we didn't turn it down. Every other participating team was the champion club of their country, but we were in on reputation rather than recent achievement.

The Hibs squad who reported back for pre-season training in July 1955 was not as strong as the team that had won three league titles a few years earlier. We had lost a few of our stalwarts and those of us who remained weren't getting any younger. However, we still had some top-class players and on our day we could beat anyone. What we needed was a bit more strength in depth. If Hugh Shaw had gone out and made a few signings, especially in defence, we would have been really formidable. Despite all our success, the big crowds we attracted, the money we presumably made from foreign tours and the income from the regular transfer of players (most recently £22,000 from the sale of Bobby Johnstone), Harry Swan was never inclined to loosen the purse strings.

We enjoyed our usual pre-season rituals. We trained on both Portobello and Gullane beaches. The *Evening News* photographed us running along Portobello Promenade and captioned the picture 'Hibs train by the silvery seas.' Down at Gullane, we were too busy running up sand dunes to see too much of the water. Sammy Kean had us pounding up the sandy inclines of Gullane long before Jock Wallace had the idea of taking Rangers there.

Then there was the usual round of five-a-side competitions. The most important was the Edinburgh Press Charities Competition, which was held at Meadowbank. It was known as 'The Scottish Cup of Fives'. We had enjoyed real success in this competition and reaped the rewards. You usually received household goods rather than money for winning but some of them were pretty valuable. We got canteens of cutlery, lengths of cloth to make suits, electric shavers – which were real luxury goods back then – and one year we even got an armchair each. I recall Bobby Johnstone saying, 'If they keep gieing us stuff like this, we'll aw have to get married.' I also remember what a struggle it was to fit my armchair into my car to take it home.

The fives were great fun. So was the annual cricket challenge against Leith Franklin and 1955 was probably the peak year of this event. No fewer than 5,000 fans sat on the grass around the boundary rope at Leith Links as we once again showed the cricketers how to play their own game. We won by five wickets and I took 2–12 as well as collecting 'three brilliant catches'. The press report also thought that my summer break had further helped my ongoing recovery from pleurisy as it considered that I was obviously very fit.

I was and I couldn't wait for the season to start. Gordon Smith had recovered from his broken leg and took over as captain again from Bobby Combe. Hibs had never had an official vice-captain up to this point but they did now. Hugh Shaw made me Gordon's deputy and I was honoured to be given this role.

Harry Swan was now president of the SFA as well as chairman of Hibs and he used his influence to get some of the big English clubs to agree to an unofficial midweek floodlit league. Newcastle, Spurs, Arsenal and Manchester City would compete with Rangers, Hearts, Partick Thistle and ourselves. I have no idea why Celtic, or indeed Aberdeen, weren't involved.

I started the season well and I was playing a slightly different game from before. In England, Manchester City had devised the 'Revie Plan'. This involved their centre forward Don Revie lying deep, playing as a creator as much as a scorer, and leaving space for his midfield colleagues to make late runs into the box. To be honest, City didn't have the patent on this. The tactic had been introduced by the great Hungarian national team in the person of their outstanding number nine Nándor Hidegkuti. Hugh Shaw suggested to me that it might surprise a few defenders if I played in a similar style and I was happy to give his idea a go.

The Scottish football correspondents didn't take long to recognise my new approach. One went completely over the top when he described me as 'an eager beaver, engineering, constructive, leading out, chasing, harassing, incisive football figure'. He must have swallowed a dictionary. Another contented himself with calling me 'The Don Revie of Scottish football'. He also observed that I was 'lying deep, starting more attacks but finishing less'. I was enjoying playing differently. I was much more on the ball and far more involved in the game.

I got my first goal of the season in a League Cup sectional match against Aberdeen and it must have been a good one because the papers called it 'an absolute gem'. When the Scottish League team was selected to play the Irish League in Belfast I was in, as were Gordon Smith and Tommy Younger. We won

3–0 and Gordon and I both scored. My goal was one of the diving headers which were my speciality. At one point in the game Tommy Younger collided with the post and knocked himself out. Big Tam was unconscious for a full three minutes before he revived. Tommy was such a character that it was hard to tell when he was being serious. As he shook his head and rose to his feet, Gordon shouted over: 'Is he all right, Lawrie?' I was telling the truth when I called back: 'I think so, but you can never be sure with Tommy.'

Tommy displayed great courage in carrying on between the posts till full time. He was also able to play again the following Saturday when we met Aberdeen. Whether he was fully recovered was something else again as they beat us 6–2.

It certainly was a very rare event for big Younger to let in that many goals. Paddy Buckley, the Aberdeen centre forward, scored a hat-trick. Paddy was a Leith lad and a Hibs supporter. Hibs might have signed him if they hadn't had me but probably couldn't see the point of signing him to play in the reserves. He was an all-action player with great pace who never stopped for the full ninety minutes. He had a real eye for goal as well. I had a lot of time for Paddy as a player, although I have to say that I did consider myself to be superior to him as a goal-scorer. Put it this way: when the Scotland selectors were about to announce their team, I always expected to be chosen at centre ahead of him.

The European Cup draw had paired Hibs with the champions of Germany, Rot-Weiss Essen. German football is always strong but it was in a particularly healthy state at that time as their national team had just won the World Cup. The right winger Helmut Rahn, who had scored two goals in the World Cup Final, was Essen's main man.

We were away in the first leg and we travelled with some trepidation. Competitive European football was a new experience for us and we weren't too sure what to expect. Before the game, Hugh Shaw told us to play cautiously for the first half an hour or so. He was concerned that if we approached the game in too cavalier a fashion, the Germans might get early openings and put the tie beyond us.

There was no lack of motivation in our ranks as it was only ten years since the end of World War II. We were quite happy to accept that the war was over and that we had to make a new beginning. It was difficult, though, to forget about the loved ones that some of us had lost in the two conflicts with the Germans which had already taken place in the twentieth century. Eddie Turnbull had served in the navy during the war and my own uncle, my dad's brother Laurence, whom I had been named after, had been killed in World War I. So we may not have been bearing old grudges, but we were harbouring poignant memories and were, shall we say, very keen indeed to win and win well.

As the game progressed, we began to realise that we were a far superior side to Essen. Players like Gordon, Eddie, Willie and me began to look at each other and say, 'We're better than this team, why are we holding back? Let's go for it.' We threw caution to the wind, took control of the game and won convincingly by the very impressive score line of 4–0.

Eddie Turnbull became the first British player ever to score in the European Cup. He added a second goal and Willie Ormond was on target too. I am delighted to say that I also managed to get on the scoresheet with one of my best goals. I picked the ball up on the halfway line, saw a gap in the German defence, ran through it, kept going and didn't stop until I had knocked the ball past the goalkeeper.

We were cheered on by 1,000 Scottish soldiers who had travelled from their barracks to lend us their support. They were all supporters of different clubs normally, but for this night only, they were all Hibees. They wore green and white scarves and hats and their presence was a tremendous spur to us.

One of the German defenders had been giving Eddie Turnbull a hard time during the match. When the full time whistle blew, Ned had a quiet word in his ear. The gist of his message was that he would see him in Edinburgh. He also promised the German that he shouldn't be looking forward to the second leg too much as he might not enjoy what Turnbull had in store for him. Eddie delivered this message in his usual direct style and demonstrated again that his naval service had widened his vocabulary no end.

He was proud of his time in the navy, as we discovered one day after a round of golf at Longniddry. One of our group had brought a German friend along with him. He introduced him to Eddie in the clubhouse after our game. Eddie gave the visitor a fierce glare and declared, 'I served in the British navy during the war in the days when ships were ships. Good day to you, sir.' The war had been over for quite some time by then, but Eddie obviously still wasn't quite ready to let bygones be bygones. Eddie clearly didn't need to be stirred up for the tie against Rot-Weiss Essen.

We knew that we had achieved something special and the next day's newspapers confirmed this. Harry Swan was quoted as saying: 'Our boys struck a great blow for the prestige of British football.' Another correspondent expressed the opinion: 'The Easter Road team has taken the greatest step for long enough in overcoming Continental supremacy in football.'

One of the German national newspapers went even further when it said, 'Last night the Hibernian team from Scotland gave the greatest display by a British team in Germany since the war.' Rex Kingsley of the *Sunday Mail* had travelled to Essen with us for the game. I don't think Rex was a Hibs supporter but he certainly admired the way we played and had a definite soft spot for our club. He took the rest of the Scottish press to task for undervaluing our victory and pointed out that a greater fuss was being made about our win in Germany than was the case at home. He didn't think that this was right and in his inimitable straight-talking style, he made sure that every Scottish football fan understood just how significant our achievement had been. We players felt a quiet satisfaction at a job exceedingly well done and a blow well and truly struck for the prestige of Scottish football. I am sure that our supporters shared that feeling with us.

We returned to domestic duty with a match against Clyde. Clyde, at that time, had international players like Harry Haddock, Archie Robertson and Tommy Ring in their ranks and were a side to be reckoned with. We didn't reckon with them quite enough as we let slip a 2–0 lead and they came back to snatch a draw which they should never have got. My goal in this game was 'touched with genius', so I was clearly on top form. This carelessly dropped point was a sign that we weren't as all-conquering as we had been at our peak. Some of the younger players who had come in – like Jimmy Thomson, Bobby Nicol, George Muir, Pat Ward and Willie McFarlane – were good enough club players but definitely not of the same standard as the internationalists they were replacing.

However, we could be unstoppable on our day and we proved this when we met the mighty Manchester United in a floodlit friendly at Easter Road. This Manchester United team would go on to be known as the Busby Babes, so they were anything but slouches. That didn't stop them leaving Easter Road having been on the end of a 5–0 hammering. We had beaten United by four goals when we demolished them 7–3 in Gordon Smith's testimonial match but now we had gone one better.

Twenty-three thousand fans turned out on the Edinburgh September Monday holiday to watch this momentous match, and they were able to witness a performance which saw 'Hibs vie with the floodlights for brilliance'. Bobby Combe missed the game through injury and young Jimmy Mulkerrin joined Gordon, Willie, Eddie and me in attack as we set about the pride of Manchester. We were four up at half-time and it could have been more. Gordon cracked a rocket against the post and the ball bounced clear. Ray Wood, United's goalkeeper, went over and kissed the post as if to say, 'Thanks for saving our bacon.'

It didn't stay saved for very long. Goals from Smith, Turnbull and Ormond brought back memories of the halcyon days of the Famous Five and I did my bit too, with a couple of well-taken goals. Young Mulkerrin impressed too. He was nippy and had a real eye for goal. He got a few goals for the Hibs first team and a host for the reserves. Jimmy's misfortune was to understudy me for a number of years and follow this by being the stand-in for Joe Baker.

United weren't quite at full strength but that shouldn't detract one bit from our performance. We were magnificent and achieved a historic result. Imagine what a sensation it would be if Hibs thrashed Manchester United by five goals today. It just wouldn't happen, unfortunately. On a personal note, I was really flying now and my pleurisy nightmare was fast becoming a memory, albeit a not very pleasant one.

Immediately after this game, Gordon, Tommy Younger and I travelled to Dublin, where we represented the Scottish League against the League of Ireland on the Wednesday night. As usual, they gave us a hard time in front of their vociferous supporters at Dalymount Park. We managed to win 4–1, though, and I continued my scoring streak by bagging our second goal. There was hardly time to draw breath as we returned to Edinburgh and faced Hearts in the first derby of the season at Tynecastle on the Saturday. We enjoyed a rare win at our bogey ground, but this time I didn't manage to get my name on the scoresheet. The honour of scoring the winning goal with four minutes left went to young Jimmy Mulkerrin.

The game had looked like ending goalless when Jimmy Thomson swung a cross into the Hearts' box. Mulkerrin won the aerial contest to nod for goal but the Hearts goalkeeper Watters parried the ball out. Quick as a flash, Jimmy fastened on to the rebound and hammered it home to send the Hibs supporting contingent in the crowd of 40,000 home happy. Actually, make that ecstatic!

Our teenage centre half Jackie Plenderleith did a great job in this match in playing the hugely talented Hearts centre forward, Alex Young, out of the game. Young went on to become a hero in Liverpool due to his outstanding play for Everton, where he earned the nickname of 'The Golden Vision'. There's even been a television play made about his impact on Merseyside. This day, however, Plenderleith was just too good for him. Jackie couldn't just defend, he was also a classy and cultured player which was very unusual for a centre half in those days.

We next travelled to Preston on further friendly duty and beat the North End, who were then a real top team, by 4–0. Ned Turnbull was having a great season, scoring goals galore, and he got two of our four. I got another and a deflected shot by Gordon Smith completed the quartet. Two very famous players were in the Preston ranks that night – Scotland right half Tommy Docherty and the legendary 'Preston Plumber', the great Tom Finney himself. Neither of them could stop the Hibs. We were in prime form at this time.

Docherty, of course, went on to manage Manchester United and Scotland and earned himself a reputation as one of football's greatest raconteurs. One of his best stories concerns himself and Finney. During their careers, players were paid slightly less in the close season than they were during the season proper. One year when Docherty went to sign on again for the new season, he was offered £16 and £14 as his terms. He asked the manager: 'How much is Tom Finney getting?' He was told: '£18 and £16.' 'That's not fair,' said Docherty. 'Oh yes it is,' said his boss, 'Tom Finney's a better player than you.' 'Not in the summer he's not,' replied the Doc as quick as a flash.

Hibs then faced Kilmarnock and beat them 2–1. Mulkerrin was again on target and I am glad to say that I managed to get the winning goal. I am not sure that I like this description of my winner too much though: 'The decider came from the wise old head of Reilly. It was from a Smith free kick and was the sort of chance in which he revels.' I agree that I got more than my fair share of headed goals but, hey, not too much of the 'old head' if you don't mind. I may have been in the Hibs first team since I was sixteen but I hadn't yet reached my twenty-seventh birthday!

It was time again to make the switch to international duty as

Tommy, Gordon and I had again been selected for Scotland. We were heading for Belfast to face Ireland in the first match of the 1955-56 Home International Championship. This was Gordon's longest run of consecutive games for Scotland and he was showing that he was well worth a place in the national side. We were joined in the team for Belfast by Bobby Johnstone.

It wasn't to prove a happy reunion when we met up again with the little man from Selkirk. Ireland managed one of their rare victories over us as they beat us 2–1 in front of 58,000 of their fanatical fans in Windsor Park. This was no disgrace for us really, because the Irish had some fine players back then. Their star performer was the captain, Danny Blanchflower. People still talk about Danny in Ireland today.

Danny was as lyrical off the field as his play was on it. He was always coming out with Blanchflowerisms such as, 'We have to equalise before the other team scores' and 'I've told the boys to retaliate first'. Danny was at his classy best this day and we found ourselves 2–0 down at half-time. We played much better in the second half. I got a goal and Gordon Smith very nearly equalised when his shot hit the bar and, according to Jack Harkness in the *Sunday Post*, 'rebounded as high as the Mountains of Mourne'. The mountains can, of course, be seen from the Windsor Park ground, which may have put that phrase into Jack's mind. He was certainly never a man for an under-statement. Moving to England hadn't diluted Bobby Johnstone's skills in any way and the wee man was declared 'the best player of the twenty-two on the field'.

Harry Swan used his position as SFA President to make his opinions on the match public. He didn't hold back either. This is what he had to say: 'The referee made several inexplicable blunders. The king of them all was when he signalled a goal which was thirty yards offside.' That sounds like a wee bit of an exaggeration to me, but our chairman's comments make Jack Harkness' use of language seem restrained.

I didn't realise it at the time, but this match at Windsor Park was to prove very significant in terms of my career. Norman Uprichard, the Irish goalkeeper, and I went for a ball together. Uprichard came out with his foot upraised. I wouldn't say that he was attempting to injure me – his main priority was self-protection. However, he certainly wasn't too concerned whether he caught me or not. And he caught me all right. His outstretched foot landed flush on my right knee, causing it to swell up. I went off for treatment then came back on to struggle through the rest of the match. After the game, my knee was still sore but I dismissed the injury as merely a minor knock and I was quite sure that I would soon shake it off.

We moved straight on to Copenhagen, where Tommy, Gordon and I were playing for the Scottish League against the Danish League on the Monday following the Ireland game on the Saturday. We won 4–0 and Gordon got a goal. The game didn't present us with any problems but the weather did.

We were due to fly straight home after the game, because Hibs were playing the second leg of their European Cup tie against Rot-Weiss Essen on the Wednesday. Thick fog delayed our flight and we became more and more agitated. No one was more concerned about the hold-up than Gordon Smith.

As Hibs captain, he felt a strong sense of responsibility and was desperate to find a way to get us home in time for kick-off. Gordon racked his brains for a solution to our problem and then came up with what he thought was a brainwave. He decided that we should charter a plane to get us back to Edinburgh. His face fell when we told him that it would cost a fortune and that Harry Swan would be unlikely to agree to stump up the money for it. We then pointed out to Gordon that if scheduled flights were grounded it wasn't very likely that a charter plane would be allowed to fly.

We had to accept the inevitable. We eventually reached London Airport at 2pm on the day of the match but, again due to mist, we couldn't get back in time for the game. Hibs managed without us as a 1–1 draw was more than enough to take us comfortably through to the next round.

Missing that game probably did us no harm as Tommy, Gordon and I had played seven games in sixteen days. Between club and international commitments, we had travelled 3,000 miles by air, sea, road and rail and spent only five out of sixteen nights in our own beds.

We returned to read more praise being heaped on Hibs' European exploits. At that time Edinburgh had two evening papers, the *News* and the *Dispatch*. Jimmy Cowe, writing in the *Dispatch*, put forward an interesting theory as to why Hibs were so successful in Europe but less consistent at home. He believed that Continental teams put the emphasis on football, while teams at home were more physical and capable of bullying us. He said, 'Teams outwith Scotland play football in the Hibs way, whereas more physical Scottish opponents can nullify Hibs' flair.' There may have been something in what he said.

I probably wouldn't have played against Essen anyway, as the injury to my knee from Belfast was still causing me discomfort. I had an X-ray and was declared fit enough to take part in our next midweek floodlit foray. We travelled to St James Park and beat Newcastle 2–1. I got a goal with 'a typically cool effort' and Bobby Combe, still as quietly effective as ever, got the winner. We had now played most of England's top sides in the first part of the season and none of them had caused us too many problems. My knee was to continue to cause me problems, though, problems which, despite my initial optimism, would never fully clear up again during my career.

Then I got a shock. The selectors left me out of the Scottish League team to play the English League and replaced me with Paddy Buckley. Paddy was in great form and scoring regularly but there weren't too many, myself included, who thought that he was a better centre forward than me. The selectors had their own agenda though and, as I have pointed out earlier in this book, their choices didn't always make sense.

I didn't allow myself to get upset and scored in our next home game against Dunfermline with one of my trademark headers.

Worryingly, the crowd was only 13,000 and it was clear that the fans realised that while we could raise ourselves for the big occasion, we weren't quite the team that we had been at our peak. The Fifers beat us 2–1 and that was further evidence of our inconsistency.

As luck would have it, Paddy Buckley had to withdraw from the match with the English League through injury and I was told to travel down to Sheffield to replace him. I headed south with a point to prove and a strong desire to do exactly that – that old Reilly determination again. I played well but we lost 4–2 to a strong English side whose goal-scorers included Nat Lofthouse and Tom Finney.

Gordon Smith scored an excellent volley and although I didn't get a goal I was happy to read, 'Reilly, the Hibernian centre, was much more like his old match-winning self.' It was a happy occasion for me because as well as being recalled to the Scottish side, I celebrated my twenty-seventh birthday. It was even happier for Tommy Younger because his wife had presented him with a daughter on the day of the game.

Gordon Smith had been injured at Sheffield so I had the honour of leading Hibs out for our next game against Airdrie at Easter Road. We again let ourselves down by drawing 3–3 after being 3–1 up. I did all right with two goals and the *Sunday Post* was sufficiently impressed with me to state that 'The Greens had a one-man forward line. Reilly was great but the rest were nowhere.' It was really frustrating. I was happy to be playing well again, but as a team we were just far too inconsistent.

Our next match, the latest in the series of floodlit fixtures, was against Manchester City at Easter Road and was to be televised live across Britain. Mindful of the sorry show we had put up against Arsenal at Highbury on our last TV appearance, we were determined to put on an impressive display.

We did exactly that, winning 2–1. Twenty thousand turned up to watch us go top of the unofficial floodlit league and we played really well. I got our first goal and Willie Ormond got the second.

City's centre half was a Scot called Dave Ewing. Big Dave was a hard player and very few centre forwards got much change out of him. Well, I did that night because the match report recorded that 'Reilly gave Ewing a torrid time.' Dave was strong and solid but not the paciest of defenders and I was able to run him ragged. Ewing of course became Hibs manager at the beginning of the 1970s and ensured himself a place in the club's folklore when he declared: 'Rangers are rubbish.'

This match saw Bobby Johnstone return to his old home for the first time since his transfer. Bobby had an uncharacteristically quiet night, but one of our younger players certainly didn't. Jimmy Thomson, at right half, was magnificent. The praise for his performance said: 'Thomson was artistic as well as strong and clever. He is heading right for the top.' Well, Tiger, as we called Jimmy, was a wholehearted player right enough and always gave his all, but he never quite made it to the level that his early promise suggested he might.

Another young player caught the eye that night as well. Hugh Shaw decided to entertain the crowd by staging a five-a-side match at half-time featuring ten of Hibs' best sixteen-year-old prospects. Among this group was a certain Joe Baker. One writer passed the opinion, 'This Baker is a bright boy and definitely one to watch.' He wasn't far wrong, was he?

On a high after playing so well against City, we travelled to Kirkcaldy and beat a very good Raith Rovers side 4–0. Their centre half Willie McNaught was an exceptionally good player. He would have earned many more Scotland caps than he did, if it hadn't been for the fact that the Rangers and Scotland captain George Young was a fixture in the number five jersey for his country for years.

I always found Willie a really difficult man to play against, but on this day I definitely got the better of him. I scored what the press described as a 'cheeky' goal after first nutmegging Willie. I'll tell you now, for putting the ball through McNaught's legs and going on to score, I should have been awarded the MBE.

Eddie Turnbull was on a great scoring run at this time and he got two of our goals, including one of his E. T. rocket special penalties. The ever-reliable Bobby Combe got the other.

Scotland's next home international was against Wales at Hampden and despite having dropped me for the game against the English League a few weeks earlier, the SFA Selection Committee picked me for this match. Make of their selection policy what you will. Tommy, Gordon and Bobby Johnstone were all in the team too, so I wasn't short of company when we gathered for the game.

Paddy Buckley's selection ahead of me for the match with the English League was still rankling and I couldn't wait to come out against the Welsh and show the Scottish public that I was as good as ever. Fifty-six thousand fans were there but, believe it or not, this was the lowest gate for a home international at Hampden since the war. Those who stayed away must have still been annoyed about our defeat in Belfast. They shouldn't have been too put out, because all four home nations had strong teams back then. Indeed, Wales – with such great players as goalkeeper Jack Kelsey, inside forward Ivor Allchurch, big John Charles and his brother Mel and flying winger Cliff Jones – had beaten England in their previous match.

They didn't beat Scotland, though. We were back to our best to win 2–0 and as Waverley put it in the *Daily Record*: 'At last, Scotland's football has once more earned the Hampden roar.' Bobby Johnstone got both our goals and they were brilliantly taken. I should have had a goal, but the English referee, Reg Leafe from Nottingham, chalked off my 'great rocket-speed header' that in the view of the press should have been allowed to stand.

I wasn't too disappointed, though, because I knew that I had played well. All the critics were singing my praises. Waverley thought, 'Reilly so much deserved to have his excellent display capped by a goal. He led the attack brilliantly and is unquestionably the Reilly of old.' John Ayres, soon to be of the

Edinburgh *Evening News*, but then with the now defunct *News Chronicle*, told his readers: 'Reilly laughed in the faces of those critics who suggested that he was on the way out.' Our old friend Jack Harkness topped them all when he declared in his usual expressive manner: 'The toast of Scotland today must assuredly be Lawrie Reilly. In the last eight days he has given two of the finest ever centre forward displays. Yet only eighteen months ago, this man was bedridden.' There you have it. Jack was never one for stating his views half-heartedly.

I did leave Hampden that night with a warm glow. It was great to be acclaimed by the Scottish support and I knew inside me that I had fully deserved their ovation as I walked off at full time. I also had the satisfaction of having made a point to the selectors. When they came to pick their next international eleven, I doubted they would be choosing Paddy Buckley in preference to me.

We then returned to floodlit league duty and kept up our 100 per cent record with a home win over Newcastle. Eddie Turnbull continued his rich vein of scoring form with another two goals in our 2–0 victory.

Unfortunately the match was marred by a blanket of fog, which not even our new top of the range floodlights could fully pierce. The referee decided that the match should be cut to thirty-five minutes each way, due to the poor visibility. Ironically, ten minutes after full time, the fog lifted and the whole pitch was clear. By that time, the crowd had gone home, so the ref didn't bring the teams back out to make up the time which had been lost.

We were playing well now, and our forward line had taken on a settled look once again after Bobby Johnstone's departure. Some people were talking about the Famous Five Mark Two and our attack now read Smith, Combe, Reilly, Turnbull and Ormond. Bobby Combe was a very different type of player from Nicker, but he had fitted seamlessly into the wee man's position and the goals were flowing for Hibs again.

Bobby scored again when we beat Queen of the South 3–2 at Palmerston. I was also on the mark and as well as my goal, I showed 'all my old magic touches'. I would need them for our next game as we were now about to face the champions of Sweden, Djurgardens, in the next round of the European Cup.

17

THE QUEST FOR EUROPEAN GLORY

Unusually, both legs of the tie with Djurgardens were played in Scotland. The Swedish season had closed down for its winter break and due to the severe weather there, they had to give up their home advantage for the first game. They switched the match to Partick Thistle's ground at Firhill and that was clearly to our advantage. The cold put paid to me as well. I went down with a chill and a throat infection and it looked like the European Cup had a jinx on me. I was desperate to play against Djurgardens but Hugh Shaw told me that, after my previous misadventure with pleurisy and pneumonia, he was not prepared to risk me.

Once again, the lads managed fine without me. We won 3–1 and Jimmy Mulkerrin, who had taken my place, again showed his eye for goal with our second. Bobby Combe, always ready to have a go from any angle, and Gordon Smith got the other two. We could have had four but Eddie Turnbull missed a penalty. It's funny, but for a man who scored an awful lot of penalties, Eddie missed a fair few as well. I suppose if you take them, inevitably, on occasion, you're going to miss them. When Eddie missed, he usually hammered the ball too close to the keeper. On this occasion, he put it wide of the goal, which wasn't like him at all.

Our display again drew high praise. None more so than, 'This was European Cup football which made Scottish League football look like Boys' Brigade stuff.' Twenty-two-and-a-half thousand people packed Firhill, which showed yet again that our supporters would turn out for the big occasion but were more selective about matches of a routine nature.

I think Hibs fans had become so accustomed to success that they were starting to pick and choose their games. A lot of Glaswegian football followers came out to cheer us on in this tie and we really appreciated their backing.

Thirty-one-and-a-half thousand of our own followers rolled up to Easter Road for the second leg and they weren't disappointed. We won again, this time 1–0, and our goal came from an Eddie Turnbull penalty. Not the slightest bit fazed by his miss in the first leg, E. T. stepped forward and crashed home the spot kick which had been awarded by Arthur Ellis, England's top referee at that time.

That was one thing about Eddie. He may have missed a few from the twelve-yard mark, but he was always willing to come back for more. He had done it again in this big match and we all valued his strength of character. If I am honest, none of the rest of the Famous Five, myself included, was ever all that keen to be the team's penalty-taker. We were always more than happy to leave that responsibility to Ned.

I also missed the second game with Djurgaardens as my illness still hadn't cleared up. Again, I was willing to give it a go but again the manager told me that he wasn't prepared to take any chances with my long-term fitness. The European Cup was proving to be a great success for Hibs but wasn't turning out to be quite so lucky for me.

We next beat Dundee 6–3 but there was quite a contrast in the crowd as only 5,000 turned out, which confirms my earlier point about our fans becoming blasé about bread-and-butter fixtures. To be fair, it was a dreadful day and the matches were coming so thick and fast – with domestic games, European games and floodlit friendlies – that most people probably couldn't afford to go to every game.

This win over Dundee put us back on top of the league and the Famous Five Mark Two was now in top form. I was back for this game but didn't score. Our attack was very impressive but I think we all knew that the defence was less than watertight. As

1955 drew to a close, now was the time for Hibs to move into the transfer market with both the league title and the European Cup within our grasp. Those who know Hibs will not be surprised to know that no steps were taken to strengthen our team.

Our title hopes were pretty much blown out of the water over the next two games. We lost 4–1 to Rangers at Ibrox and our defensive frailties were exposed again. Mind you, we felt that the referee did us no favours at all. He awarded Rangers two questionable goals which turned the game. It wasn't the done thing for journalists to criticise officials whose decisions went in favour of the Old Firm, but Jack Harkness let rip in the *Sunday Post* after this match. Comparing the referee to a character from *Alice in Wonderland*, Harkness wrote, 'the referee's decisions just got curiouser and curiouser.' I got booked for protesting over one of these decisions, a highly contentious penalty award, and that was a very rare occurrence for me. The *Post*'s main man's opinion on my caution was, 'Human nature can only stand so much.' He was absolutely right. In my opinion, the performance of the referee that afternoon would have tried the patience of a saint and I certainly wouldn't place myself in that category.

If that wasn't bad enough, we were hard done-by again in our next game. We met Celtic at Easter Road and trailed 3–2. We were pressing for an equaliser when the referee blew for time with a full four minutes to go. Mr Harkness was covering this match as well and he summed up most people's feelings after the game when he said: 'The referee was grand apart from his time-keeping. With Last Minute Reilly around, anything is likely to happen.'

Quite! We had no option but to keep going. We did when we hammered Stirling Albion 6–1. All of the forwards except Eddie were on target, but the fluctuations in our gates continued. Only 10,000 had turned up for the Stirling match, compared with the 32,000 who came out to see Celtic.

Maybe they were saving their money for the New Year derby match, because when Hearts came first footing to Easter Road on the first day of 1956, a massive 60,000 filled the ground. They saw a great match and one of my best-remembered goals.

I chased a ball up the slope and caught it just before the corner flag on the left wing. I hit the ball first time with my left and it flew across the goal, over Willie Duff the Hearts goalkeeper, against the far post and into the back of the net. The crowd went wild and so did I. After the game I told everyone that I had meant it but my secret's out now. It was intended for a cross and, in all honesty, it was a bit of a fluke. I wasn't caring back then, though, because any goal against Hearts is sweet and that one was very sweet indeed.

The game finished 2–2, but we missed a golden chance to win. In the last minute, I fired in a shot which Duff parried but couldn't hold. The ball spun along the line and Bobby Combe, coming in on the rebound, fired it over the bar from a couple of feet out. The *Daily Record* asked: 'How did this miss happen? Sixty thousand fans don't know and Bobby Combe can't understand.' You would have put your house and your life savings combined on Bobby to put that one in. It could not have been more unlike him, but that was the sort of luck which Hearts carried against us in those days.

Aberdeen, as reigning champions, quite often caused us problems at this time and they did so again when they beat us 3–1 after the Hearts game. We then bounced back to beat Kilmarnock 1–0 at Rugby Park. I scored our goals in both these games so I was still in pretty prolific form.

Then Hugh Shaw made an interesting move. Willie Ormond was injured again – although it wasn't too serious this time – and our manager decided to move me to the left wing to replace him. He put Jimmy Mulkerrin at centre forward in my place. Shaw's logic was that Mulkerrin was an excellent player and the obvious replacement for any forward who was injured. I understood that part of it but I wasn't so sure that it was a good move to stick the best centre forward in the country on the wing to accommodate the second best centre forward at the club.

I had a private conversation with the boss and he assured me that as soon as Willie was fit again, I would be back in my usual position. That was good enough for me. We then went out and hammered Motherwell 7–0. All five forwards scored, with Eddie Turnbull leading the way with a hat-trick, so Mr Shaw probably allowed himself a quiet smile of satisfaction that night.

Then on 30 January 1956 came one of the happiest events of my life. Kitty gave birth to a son, whom we named Lawrance John. His first name was after me and his second after my dad, so I had covered all bases. I mentioned earlier that I had been called after my Uncle Laurence. Unfortunately when my dad had registered the birth, the registrar had entered my name on the birth certificate as 'Lawrance'. My dad didn't notice this wrong spelling until he got home and by that time it was too late to change what was, after all, a legal document.

I saw no reason, therefore, to change anything when we named Lawrance. Mind you, although every paper reported the birth only one managed to spell the new arrival's name correctly. All the rest went for the conventional spelling. Lawrance weighed in at nine pounds. The press took the opportunity to wonder if the number nine might be significant, speculating on whether Lawrance would follow in his dad's footsteps and wear the number nine jersey at Easter Road.

Lawrance arrived a day or two early and this was another angle for the newspapers: they all declared that he definitely wasn't Last Minute Reilly Mark Two. Lawrance did grow up to be a good footballer but, like a lot of sons of famous fathers, he had to put up with being constantly compared less than favourably with his dad. He eventually turned his attention to rugby and cricket and proved to be very good at both games. Indeed, in his fifties now, he still plays cricket most weeks in the summer.

One of the interviewers who was asking me about Lawrance threw in another question. He asked if I was enjoying playing on the left wing and if I would be happy to keep playing there long-term. No one would be in any doubt about where I stood on this particular issue when he reported my answer verbatim next day. I told him 'No! No! No!' Hopefully that was conclusive enough.

After all the excitement of becoming a dad, I had to get my mind back on football because it was Scottish Cup time again. We knew we weren't quite the team we had been but we still entertained hopes that this might at last be our year to lift the trophy which we were so desperate to win. Well, we didn't even come close. Raith Rovers knocked us out in a first-round replay. We went down 3–1 at Stark's Park and the fact that I was back at centre forward and scored our goal was absolutely no consolation to me as we crashed out.

The next day's papers didn't miss us. One report started: 'Hibernian have said goodbye to the Scottish Cup for yet another year. The glamour team from Easter Road are out in the cold again as their amazing hoodoo strikes once more.' All season the Famous Five Mark Two had been hailed as nearly as good as the original version, but now the knives were really out. One journalist went too far when he proclaimed, 'The Hibs forwards have too many birthdays but not enough fight.'

Hugh Shaw immediately sprang to our defence. He said: 'That is not true and it is totally unfair.' So who was right? As with all arguments, there was truth on both sides. Our forwards weren't getting any younger. Gordon, Bobby Combe and Eddie were all now into their thirties. They were still top players but very few players are as good at thirty-two as they are at twenty-two and that's a fact. However, we were more than good enough to beat Raith Rovers. It was a cold day, they got stuck in and knocked us off our stride and our defence was less than watertight. That was the story of our latest Scottish Cup disaster. Hugh Shaw should have signed a couple of experienced defenders earlier in the season. This hadn't happened and now we had paid for it.

There was nothing wrong with the fitness levels of the senior members of our team. Gordon and I were so committed to looking after ourselves that we never touched alcohol. Well, to be fair, Gordon did take a drink once. It was a particularly cold winter's day and Jimmy McColl persuaded him to have a small tot of whisky to fortify him against the weather before he went out. I don't think that he ever repeated that exercise. Interestingly, the same writer who made ageist comments about our forwards concluded in his report that 'the youngest members of the Easter Road defence folded and crumbled under pressure'. He clearly didn't realise the contradictory nature of his words.

We then lost away to Falkirk in the league. It must have been some game because the match report stated: 'If Marilyn Monroe had strolled on to Brockville wearing tights and playing the bagpipes, no one would have noticed as this game was such a ripsnorter.' There's no doubt that that particular reporter was indulging in more than a little journalistic exaggeration.

It was almost time for the draw for the semi-finals of the European Cup. Harry Swan made it clear that he wanted Hibs to be paired with Real Madrid. Was our chairman being bold and looking for the ultimate football challenge? No, he just wanted to make as much money as possible, as he freely admitted. Swan declared that Hibs' coffers needed a boost because of the club's 'heavy financial commitments'.

I am not sure just what these commitments were. Hibs had enjoyed big gates for years, had taken in a fair bit of money in transfer income and, as far as I know, had made money from their summer tours. They certainly hadn't handed out a fortune to their players. I played for Hibs for fourteen years and in all that time, the highest weekly wage I was paid was £16. That was hardly likely to bankrupt the club.

Anyway, Mr Swan didn't get his wish as we came out of the hat with Stade Rheims from France. They were a good side and we would play the first leg in Paris. We found a bit of form in the league by beating Dunfermline 7–1. I got a couple and Eddie continued his phenomenal goal-scoring form with another hat-trick. This inconsistent form must have infuriated our fans as much as it irritated and puzzled us.

We switched back to international football with a match

against South Africa at Ibrox. Tommy Younger, Gordon and I all teamed up in the dark blue once again and 54,000 saw us win 2–1. I was pleased to get another international goal and to read next day: 'The Hibernian centre forward was in good form, with his quick-thinking football and darting runs.'

My reward for this was to be dropped by Hibs for their next league match against Raith Rovers. Tommy Younger was also left out. My knee was a bit sore so maybe that was why Hugh Shaw gave Jimmy Mulkerrin a run in my position. I have no idea why Tommy wasn't selected. He was furious and banged in a transfer request. This was the third time that Tommy had asked for a move. It always puzzled me that Tommy should want to leave Hibs knowing that he wouldn't earn any more money anywhere else. I never asked him his reason and he never told me. It was his business and although I admit that I was curious, I left it at that.

There was a real boost for Hibs when we travelled to Bayview to play East Fife. Archie Buchanan, who had been out for over a year with a broken leg, was back at last. We had really missed Archie and his return would definitely strengthen our team.

Games in Fife were always tough and tousy back then and we learned from our cup defeat at Kirkcaldy and matched like with like. As the match report said, 'Hibs discarded finery for fight.' Mind you, it then added, probably fairly, 'It's a pity they didn't show the same fire and fury in the cup.'

When we next beat Queen of the South 4–1, Archie Buchanan made one of my two goals with a perfectly placed free kick. It was good to have my old mate back.

The season's top game against England was just around the corner and this year the match would be back at Hampden. Once again Tommy, Gordon and I were in but Gordon found himself in a new position. Graham Leggat, the Aberdeen outside right, had enjoyed a superb season and the selectors wanted to give him a chance. They didn't want to leave Gordon out though, so, to accommodate Leggat, they moved our captain to the left wing.

I had to laugh when I heard this. For years, the selectors had ignored Gordon when he was at his absolute peak and chosen Willie Waddell of Rangers instead. Gordon was still a fine player now, but he was not quite the man he had been during Hibs' greatest years. However, he was now being chosen for every match and being fitted in out of position to avoid leaving him out. I often thought that, contrary to people's perceptions, Gordon's biggest rival was not Waddell but the SFA Selection Committee with its idiosyncratic choices.

Before we could think about gaining revenge on England for the 7–2 defeat they had inflicted on us at Wembley the previous April, we Hibs players had some European Cup duty to attend to. We travelled to Paris and met Stade Rheims in front of a 35,000 all-seated crowd. In Scotland at this time, most fans watched matches standing on the terracing, so to see all the supporters at this game comfortably seated to watch the action was definitely different. Rheims were a fine side and their best player was Raymond Kopa. He was a clever, mobile forward, full of ball skills, who popped up all over the field and could score goals as well as make them.

We played really well in this match and dominated possession. We made a lot of chances but sadly we missed them. We were one down going into the final minute of the game. We could have, and probably should have, shut up shop and settled for a narrow defeat but we felt that we could equalise. After a period of sustained Hibs' pressure, we mounted one last attack. Unfortunately the move broke down and Rheims showed how good they were on the counter by working the ball quickly to Kopa who had drifted out to the left. He slid a great pass to one of his colleagues and in a flash we were two goals down.

Chants of 'Kopa, Kopa' rolled round the ground. We felt like shouting something else. We were used to scoring last-minute goals against other teams but this time it had happened to us. It wasn't a good feeling. We were really down as we left the field and the flight back wasn't the cheeriest journey we had ever made. However, by the time we landed back in Edinburgh, our spirits were starting to lift. We knew that we could overcome a two-goal deficit at Easter Road and reach the first ever European Cup Final. Gordon Smith told the press pack waiting to greet us at the airport, 'It's a pity that they got a second goal so late on. We could have and should have won. The second leg will be a thriller.'

On our return, we beat St Mirren 2–0, despite finishing the game with nine men. Eddie Turnbull was off injured for sixty-five minutes and Willie McFarlane was sent off. The ref looked at first as if he was just going to caution Willie. He then changed his mind, put his book away and ordered him off.

It was rare for players to be dismissed for just one foul in those days and McFarlane's face was a picture as the referee pointed to the dressing room. His nickname was 'Packy' and as he went off, one of the lads shouted, 'Packy's been sent packing.' That didn't improve Willie's mood one bit. With Eddie off, Willie Ormond took the penalty which we were awarded. Unfortunately he missed it, but he proceeded to score two cracking goals to win the game for us.

Our game with England came next and we were agonisingly close to getting revenge for the seven-goal thumping Matthews and Co had inflicted on us a year earlier. Graham Leggat marked his debut with a fine goal and we thought we were home and dry until Johnny Haynes popped up with a last-minute equaliser. Once again, Last Minute Reilly had had to suffer the pain of his team losing a late goal. That was definitely not the established order of things and I didn't like it one bit.

I did like Rex Kingsley's match report, though. He said: 'Smith and Reilly played really well. In fact, Reilly did the work of three forwards.' Thanks, Rex. Comments like this proved to me that I had now fully regained all my old strength and running power. The hard-hitting columnist was less kind to Bobby Johnstone. He took him to task for, 'carelessly losing the ball for the move which led to England's equaliser'.

Incidentally, 132,817 fans had Hampden bursting at the seams for this game. Since the turnstiles weren't computerised then, you have to wonder who had the job of counting all those tickets to come up with such an exact final figure by the end of the match.

We played in front of another huge crowd when Rheims came to town for the second leg of our European Cup semi-final. Forty-five thousand were inside Easter Road for a massive game. We really thought that we could win and again, especially in the first half, we created chances galore. We just could not put them away, though. They had a great goalkeeper in Jacquet and 'an iron curtain defence'. They also had Kopa, who broke away to create a second-half goal which ended our resistance. Even now, fifty-four years later, I can categorically state that the 3–0 aggregate margin for this semi-final tie greatly flattered Rheims. They were a very good side but we were definitely better than them. We just missed too many opportunities which we would normally have taken over the two legs and as I have mentioned on a couple of occasions in this chapter, we weren't strong enough defensively at this time.

Defeated dressing rooms are always quiet places, but the home dressing room at Easter Road was deathly silent that night. We knew that we had missed out on a great opportunity to make Scottish football history and we were hurting to our bones. Rocky Marciano had just retired as undefeated world heavy-weight boxing champion. Not even one of Rocky's most jaw-crunching punches could have numbed us quite as much as our undeserved exit to the champions of France had just done. Stade Rheims went on to lose the final to Real Madrid, who rubbed salt in their wounds by signing Kopa after the game. Would we have beaten Madrid if we had reached the final? We might well have done. We would definitely have beaten them if this competition had been played in 1951 rather than 1956.

Our season was effectively over now and we had to rouse ourselves for the visit of Rangers to Easter Road on the Saturday after our midweek defeat to Rheims. The crowd of 20,000 showed that our fans saw this game as a bit of an anti-climax after our European Cup exit. It's not often that you can say that about a Hibs–Rangers game. We drew 2–2, with goals from Eddie Turnbull (yet again) and myself.

I scored again when we travelled to Dundee but they beat us 3–2, with the help of yet another last-minute goal! Then came a much needed boost. We went to Parkhead and chalked up a convincing 3–0 win. Celtic didn't lose at home by three goals very often and it was even less usual for someone to score a hat-trick against them on their own pitch. That is exactly what I did that day, though.

Jock Stein was injured and Bobby Evans had switched to centre half for the day. Bobby and I were long-time pals from Scotland duty but I showed him no mercy. The only way I can describe my display is to say that I gave Bobby the runaround. Bobby finished his career by making the move to central defence permanent. He did really well there for Celtic, Chelsea and Scotland. He didn't have the happiest of afternoons when he came up against me at Parkhead in the spring of 1956, however.

Two of my goals were headers, as I continued to use my ability to jump higher than defenders. It wasn't just about being spring-heeled, mind you. Timing played a big part too. I was able to be at the height of my jump when the centre half was coming down from his. I don't think that that is a skill which can be taught. It is just a natural gift you either have or don't have.

A couple of my goals were laid on by a young right winger called John Fraser. John was deputising for the injured Gordon Smith and gave Sean Fallon, the Celtic left back, a really difficult afternoon. John went on to captain and coach Hibs and played most of his career at right back. He started off in the forward line, though, and he was a dangerous attacker. He is a good friend of mine and we still keep in regular touch. In fact, John lives just along the road from me.

I wasn't our only star. Tommy Younger had a tremendous

game. His performance was described as 'superbly invincible' and you can't say fairer than that. It was a funny game, this one, a little bit like the Coronation Cup Final in reverse. At Hampden, we had dominated the game but their goalie Johnny Bonnar had kept us out. This time, we played more on the counter and big Tommy was the keeper who was in unbeatable mode. I know which of the two games we would rather have won, though.

Scoring a hat-trick in a Hibs win at Parkhead was quite an achievement and I was proud of my performance. No other Hibs forward repeated my feat until Neil Martin got a treble in the first Hibs–Celtic game after Jock Stein had left Hibs to return to Celtic Park in 1965. Neil has since told me that he felt Stein's abrupt departure from Easter Road left the club in the lurch at a time when they were well placed to collect a couple of trophies. Playing out of his skin and inspiring a 4–2 Hibs win was Neilly's way of making a point to big Jock.

Bobby Evans was the first to shake my hand at full time after my Parkhead treble and this didn't surprise me one bit. Bobby and I had been close friends from the minute we had come into the Scotland team together and as well as being a great player, he had always been a true sportsman.

Evans and Reilly were usually roommates on Scotland trips and this arrangement had caused us a bit of bother on one occasion. When we had returned to our hotel room after a round of golf, we discovered that it had been turned upside down by a couple of teammates who thought they were very funny. It was in a real mess and it took Bobby and me ages to get it back into a habitable shape again. We were sure that we knew who the culprits were. Our fingers of suspicion pointed at Sammy Cox and wee Jimmy Mason. We decided to outsmart them and get our own back. Over coffee in the hotel lounge, I casually asked Jimmy and Sammy what room they were in. 'Twenty-one, the same as my age,' replied little Mason. As soon as we could, Bobby and I made our excuses and headed for that room. We gave it a good going over and left, congratulating ourselves that we had more than gained revenge on Messrs Cox and Mason. Imagine the shock we got when we learned that Mason had hoodwinked us and that room twenty-one actually belonged to the Chief Constable of Glasgow, who was a member of the official SFA party for this game. For a while, Bobby and I thought we would end up in jail but in the end it was all smoothed over.

We followed our victory over Celtic by winning another away game when we took care of Stirling 3–0. Eddie Turnbull was a scorer once more and John Fraser opened his account for the first team. Then it was back to international duty as we prepared to meet Austria again, this time at Hampden.

Gordon Smith had to miss the game with his injury but Younger and I were in again. After our great win in Vienna the previous year, expectations were high, but we didn't manage to hit those heights again and had to settle for a 1–1 draw. Alfie Conn of Hearts got our goal and Waverley in the *Daily Record* called the Scotland attack a 'washout' but made me feel better by adding, 'Only Reilly was above censure.'

That brought our domestic season to an end and it had been a disappointing one. We had fared poorly in both cups and had fallen away badly in the league after showing early promise. Only our European Cup adventure had made our season special and with a bit more luck in that semi-final with Rheims, it could have been very special indeed.

We still had more football to play, as Hibs were embarking on another of their close season tours. This time we were going to France and Switzerland which, I am sure you would agree, was a pleasant way to finish off our campaign. We began with a 3–2 victory over Rouen. Gordon was still injured so I had the honour of leading the boys out. We played well and Rex Kingsley, who had accompanied us, headed his match report: 'Hibernian's Speedy Football Creates Fine Impression in France'. That was nice – and so was the fact that I scored a couple of goals.

According to Mr Kingsley, 'Reilly was in terrific form despite the Rouen centre half draping himself all over the wee fellow's back most of the time.' Man marking never caused any difficulties for me. The next part of our trip wasn't going to pose any problems either. We were moving on to play Marseilles, but before that game came round Hibs had fixed up a five-day Riviera break for us further along the coast.

We had a tremendously relaxing few days, recharging our batteries after another long, hard season. The scenery was very good indeed. as Rex reported: 'I am sitting under a coloured umbrella in my shorts, sipping an ice-cold drink. My rambling eyes take in a sea of utter and breathless beauty. They also take in beauties who wiggle tantalisingly past wearing sunglasses and sandals.' I am sure that they were wearing a bit more than that but the *Sunday Mail* man was clearly enjoying himself. To be honest, everyone was having a great time.

Kingsley found time to offer some advice to Tommy Younger in his column. He wrote: 'Tommy, you must be crazy to want to leave a team which pays for you to come to a place like this *and* gives you spending money.' Tommy, though, was still determined to leave his hometown club and make a fresh start down South.

All too soon it was back to business for the game against Olympique Marseilles, the team with which former Hibs great Franck Sauzee was to win a European Cup medal many years later. Two thousand French fans turned up to watch our training session the day before the match and the Marseilles president was so impressed by us that he immediately went out and signed two new players to play against us.

His move into the transfer market worked, as Marseilles beat us 3–2. I scored again and Willie Ormond – 'this truly great and deadly little winger' – got the other. Marseilles certainly knew how to mix it and in his match report Rex, as was his wont, didn't hold back. Listen to this: 'I have never seen anything like the blatant obstructions, hacking, kicking that would have split a head open, arm-pulling, tripping and players shaping up to each other with their fists as I saw in this French seaport.' He finished by writing: 'Despite all that, it was a great game.' It was, and Hugh Shaw was so impressed with Marseilles that he invited them to come to Easter Road for a return match the following season. He concluded his less-than-politically-correct invitation as follows: 'They play very fine football, despite their Continental shortcomings of resorting to pushing, elbowing and obstruction when things aren't going well for them.'

The referee in this match didn't impress as much as the Marseilles team, as the match report was headed: 'The Referee was a Buffoon'. I don't know about you, but I think that sounds just a little bit harsh.

We now travelled on to Strasbourg and if we had enjoyed a little luxury during our time on the Riviera, we came right back down to earth as we undertook an eleven-hour train journey in sweltering heat. When we got there, our tiredness showed. We were held to a 1–1 draw by a team we would normally have defeated comfortably. Once again, French opposition didn't take any prisoners.

Alec Young laid it on the line in the *Daily Mail*: 'Lawrie Reilly was Strasbourg's target here tonight and I bet the centre forward will be feeling the effects tomorrow. They had it in for Lawrie right from the start and the centre was floored in almost every tackle.' He was right too. My reputation as Hibs' danger man had obviously gone before me and I was literally kicked black and blue. I had no shortage of bruises or aches and pains the next day. Continental teams were capable, then as now, of playing very silky soccer. They could also mix it with the best of them. Willie Ormond continued his great tour form by getting our equalising goal.

Our tour ended in Switzerland, where we lost 2–1 to Basle. The referee in this match was apparently even worse than the one in Marseilles. In the opinion of Rex Kingsley, he was a 'Music Hall comedy Swiss referee who awarded countless free kicks to Basle and even gave a penalty for handball against Hibs goalkeeper Tommy Younger!' You could never accuse Mr Kingsley of mincing his words. It doesn't sound like he considered the referee to be the most impartial of officials. Rex's last word on the tour showed that he knew a bit about the game. Referring to our young defender John Grant, he said: 'Grant has poise and precision and may play for Scotland one day.' He went on to do exactly that, winning his first cap two years later.

We returned home tired but happy. It had been an eventful season, when we had made history by being the first British team to compete in the European Cup. We had come close to making much more major history by winning it. We still had the nucleus of a fine team, although we had lost some our stalwarts through retirement and the transfer of Bobby Johnstone had been a blow. What we needed before the start of season 1956-57 were a couple of top-quality signings. What we got was the transfer of Tommy Younger to Liverpool. The papers tried to excuse Hibs by saying: 'It is not in the interests of a club to hold on to an unhappy player.' Agreed, but Harry Swan and Hugh Shaw could always have made Tommy happy and kept him at Easter Road!

Tommy was gone, though, and the absence of Scotland's number one was going to make the new season very challenging indeed.

18

A TIME OF TRANSITION

I used to really enjoy the close season. We took part in a whole range of different activities, which made a change from the non-stop routine during the season of training, travelling and playing. We also got a chance to rest and recuperate from full campaigns, which were made even more lengthy by pleasant but tiring summer tours. June and July were always months of optimism when we considered what the new season might bring. We usually entered pre-season training confident that we could achieve something in the months ahead.

I started the time between seasons 1955-56 and 1956-57 by paying a visit to Bonnington Primary School. The school had just won the Leith Schools Cup and the Mackie Shield, which gave them a clean sweep of the trophies available to them. The head teacher there was my old mentor Bob Pryde. He asked me to come along and present the boys with souvenir photographs of their trophy-winning season and I was delighted to do so. The young players had lots of questions for me. They all wanted autographs and seemed delighted with my visit. I enjoyed it too. Bonnington Primary School recently closed down. I don't know if they ever managed such an impressive haul of trophies again.

Next came our annual 'test match' with Leith Franklin on the cricket field at Leith Links. We won again to go 5–1 up in the series and I put in my best all-round performance to date. I took two wickets, held a catch and saw us home with a score of fourteen not out at the end. John Fraser didn't have the best of the days, as he dropped two very easy catches. The papers consoled him next day by making the point that some people may be cut out for one game but not necessarily for another. He took a bit of stick from his teammates, I can tell you. I am not sure whether John was a decent cricketer who just had a bad day, or if this performance was a true reflection of his talents in the summer game. What I do know, though, is that he was a first-class bowler and continues to demonstrate his prowess on the bowling green to this day. I think it's a shame that Hibs and Leith Franklin don't restart their annual cricket fixture. They could charge for entry and give the money to charity. I am sure that the fans would turn up in numbers on a warm summer's night to watch something a bit different.

Another summer diversion was, of course, golf and the players of Hibs and Hearts competed in a competition called the Allison Trophy. The men from Easter Road came out on top. John Paterson, shot sixty-eight and I followed him in with a sixty-nine. Because I had a handicap of four then, I was declared the winner with a nett score of sixty-five. Another fine Hibs golfer was Willie Clark. Willie was the full back who went in goal when we beat Celtic 4–1 with ten men, and Eddie Turnbull scored a hat-trick of penalties. He loved his golf and lived a fine long life. I attended his funeral recently after he had passed away at the age of ninety.

All too soon the close season fun came to an end and it was back to the serious business of pre-season training. We used to kick our training off with a run from Easter Road to the top of Arthur's Seat and back. I think Arthur's Seat is 800 feet high, so it was a good way to get the cobwebs out of our system. This time, as we emerged from the stadium, two fourteen-year-old lads fell into step with us and informed us that they were going to join us in the run. They were a couple of Hibs supporters called Tom Owens and Bruce Milne. The press photographers waiting outside the ground to take the traditional 'back to training' photographs thought this was great and snapped away as the Hibs squad and the two lads set out along Albion Road.

Well, I have to say that the two teenagers matched us stride for stride and were still going strong when we got back to Easter Road. We rewarded them with autographs and cool drinks. By my calculations, Tom and Bruce will now be sixty-eight years old. I wonder if they are still supporting the Hibs? Mind you, we didn't just run up Arthur's Seat in pre-season training. If Hugh Shaw thought that we had played badly in a match, he would send us up there on the Monday morning afterwards as a punishment.

The traditional curtain-raiser to the season proper back then was the Edinburgh Select match. A team composed of players from both Hibs and Hearts would meet a top English team and the proceeds would go to a good cause. This season the visitors were Birmingham City and we beat them 2–1. I scored the winner from a cross from Gordon Smith and the goalkeeper I sent the ball past was none other than England's last line of defence Gil Merrick. I never seemed to have any problem beating Gil in international matches and now I had done it again in a club game. The City of Edinburgh Council could do worse than reintroduce the Edinburgh Select game. I am sure that Hibs and Hearts fans would still be attracted by the prospect of their teams playing together against English opposition, as a change from being locked in battle for local bragging rights.

The winners of the Select game each received £10 in savings certificates. You could leave your certificates in the post office to gather interest or you could cash them in right away. I am not sure now which option I took, but I do know that some of my teammates couldn't convert the certificates into cash quickly enough.

Hibs' biggest problem as the League Cup qualifying sections got underway was replacing Tommy Younger. We had three young goalkeepers – Jackie Wren, Jim Rollo and Jim Proudfoot. We didn't really think that any of them came close to Tommy's standards but Hugh Shaw hadn't signed an experienced keeper in the summer, so we would have to make do with what we had.

We got off to the worst possible start, losing 6–1 to Hearts at Tynecastle. Hearts were now a very strong team. They had won the League Cup in 1954-55 and the Scottish Cup in 1955-56 and were now targeting the League title. They still had their Terrible Trio of Conn, Bauld and Wardhaugh; they had fine full backs in Bobby Kirk and Tom McKenzie; John Cumming was an international class left half; and in Davie Mackay and Alex Young they had two of the best young players in Britain. They also had Ian Crawford on the left wing. Hibs had freed Crawford and he would make us pay for that on a number of occasions over the years. Crawford was among the goals in this our latest Tynecastle humiliation and Jackie Wren between the posts for us showed his inexperience.

Some of the rest of us took stick in the media for having too much in the way of experience. It was pointed out that our attack had sixty years of service to Hibs between them – and that, in the opinion of some critics, was just too many games under our belts.

We lost our first four League Cup games, including the return match with Hearts at Easter Road, and I didn't score until we met Partick Thistle at Firhill, where I got off the mark in a 2–2 draw. Things then looked up when we beat Falkirk 6–1. Enough of our fans had kept the faith for a 20,000 crowd to turn out for this final meaningless League Cup sectional match. I kick-started my season properly with a hat-trick and a display which drew lots of praise. Although I wasn't quite twenty-eight years old, my hair was starting to grey, which elicited the following comment in one of the Sunday newspapers: 'Reilly was a greyish-haired five feet seven inches of concentrated soccer genius who blazed through the game with lightning-like darts, dribbles and flying headers.' They don't write like that any more, do they? By the way I was nearer five feet eight than five feet seven!

As the league matches got under way, Hugh Shaw moved to sign a goalkeeper. He brought in Lawrie Leslie from Newtongrange Star. This told us that our manager wasn't happy with the goalies he had. The fact that he had raided Junior football, though, let us know that Harry Swan still wasn't for loosening the purse strings. The press made a big thing of Lawrie and me having the same first name. I suppose you could say that Hibs had 'The Two Lawries' long before the BBC had 'The Two Ronnies'.

Unfortunately Leslie was doing his national service in the army so wouldn't always be available. When Tommy Younger had been stationed in Germany, he had managed to fly home on leave almost every weekend. Tommy had been an established player though and Lawrie, just starting out in his career, would find the army authorities to be less flexible.

Talking of Tommy, he returned to Easter Road to play for Liverpool in a floodlit friendly. Young Leslie made his debut in our goal and showed great promise. He couldn't stop us losing 2–1, though, as our inconsistent form continued. We lost our next two games 5–1 to Spurs and 2–0 to Queen of the South. Proudfoot and Wren kept goal in these games and it was obvious that when Leslie wasn't available we had problems between the sticks. We had quite a few problems, in fact, and were obviously a team in transition. New players like John and Hugh Higgins, Jimmy Harrower and Davie Gibson had come in. Their talents varied but none of them at that time was of the class which Hibs fans had become accustomed to in the post-war years.

Next came our third match with Hearts in a couple of months. The first league derby of the season was at Easter Road and I had a problem. Captain David Sinclair – who had looked after me so well aboard the SS *Gothland* when I had taken a cruise to recuperate from pleurisy and pneumonia – had asked me to give away his future daughter-in-law on her wedding day as her parents were in New Zealand. I had been happy to agree but unfortunately the wedding had been rescheduled from its original date to the day of the Hibs–Hearts game.

I was determined to make both, so I left the church after performing my nuptial duties at 2.30pm, jumped into one of the wedding cars and headed for Easter Road. I leapt out opposite the players' entrance, still in my wedding tails, to draw amazed looks from supporters making their way into the ground: 'Look at Lawrie – what's he dressed up like that for?' was the first comment I heard. Hugh Shaw wasn't a man to get too fussed about things, though, and when I raced into the dressing room, he simply said: 'Hurry up and get changed. Ye cannae go oot on the field dressed like that.'

I was in my kit in time to lead the team out. I was captain in a derby for the first time as Gordon Smith was out injured. We played really well, but to the despair of ourselves and our supporters we lost to Hearts again. The papers reckoned that I had played the 'game of my life'. I did score but we lost 3–2 and Jock Buchanan, another of the young players coming into the team, missed a sitter in the last minute. That maybe had something to do with the fact that Jock, who was a centre forward, was doing his best to fill in for Gordon in the unfamiliar right wing position.

This time Rollo was in goal and again Tommy Younger's absence was keenly felt. The fact that we were changing our goalkeeper virtually every game told its own story and Harry Swan's folly in selling Big Tam was clear for all to see. We didn't play badly in this match. In fact we played much better than we had done in the two League Cup derbies but, as was often the case at that time, we didn't get much in the way of luck.

Newcastle were our next floodlit friendly visitors and, whereas once we had been invincible in these games, we lost again. Their centre forward Jackie Milburn got the winner. 'Wor Jackie' as he was known on Tyneside, was one of the very best. He was a big, powerful man and an out-and-out goal scorer. People have often asked me how I compare myself with Milburn. I would say I had more of an all-round game, but the Geordie legend was deadly in front of goal. When he retired they erected a statue of him outside St James Park. He deserved it too. As well as being a great player, he was a really nice man. Jack and Bobby Charlton were related to him and his brother Stan played for Leicester City, so there was obviously a lot of footballing talent in the Milburn genes. To date, nobody has suggested putting up a statue of the Famous Five outside Easter Road. It wouldn't be a bad idea, mind you!

Gordon Smith was back for our next league game against Queen's Park and as we ran out a fan shouted, 'With Gordon back, we'll take six off this lot.' We didn't. It was 1–1. Our next game against Raith Rovers ended in the same scoreline. Gordon got injured again, and only that very rare phenomenon, a right-footed goal from Willie Ormond, enabled the ten of us who finished the game to snatch a draw. We were really hanging on for full time, and when one of the journalists in the press box shouted down to Harry Swan, sat below him in the Kirkcaldy stand, 'How long is there to go?' our chairman replied: 'Too long!'

At this point, I took a major step to secure my future. A friend of mine, Jimmy Malone, worked for Scottish Brewers and he suggested that I should buy a pub. It seemed like a good idea and I spoke to the brewery. They made it clear that if I could come up with a decent deposit, then they would provide a loan to cover the balance of the purchase price. I was happy with that and we didn't take long to shake hands on a deal.

If that was good news off the field, things were not going well on it. Crowds at Easter Road were now dropping and any money Harry Swan had made from selling Bobby Johnstone and Tommy Younger was being used up to make good the shortfall in cash coming through the turnstiles. Swan was defiant and declared, 'We're building a sure foundation for the future.' Not everyone was in agreement with our chairman on that one.

When I played my first game of the season for Scotland against Wales I still couldn't get myself onto the winning side. It was a 2–2 draw. I did score, though, and my performance was described as 'inspiring'. I moved on from Cardiff to London where we drew 3–3 with Spurs. We should have won, because Willie McFarlane missed a penalty in the dying seconds. He also missed the chance to be known as 'Last Minute McFarlane'. Eddie Turnbull had decided to take a break from spot-kick duties and Packy had been doing well up to this point, but he failed to win the match for us. I was again on target and the Russian ambassador who sat in the stand was full of praise for my display. The next day's headline read: 'Reilly Impresses Man from Moscow'.

I was more intent on impressing the men and women from Leith, but our next game was another defeat. We lost 5–3 to Rangers at Ibrox and the *Sunday Mail* journalist Willie Allison, who would go on to be Rangers' press officer, declared that: 'The wily Reilly proved himself to be Scotland's best.' That was praise indeed from a man who never hid his allegiance to Ibrox. I didn't need newspaper reporters to tell me that I was playing well, though. As a team, we had declined. There was no doubt about that, although we could still raise our game on our day and we were probably just two or three signings away from being good enough to compete for trophies again. On an individual level, I knew that I was still the best centre forward in the country. The game I had played against Hearts after rushing from the church had been one of my very best and I hoped that there was more to come.

The Scotland selectors obviously agreed with my assessment of my form, because when it was time to go back to international duty for the match against Ireland at Hampden in the Home International Championships, I was once more chosen to lead the line. I got a bit of a shock when I opened my post a few days before the game. I had received a letter from someone signing himself as 'Mr X'. He was offering me £150 to feign injury and make myself unavailable for the Ireland match. I dismissed it as the action of a crank and threw the letter into the fire. I took the whole thing so lightly that I didn't even consider telling Sir George Graham or Hugh Shaw about it.

I went ahead and played of course and laid on the winning goal for a young right winger from Rangers who was making his debut. Alex Scott was a flyer and he certainly got his international career off to a flying start with the only strike of the game. Alex's brother Jim served Hibs well with his silky skills for many years and Alex himself signed on at Easter Road towards the end of his career.

In the weeks following this game, 'Mr X' made his unwanted presence felt again by making a number of abusive and threatening phone calls to our house. I took it in my stride but it was upsetting for Kitty. We eventually decided that enough was enough and reported the matter to the police. A quick change to an ex-directory telephone number did the trick and we thankfully never heard any more from our mysterious caller.

Then came a Hibs' performance which was just like old times. We went to Bayview and thrashed East Fife 6–1. Eddie, Willie and I were all on target, which proved that there was still life in our experienced legs. This was the end of 1956 and the new style of music which was being pioneered by Elvis Presley and Bill Haley was very much in the forefront of everyday life. This was reflected in the *Sunday Post* match reporter's description of our improved performance. He said: 'Rock and roll blasted from the loudspeakers and Hibs razzle dazzled on the pitch.'

The Monday after this game, I officially opened my hostelry. The pub was in Mitchell Street in Leith, quite close to the bowling green at Leith Links. I called the pub 'The Bowlers' Rest', although people were soon talking about going down to 'Reilly's'. A few of my footballing friends came along to the opening and the first recipient of a drink was my old Scotland pal, Willie Woodburn. Big Ben asked if his drink was on the house. I told him that it was as long as he proposed a toast to Hibs. Tommy Preston, Eddie Turnbull, Willie Ormond and John Paterson all came along too. John worked in the whisky trade after he retired so he and I often did business together. I would train during the day and work in the pub in the evenings and I enjoyed it. I met a lot of people and made a lot of good friends and business contacts. I built up a regular clientele, most of whom were Hibs fans and well behaved. If anyone stepped out of line, I was quite happy to be a strict mine host and deal with them, but most of the time there were no problems at all.

We even had a Rangers Supporters Branch bus which called in before Hibs–Rangers games at Easter Road. They would park their coach outside the pub, have a couple of drinks before the game, walk up to the ground, have one for the road after the match and then head back to Glasgow. Despite the intense rivalry between our two teams, they always got on well with the Hibs fans in the pub and there was never any trouble. The walls of the bar were decorated with footballing photographs from my career and that went down well with the regulars.

Back on the field, we managed another good away win at Airdrie, where we chalked up a 5–3 victory. The result was spot-on but I wasn't. When we got a penalty, Eddie Turnbull didn't want to take it and Willie McFarlane wasn't playing, so I stepped forward. I hit the bar but the ball bounced out. Later in the game, we got another spot kick and Eddie decided that enough was enough and that he was putting himself back on penalty duty. Eddie's shot also hit the bar but from there it flew into the net. I got two goals in this game so only my own poor penalty-taking stopped me notching up a hat-trick. Little did I know it at the time but I was never to score three goals in one game for Hibs again.

Gordon Smith made his third comeback from injury of the season in this game, but broke down again. Gordon's continued absences weren't helping our cause. Lawrie Leslie was available to play in goal in this match and again did well. Although he conceded three goals, he had no chance with any of them and was described as 'looking the dazzling part'. There was absolutely no doubt that Leslie was the best of our new crop of goalkeepers.

Talking of goalkeepers, we had the pleasure of Tommy Younger's company at training over the next few days. Big Tam's wife was about to give birth to their second child and they had come back up to Edinburgh to make sure that their child came into the world in their own country. It was good to have the big man back. Most of us wished that he had never left in the first place.

Tommy even found time for a game of golf during his visit. Tommy loved the game and he and I often played together. Once when I was on holiday, Tommy scored a hole in one at the fifth at Longniddry which was a difficult par three bordering on a par four. When I got back, he and I played there the following week. Tommy kept going on about how he intended to repeat his feat of the previous week. When we reached the fifth, I bet him that he wouldn't even get his drive on the green. He accepted immediately and, to my delight, proceeded to hit his tee shot well wide of the putting surface.

We next met Celtic at Easter Road in the last match of 1956. We used to get 60,000 for this game but this time only 31,000 turned up, which shows that the fans knew that things weren't completely right with Hibs. It was a great game, though, an exciting 3-3 draw, which saw me snatch an eighty-first-minute equaliser. It was not quite Last Minute Reilly, more Late On Reilly.

Round about this time, a colour magazine did a feature on me. It revealed that my grandfather Barney Reilly had looked at me in my pram as a baby and said, 'That boy will play for the Hibs.' He was right, but there again if anyone was qualified to make such a forecast, it was him. He had come across to Scotland from County Cavan in Ireland and had lived originally in Blackfriars Street in Edinburgh's Old Town, before later moving to Stockbridge. He was a member of St Patrick's Parish and, I believe, involved in the rebirth of Hibs in 1893 after the club had gone out of existence temporarily in 1891. I am proud of that and proud of the fact that he passed his love of Hibernian FC on to my dad, who in turn passed it on to me. I, of course, made sure that my own son Lawrance was also raised as a Hibs fan.

New Year's Day 1957 was a happy one for Hibs fans. We met Hearts for the fourth time that season and at last we managed a win. Eddie Turnbull gave us the lead with 'a blistering shot' in just twenty seconds and John Fraser, who was deputising for the still injured Gordon Smith, scored our second after half-time. John and I took it upon ourselves to continually switch positions during this match and it worked, as John's goal came from the centre-forward position. Hugh Shaw rarely gave us any such tactical advice but he was always happy for us to use our own initiative.

For once we got some luck against Hearts as the maroons hit the woodwork no fewer than four times. It was nice to put our Tynecastle hoodoo to rest. It wasn't quite so nice for our city rivals, though, as this defeat dealt what proved to be a terminal blow to their hopes of winning the league. Mind you, they did win it twice in the next three years.

We built on this win to beat Aberdeen 4–1 at Easter Road. Lawrie Leslie continued in goal and that helped. Willie Ormond got two fine goals including 'a back heel of the leather into its billet' – which takes some beating in the flowery language stakes – and I got a goal and put in a fine performance. I was pleased to read: 'The star of the Hibs side was Reilly who is in great fettle these days.' I might have become a dad, my hair might have been greying and I might also have taken up the publican's trade, but I was proving that I could still play. What the journalists and fans didn't know was that my knee still wasn't fully right. I could play through the discomfort it gave me during games, but I knew that I would suffer pain afterwards.

The writer of this piece, though, wasn't fully convinced by our performance as he recorded: 'A 4–1 win over Aberdeen looks good but I am not rushing into print to say that the Hibs are definitely back.' He was right to have his doubts because we then proceeded to lose our next two matches. Lawrie Leslie was once more unable to get his release from army duties so Jackie Wren returned in goal. This may have been a factor in what followed, but it wasn't the only one. We had too many players who weren't consistently good enough. On our good days, the nucleus of the team could carry the rest, but on other days we struggled.

We were about to face Aberdeen at Easter Road again, this

time in the Scottish Cup. We had met the Dons three times in this competition in the ten years it had been played since World War II. Now we had drawn them once more. We had beaten them comfortably the previous week, on paper at least, so we should have been going into the game feeling optimistic. We were but our high hopes weren't justified. This game proved that our personnel may have changed but our luck in the Scottish Cup hadn't. We didn't turn up in the first half and everything Aberdeen hit went in. We found ourselves turning round 4–0 down yet still feeling we were in with a chance.

We played much better after the break. We poured down the slope, showed some of our old form and pulled back three goals. The all-important fourth one, unfortunately, eluded us. It wasn't as though we didn't have chances. We had plenty of them. It just wasn't Willie Ormond's day because the wee fellow himself could not only have saved the game but could have won it for us.

John McPhail, the former Celtic centre forward, was now writing for the *Daily Record* and his report summed up our second-half performance pretty well. He said, 'Lawrie Reilly had the game of his life, Gordon Smith's touchline display was reminiscent of his vintage best but Willie Ormond missed around six scoring chances.' No one felt worse than Willie. He was usually reliable in front of goal but this hadn't been his day.

We had good reason to feel sorry for ourselves but the bottom line was that we were once more out of the Scottish Cup. Things at Easter Road weren't about to improve either. As I mentioned in the chapter on my re-signing dispute with the club, players were eligible for a benefit after five years of continuous service with one team. The club didn't have to pay up but it usually did. Hibs, in the past, always had. Now we had a number of players who were due for benefits again. Harry Swan said Hibs couldn't afford to pay. He came out with: 'All our players are underpaid but we need more cash coming through the turnstiles.'

I wonder if our chairman was starting to reflect on his policy of selling top-quality players and replacing them with home-grown youngsters. That's fine if the young players who come through are good enough. In the previous four years, Hibs had signed thirty-eight players. Of these, only Tommy Preston, John Fraser, John Grant and Jackie Plenderleith had established themselves in the first team. To be fair to Mr Swan, one top-class and one exceptional player in Johnny McLeod and Joe Baker would come through in the next year.

Archie Buchanan was due a benefit but Harry Swan offered him a free transfer in lieu of his payment. Archie reluctantly accepted. He hadn't been able to re-establish himself as a first-team regular after his cartilage operation and leg-break but everyone at Easter Road was sorry to see him go. No one was sorrier than me as Archie and I went back a long way and had always got on really well off the park.

Willie Ormond was due a benefit as well and was also told that the club couldn't afford to pay it. His response was to ask for a transfer. This was really an act of protest on Willie's part as, like the rest of us, he loved life at Easter Road. In due course, his transfer request was forgotten about.

I was in the headlines too, but for a different reason. I had only scored fourteen goals so far in season 1956-57. This was a good bit less than my normal quota. There were reasons for this. I was definitely getting less service than I was used to – the decline in the team's quality had seen to that. My knee problem was also contributing to my reduced output on the goal front. As I mentioned earlier, although I had kept playing since my clash with Norman Uprichard at Belfast, my knee had never felt right. The best way I could describe it is that when I tried to run full-out I felt like a car trying to accelerate with its handbrake partially on. I could still sprint, but I couldn't stretch out full-throttle. Also, after every game, fluid gathered on my knee and I couldn't train properly for a couple of days until the swelling had gone down.

Now there was press speculation that I might not be chosen for Scotland when the annual match with England came round. We were going back to Wembley and if I was selected it would be the fifth time in a row that I had walked out at England's national stadium. That would be quite a record and I didn't want to miss out on it. All my life, my response to a challenge had been to bring out the best in myself and that is what I did now.

I started with a fine display and a goal in a 3–0 home win over Dundee. This persuaded one reporter to write: 'Reilly is still the best centre forward in Scotland. If he doesn't go to Wembley, there ain't no justice.' That was more like it.

Next, we played East Fife. This match was unusual as it was the first match played under floodlights at Easter Road on a Saturday night. The reason for this was that Falkirk and Raith Rovers were playing a Scottish Cup semi-final at Tynecastle in the afternoon and the police didn't want to have to cover two matches at the same time. The change of time did us no harm as we ran out 4–0 winners. I scored a good goal with a left-foot shot and the *Sunday Post* thought, 'Reilly wrote his ticket to Wembley with his left foot.' I hoped that I had done exactly that. If I was selected to make the biennial trip to London's premier stadium, it would be a triumph of will. I had forced myself to ignore the niggles in my knee and had given everything I had to keep my place in the Scotland team for the game which meant so much to me.

Ever since I had come into the Hibs team, one of the supporters had shouted regularly, 'Gie the ba to Reilly.' He had a loud voice and other people in the crowd would take up the shout with him. This call hadn't been heard much in season 1956-57, but this night against East Fife, as my determination saw my best form return, it rolled round the terraces again.

My improved form did indeed see me included in the Scotland line-up for Wembley. I almost ended up missing the game due to a complete accident. On the day before the game, we were in the dressing room at our training ground. Tommy Younger and Tommy Docherty were larking about with a cup of water. The cup went flying out of the Doc's hand and fell to the floor. It shattered and a sharp piece ricocheted across the room and embedded itself in my foot. There was blood everywhere and, of course, doubt about whether I would be fit to play next day. Dr McMillan, the team doctor, removed the shard of china, cleaned my foot up and inserted stitches. He told me that we would wait and see how I was the next day.

When Saturday came, my foot was really sore and I had difficulty walking, let alone running. When our team coach pulled up at Wembley, I got out and hobbled towards the dressing room. I heard one Scots fan say, 'One thing's for sure – he'll no be playing the day.' Well, he was wrong. Dr McMillan offered me a painkilling injection and I decided to take it. The foot was agony before he inserted his needle into it, but the pain very quickly receded. I never felt a thing during the match and I have never felt it since. The injury must have had a subconscious effect on me, though, because I wasn't at my best.

We lost 2–1 and England's winning goal came from a very special player. Big Duncan Edwards, then only twenty, smashed home a twenty-yarder to take the game away from us. Less than a year later, of course, Duncan, along with many of his Manchester United colleagues, lost his life in the Munich air disaster.

I heard about the plane crash as I came off the course after completing a round of golf at Gullane. The tragedy had a huge impact on the whole country, but it was particularly poignant for those of us at Easter Road. Because the Manchester United manager Matt Busby had played for Hibs during the war, there was a close bond between the two clubs. We played United regularly and we had got to know their players quite well. The last time I had seen Mr Busby, he had put his arm round me and said, 'How are you getting on, son? How would you like to play for Manchester United?' As I have made clear in this book, I never had any desire to leave Hibs or to play in England. If I had decided to move south though, the only team I would have considered would have been Manchester United. Now the great manager was in a Munich hospital fighting for his life. Thankfully he pulled through. Indeed, he went on to lead his team to a great triumph in the European Cup when they beat Benfica at Wembley in 1968. I can only begin to imagine what went through his mind on that night of many and mixed emotions.

This was the first time I hadn't scored for Scotland at Wembley. I was involved in a move that should have led to an equaliser when I shoulder-charged the England goalkeeper Alan Hodgkinson and he dropped the ball. Willie Fernie knocked the ball in but the referee gave a foul against me. Shoulder-charging was commonplace then and, as long as the contact was shoulder to shoulder, perfectly legal. There was no doubt in my mind that the contact between Hodgkinson and myself had taken place in exactly that way but the referee didn't agree. Rex Kingsley in the *Sunday Mail* didn't agree with something else. He was most unhappy about how England approached the game. Outspoken as ever, he declared, 'Thirty thousand Scottish fans regularly booed coarse English tackling.'

I didn't realise it at the time, but this was to be my last game for Scotland. After the Wembley game, we had World Cup qualifiers coming up but I had to count myself out of them and accept that it was time to do something about my knee injury. I had a cartilage operation and admitted publicly for the first time that I had been labouring under a handicap since sustaining the injury in Belfast eighteen months earlier. Because I knew that my ability was unimpaired, I had tried to convince myself that I could go on playing for a long time yet and maintain my normal high standards. I had told myself that my knee pains would eventually go away. I now finally forced myself to face up to the fact that I had a serious long-term injury and it was time to try to do something about it.

Nowadays such an operation would probably be performed using keyhole surgery and post-operation discharge would be immediate. Back then, I was kept in hospital for three weeks to rest my leg after the doctor had done his work. The doctor who performed the operation was Sir John Bruce, an eminent surgeon and a member of the Hibs board.

I was advised to take a holiday to help my recuperation so Kitty, Lawrance and I set off for two weeks in the exotic location of Lossiemouth. The 'Moray Riviera' as it was known back then had fine golf courses and bracing sea air but people probably wouldn't see it as their first-choice holiday destination these days.

We enjoyed our stay and, while we were there, we visited the local boys' club. There was a great turnout and I answered questions and signed autographs. My visit proved so popular that the local paper declared that every shop in the area was sold out of autograph books. The boys' club marked our visit by kindly presenting Lawrance with a football which, of course, pleased him no end.

Lawrance used to love his family holidays and he particularly enjoyed our regular trips to Torquay. We would leave home at 5am and drive to Devon with the minimum of stops. We usually reached the 'English Riviera' at around 5pm. As you can see, we managed to take a few 'Riviera holidays' without actually leaving Britain! The highlight of our Torquay trip for Lawrance was invariably when we passed through Wolverhampton. I would stop outside the Wolves stadium at Molineux and let him look at it. He was always delighted.

When I came back from Lossiemouth and began the long road back to fitness, I would have been delighted to return to action at the beginning of season 1957-58, fully recovered from my operation. As the summer progressed though, I realised that I would need to show a little patience as my knee was taking its time in returning to normal.

19

CALLING TIME ON MY CAREER

When the new season came round, I wasn't quite ready for action. I had made progress and I was feeling optimistic. I told the press that I felt 'as fast as ever'. There may have been an element of wishful thinking in that assessment. There was speculation about who would fill in for me at the start of the season. The two contenders were John Fraser and a seventeen-year-old called Joe Baker. Harry Swan went on the record to state, 'Baker is Hibs' best find for years.' He was absolutely right.

When I had made my comeback after pleurisy, my first game back had been against Hearts' reserves. Coincidentally, when I came back this time, the Tynecastle second string was again the opposition. I ended this game on the right wing because my knee had taken a knock earlier in the game. I was allowed to finish the match which, looking back, seems ridiculous. There was nothing to gain by keeping me on and I could have done a lot of damage to my knee.

I can't have done it too much harm, though, because I was back in the first team against Airdrie a few weeks later. We won 4–0 and I got a goal and a tremendous ovation. The fans were obviously pleased to see me return and I was delighted to be back. The match report stated: 'Lawrie Reilly came back into the Hibs team and brought all his old magic with him.' That was good. What wasn't quite so good was that I had played with my knee heavily bandaged. The fact that the knee still needed support and protection, despite surgery, wasn't encouraging.

I was then moved to inside right to accommodate the precocious Baker Boy at centre forward. We beat Queen's Park 2–0 and young Joe scored both goals. One journalist wrote after the game: 'Baker's class is obvious and he should soon be one of the best.' You could only agree. I got on well with Joe from the start. Although he had been born in Liverpool and later played for England, he considered himself Scottish through and through. He spoke in a broad Lanarkshire accent and told us he came from 'Wishae'. We used to kid Joe about the way he spoke but it didn't bother him one bit. He was a confident lad and he had every right to be. He clearly was something special.

Because of Joe's dynamic entrance to the team, I was no longer first-choice centre forward. This encouraged Sunderland to make a £15,000 bid for me. Rex Kingsley thought that Hibs would reject that offer but he wasn't entirely certain. His opinion was, 'It wouldn't shake me as much as it would have done before I saw the wonder boy Baker.' There was no chance of me leaving Hibs, though, and Sunderland soon realised that and cooled their interest. The fact that they had thought Hibs might be prepared to let me go gave me food for thought. Six months ago, the club would have considered me indispensable. Now with a new star on the scene, my position looked to have changed. I had been in the game long enough to know that there is little sentiment in football. Being the strong-willed person I was, though, I was determined to show that I was still very much the best centre forward at Easter Road. The only problem was that the state of my knee would play a big part in deciding whether I could get back to my best again.

I was now moved to the right wing as Gordon Smith was injured again. We beat Third Lanark 3–0 and it was reported that 'Baker brought the house down when he beat three men to score the third goal'. I was still at outside right when we went to Kilmarnock and won 4–1. Johnny McLeod, making his debut on the left wing, scored two goals and a new order was beginning to emerge. I was the only member of the Famous Five in the Hibs attack in this game.

Gordon came back in for our next match against Motherwell, which we lost 3–1. In truth, though, neither of us was fully fit and it showed. The journalists who had praised us for years were now starting to change their tune. The verdict after this defeat was 'Smith and Reilly were shadows of their former selves.' That hurt. What came next hurt even more. Both Gordon and I were dropped.

I didn't like it but I couldn't complain. My knee was still causing me problems. Fluid continued to form on it after every game and the operation had clearly not been fully successful. The game from which Gordon and I were dropped saw Hibs field an attack without a member of the Famous Five for the first time in nearly six years. One newspaper published a few statistics about the Five. We had played over 1,600 games for Hibs between us, had scored 700 goals and had been capped 120 times for Scotland. That is quite a record and I am happy to let it speak for itself.

I was back in the team for the first Scottish Cup match of the season against Dundee United at Tannadice. We scraped a goalless draw, but my form hadn't improved. One rather cruel critic wrote: 'The tornado that was Lawrie Reilly is now a gentle breeze.' It wasn't pleasant to read but it wasn't wrong either. When you have had success and praise throughout your career, stuff like that is hard to take. In my heart of hearts, though, I knew that my knee was going to continue to handicap me. I have never been a man to settle for anything other than the best, so I took a momentous decision and announced my retirement. It saddened me to have to do so but I could see no point in soldiering on as things were. I issued a statement which summed up perfectly how I felt. It said: 'I can no longer play my best football. I am not prepared to be a second-rater or risk crippling myself.'

The tributes flooded in. Gordon Smith was in hospital recovering from an ankle operation and he wrote to me. Here is an extract from Gordon's letter: 'It certainly makes me very sad that I will never play with you again. When I think of the wonderful games that we have had together and the service which you have given the club, it is a tragedy that it has had to end this way.' That meant the world to me.

Edinburgh Thistle, my old juvenile club, presented me with a beautiful clock and that touched me as well, but I still had one game to play. I rested my knee to make sure that when I ran out at Easter Road for the last time, I would be able to finish on a high note and do myself justice. That was really important to me.

We were playing Rangers and I was captain for the night. The papers had previewed the game with the headline 'Last Time Reilly' and I wanted that last time to be a special one. What an ovation I got when I led the team out. It was a cold April Monday night but 24,000 had turned out to bid me farewell.

Because my knee had been under no pressure for a couple of months, I was able to move more freely than had been the case earlier in the season. I was determined to go out with a bang and I certainly managed to do that. We won 3–1 and I got the second goal. Listen to this description of it: 'Reilly got possession and shot home a low drive. How the crowd roared. The windows of Abbeyhill shook with the noise.' At full time, both teams lined up at the tunnel to clap me off the field. I had a huge lump in my throat as I looked up into the old centre stand to where Kitty, Lawrance and my mum and dad were sitting. I knew that they would be as happy for me as I was for myself. I felt a mixture of emotions but I was mostly proud that I had finished my career on a high. It meant a lot to me that people would remember me as the great player that I had striven to be throughout all of my time at Hibs.

One report summed this moment up perfectly when it stated: 'Lawrie Reilly left the field with the cheers of the crowd ringing in his ears as a crescendo of thanks for a great career. Both teams sportingly and respectfully lined up to clap the grey-haired maestro from the field for the last time.' I am happy with that.

I was still only twenty-nine, despite the grey hairs, but I knew that I had made the right decision. My knee would never again allow me to play to the standards I had always set myself and going out at the top was the correct thing to do.

The press love a good story, though, and now they had one. Despite Hibs' tribulations in the league, the club had reached the Scottish Cup Final. Inspired by Joe Baker, we had beaten Dundee United, Hearts (my teenage successor had knocked in four goals at Tynecastle), Third Lanark and Rangers and would face Clyde in the final on the Saturday after my final game against Rangers.

The papers now began to suggest that I should play up front with Joe at Hampden. Headlines like 'Last Game Reilly' began to appear and the speculation reached fever pitch. Just when it looked like Hugh Shaw was going to have to make a big decision, fate took a hand. I went down with tonsillitis and had no chance of making the final. While I would have loved to play at Hampden and end my career on the very highest of highs, I was quite relieved in a way that our manager didn't have to make that decision in the end. If I had played, John Fraser or Andy Aitken, who had both played well all through the competition, would have had to drop out. That just wouldn't have been fair on them.

In the event, I listened to the Scottish Cup Final on radio at home as I wasn't well enough to travel. There were over 97,000 supporters inside Hampden and the vast majority were bedecked in green and white. If we thought that we were going to end our Scottish Cup hoodoo at last, we were wrong. Sadly, Clyde won 1–0 with the help of a deflected goal from their centre forward Johnny Coyle. Hibs had again come up short at Hampden and what had promised to be a day of celebration ended as a day of mourning.

I was pleased that my centre-forward position was in good hands for the future as we had one of the very best in young Baker. Eddie Turnbull was now playing right half and his form was good enough to earn him a place in Scotland's party for the

1958 World Cup Finals in Sweden. Willie Ormond was also back in the team and Gordon Smith would return the following season. We had very promising young players in Johnny McLeod, Davie Gibson and Andy Aitken, so the future looked bright.

Harry Swan saw it differently, though, and these players along with Jimmy Harrower were all to be sold to English clubs, while Joe Baker was eventually sold to Turin. If these players had been kept, Hibs could have scaled the heights again but it looked like money in the club's coffers was the chairman's main priority as the 1950s gave way to the 1960s.

As for me, I had my testimonial game to look forward to. Hibs had only agreed to this game after the intervention of Sir George Graham. By saying that they would allow me to use Easter Road for the match and that they would provide the opposition for an international select put together by Sir George and myself, Hibs were able to strike a compromise that kept me happy and allowed them to maintain the position that they weren't organising a testimonial for me.

Having fought so hard to get a testimonial match, I was only interested in ensuring that the event was a success and that it helped to secure my future. There were difficulties from the outset. Hearts refused to release Jimmy Murray and Willie Bauld, who had both agreed to play for the select team. Stanley Matthews had said that he would come up and take part too but he was ruled out through injury. On the day of the game, the SFA dropped a bombshell when they told me that I would not be allowed to play in my own testimonial. Their secretary Willie Allan said: 'You cannot play in the game because you no longer come under the jurisdiction of the SFA as you have retired from the game.' Allan added: 'Lawrie knows that the SFA ban is not a personal one on him. It is a matter of having to act according to our constitution.' What I did know was that I was being prevented from playing in a game which meant a huge amount to me by red tape and bureaucracy.

There was worse to come. The weather on the day of the game was abominable. There was a strong biting wind and icy rain poured down all day. The elements couldn't have done more to encourage people to stay at home. In the event the crowd fell below 10,000. If I had played and it had been a decent night, I am certain that there would have been a much bigger turnout. The weather-affected attendance also meant that the proceeds of the game were less than I had hoped for.

All of this was disappointing but the match itself wasn't. The international select team was a strong one featuring such great players as George Farm in goal, Willie McNaught, Tommy Docherty, Ian McColl, Bertie Peacock, Willie Fernie, Jackie Mudie and Billy Liddell. Also in the select team was my old teammate Bobby Johnstone, who had come up to play in my game. Bobby scored a penalty and the photographs in the papers showing Lawrie Leslie diving to try to keep out Bobby's shot reveal how bad the weather was. Lawrie is wearing tracksuit trousers, big gloves and, by the looks of it, two sweaters.

Hibs won a very open and entertaining game 9–3. Gordon Smith, Willie Ormond and Joe Baker all got two goals each. Eddie Turnbull was also on the mark. Ironically, the only member of the Famous Five not able to play in the Lawrie Reilly Testimonial Match was Lawrie Reilly!

The Hibs Supporters' Association also wanted to mark my retirement and they did so in style. They staged a rally in the Usher Hall and the event was a sell-out. Two-and-a-half thousand filled every seat (it couldn't rain in the Usher Hall!) and stars of stage, screen and football came along to pay tribute to me.

I was given a top-of-the-range cine camera, which was considered to be cutting-edge technology at that time and I was very moved by the whole occasion. Matt Busby had promised to come up and make my presentation but, in the event, he wasn't able to do so. He had been part-time manager of Scotland in the autumn of 1958 and had showed how good his judgement of a footballer was by selecting an eighteen-year-old from Huddersfield Town called Denis Law for his first match in charge. However, post-Munich, Matt's health still wasn't good and his doctors had discouraged him from taking on any unnecessary travel. This had caused him to resign his Scotland post and prevented him from attending my rally. Jimmy Hoy, the MP for Leith, made my presentation instead and like others that night had very kind words to say.

When I stood up to respond, I looked out at the packed hall, thought of my family sharing this great night with me and said, with tears rolling down my face, 'Thank you all so much. This really is a wonderful day for me.' It was simple but sincere as was my comment on my successor. I told the crowd: 'There are no heights that young Joe cannot reach in the game.' I meant every word of it and I wasn't wrong, was I?

That was a truly memorable occasion for me and there had been many equally special times for me in the green and white of Hibs and the dark blue of Scotland over the years. Thanks to a stubbornly troublesome right knee, these days were gone now and I had to turn my attention to the rest of my life. It was going to be very strange indeed to adjust to an existence that didn't involve being fully focused on the game which had assumed so much importance in my adult life to date.

20

LIFE AFTER FOOTBALL

As footballers across Scotland went on their close-season break in the summer of 1958, I began to come to terms with life after football. Initially, it seemed like a daunting prospect. I had signed for Hibs at the age of sixteen and now, nearly fourteen years later, I had to make a life for myself which didn't involve the camaraderie and enjoyment of training at Easter Road and the excitement and fulfilment of playing and winning with Hibs and Scotland.

I was surprised by how quickly I was able to put my old life behind me and embrace new challenges. I think the state of my knee helped me to do this. I knew that it would never be right again and that playing regular professional football just wasn't an option for me any more. Even now, more than half a century after hanging up my boots, my right knee still causes me problems.

During my time out with pleurisy and pneumonia, I had written some articles for the *Daily Mail*. I commented upon current matters with Hibs and Scotland as well as giving my views on the general footballing topics of the day. I enjoyed it and, to this day, I am happy to give my opinion on anything to do with the game of football. I had also written some coaching columns offering players below professional level some advice on how to improve their skills.

When I retired, the *Scottish Sunday Express* approached me to share my recollections of some of the highlights of my career with their readers. It was a pleasure to do this and it led to me being offered work with the *Daily Express*. Every Saturday, I would go and watch a secondary school match in Edinburgh. I would have my photograph taken with both teams before the match and write a match report after it. As well as reporting on the match, I would evaluate the performance of each player, commend him on the better aspects of his performance and provide some advice on how he might develop his game in future. This proved tremendously popular and I think that a lot of schoolboy players and their families enjoyed meeting me and reading my comments on their footballing ability.

I was very busy too, of course, with running The Bowlers' Rest – so busy, in fact, that I had to give up my journalistic work. I just didn't have the time for it. The pub was really popular and I enjoyed the daily chat and banter with customers. Pouring a pint is the nearest I have ever come to an alcoholic drink in my life so you might think that going into the licensed trade was a strange choice for me. I didn't think so. Lots of footballers opened pubs when they retired in those days and I have always been sociable and enjoyed company. A lot of nice folk came into my hostelry and I formed lifelong friendships with people who drank in my bar or who came into it on business. I ran 'Reilly's' for thirty-six years before selling it for a good price in 1992. I was coming up for sixty-four then and ready for retirement. I had enjoyed my time as a mine host but I was looking to have more free time for myself.

A lot of my free time has always been devoted to playing golf. I had taken up the game at an early age, found that I was good at it, worked hard to become even better and thoroughly enjoyed the challenge and companionship of life on the fairways.

I had a fair amount of success. I won a number of tournaments and was club champion at two separate clubs. I twice won the championship at Broomieknowe in Bonnyrigg and took the honours once at Longniddry in East Lothian. I also achieved no fewer than six holes in one. The first time I holed my tee shot was at Dunbar and courses beginning with 'D' were lucky for me as I also managed aces at Duddingston and Dalmahoy. The other courses where I only needed one shot were Longniddry, Gullane and Whitecraigs in Glasgow.

Someone once told me that Jack Nicklaus never achieved a hole in one in his tournament career. I am not sure if that is true, but if it is then maybe that's something I have over the great man.

When I became champion at Longniddry, the player I beat in the final was Alex Harvey, son of the Hearts manager Johnny. Alex and I had some great matches over the years. One of our contests went to sudden death and required no fewer than nine extra holes before Alex rolled in a birdie putt to win.

The barman at Longniddry told me a good story not so long ago. A party of golfers from England had just completed a round and were having a drink in the clubhouse. One of them looked at the honours board and saw my name. He asked if this 'L. Reilly' was the one who had played football for Scotland. When he was told that it was indeed the very same man, he introduced himself as Ivor Broadis. Ivor had scored two goals for England against Scotland at Wembley in 1953 – the match at which I had scored both the Scottish goals in a famous 2–2 draw. That was the game in which my equaliser in the dying seconds had earned me my 'Last Minute Reilly' nickname. Ivor asked the barman to pass his best wishes on to me, which he duly did.

I was also the prime mover in forming a golf club for ex-Hibs players. We had regular games at Longniddry and it was great fun. The standard of golf was generally good. Our matches were always competitive but we all got on really well together and very much enjoyed keeping in touch with each other even though our playing days were over.

Eddie Turnbull, Gordon Smith, Willie Clark, Tommy Younger, Tommy Preston, John Paterson, Willie McFarlane and others all played. We had a few laughs, I can tell you. Big Tam had been some character when he played and he was even more ebullient when he retired. He had carved out a successful business career for himself in gaming machines and was doing well enough to be able to treat himself to a Rolls-Royce. Tommy used to drive me down to the East Lothian coast in his Rolls every week for the golf. After the game, though, he was inevitably the life and soul of the nineteenth hole. With a big cigar in one hand and a glass in the other, he would have everybody in stitches with his quips and stories. When it was time to head for home, he always asked me the same question. 'Lawrie, I've had a wee drink. Would you mind driving the Rolls back up the road?' I was always happy to oblige.

Tommy was a real character. He used to smoke Montecristo cigars. They cost £10 each and he would get through three of them in the course of a round of golf. His wife told me once that he kept a box of Montecristos beside his bed. When he woke up in the morning the first thing he did was to wipe the sleep out of his eyes. The second was to take a cigar out of his box and light up.

Mind you, the atmosphere between Eddie Turnbull and big Younger became a bit strained when Eddie left his job as Hibs manager. Tommy was on the board at the time and Eddie was convinced that he had had a hand in his departure. Personally, I think that Tom Hart was the man who was instrumental in Eddie stepping down as Hibs boss. Anyway, Eddie refused to play in the same foursome as Tommy for a while and things were a bit difficult. Normal service was soon resumed, though. Tommy Younger was a man nobody could dislike.

When we were playing for Hibs, Gordon Smith had been a quiet, reserved man. He always roomed with Bobby Combe on trips away and Bobby was his closest friend at the club. During my time at Easter Road, I had never been in Gordon's house. That all changed when we retired and started our golfing get-togethers. I became a regular visitor to Gordon's home, especially if we were playing at North Berwick, where he lived, and he would visit us as well. It was great to see Gordon coming out of his shell.

Gordon got bit of a shock when we were playing at North

Berwick once. One of our former Hibs colleagues lined up a drive on a hole where a low wall ran across the course about twenty yards in front of the tee. He hammered the ball but it didn't rise too much and clattered into the wall.

From there it rebounded back towards us and hit Gordon in the neck. If it had struck his Adam's apple it could have seriously endangered him. Fortunately it caught him on the side of his neck and did no serious damage. Gordon made light of it but he did need to have his injury bandaged after we finished our round. Gordon grew to love his golf and it would have been a terrible tragedy if the man who, in my opinion, was the best right winger ever born in Scotland, had been seriously injured taking part in one of his favourite post-retirement hobbies. Thankfully that wasn't the case.

We used to play an annual match with the former players of Dundee. One year we would go over to Rosemount and the next they would come across to us at Longniddry. Doug Cowie, one of their all-time great players, was always a keen participant in these contests, but he wouldn't have been too happy with the results of them because we usually came out on top.

I also used to take part in a golf tournament in Spain every year. It was a team competition at the Aloha course in Andalucia. Each team had four members but only the three best scores counted. My regular teammates were three friends of mine, Jimmy Armstrong, Wilson Morton and Bob Pringle. One year we played particularly well and Wilson, Bob and I were all in the clubhouse with scores which were clearly going to win the trophy for us by a wide margin. Jimmy didn't know that as he stood over his second shot on the eighteenth fairway. We shouted to him, 'Jimmy, you need to get down in two for us to win.' He nodded and concentrated like mad to finish his round with only a couple more shots.

You should have seen his face when we told him that we had only been winding him up and that we had actually won by nine strokes. You might not have wanted to hear his language, though!

Funnily enough I bumped into another of Edinburgh's famous sons on that same Aloha course. One year, Sean Connery was playing in the annual team tournament there. He told me that he remembered me not just from my days playing for the Hibs but from his days as a milkman in the west of Edinburgh. He said that he used to see me in the streets around Bryson Road when he was doing his deliveries. He wasn't in the best of humours that day. Like me, he took his golf seriously and played to win. He wasn't going to win this tournament, though, because his team-mates had let him down by playing poorly. He wasn't slow to express his opinion of them and he didn't mince his words either. I felt like saying to him, 'I didn't know that 007 could curse like that!'

I also used to holiday in Florida and play golf there. I played at the outstanding Lake Nona course, where the professionals play in the Tavistock Cup.

One of the many things I like about golf is that it is such a sporting game. Golfers usually play to the rules and that is very important to them. Sportsmanship was important to me as a footballer too. I am proud to say that I was never sent off. I did pick up a few bookings but never for foul play. My name was always taken for having too much to say to the referee. Unlike Mr Connery, I never used foul language. I usually just asked the refs if they had considered booking an eye test because it seemed to me like they could do with one. I played golf until recently but decided to give the game up when I couldn't play to the high standards I had always set myself any more. To say that I have a competitive nature is an understatement. If I can't play to win then I don't want to play at all.

I remember after a tournament once, we had a social function in the clubrooms in the evening. One of my regular golfing partners, Raymond Scoular, tapped me on the shoulder and said, 'Lawrie, I've been watching you for the last few minutes and you have been staring at the ceiling. What's on your mind?' I replied, 'Sorry Raymond, I can't stop thinking about the three putts I took at the fifth hole. If it hadn't been for that I would have won the competition.' That was me and golf and when I couldn't compete at the top of the leaderboard any more, I decided to put my clubs away.

I formed a lot of great friendships through golf. What is really nice is that lots of people have told me that they have valued their relationship with me and found me a loyal and supportive friend. That means something to me.

During my retirement years, my marriage to Kitty came to an end. In the mid-1970s, an attractive lady in her thirties came into my pub with her friend for a drink. We had a chat and found that we got on really well. She had been widowed and her name was Iris. Like me she had been in the licensed trade although she had sold her pub by this time. We began to see each other and eventually decided to get married. Our wedding took place in 1981 and twenty-nine years later we are still together and still very happy indeed.

Iris and I have had some great times and we have particularly enjoyed the many and varied holidays which we have taken. For some years, we had our own holiday apartment in Spain. We sold it when we decided that we didn't want to keep going back to the same place every year for our holidays.

We have now been to a whole host of different countries and found something special in all of them. We have visited Hong Kong, Singapore, Thailand, California, Florida and New York. In recent years, we have really enjoyed the Italian Lakes.

Iris had a son and a daughter from her first marriage so I found myself with a stepson and stepdaughter, both of whom I get on with very well. I also now have six grandchildren. Laura and Sam are twenty-two, the two Emmas are nineteen and twenty respectively, Clare is also nineteen and Stuart, the youngest, is just sixteen. Stuart likes his golf and hopes to be a professional one day.

My son Lawrance is now in his fifties. He is a son to be proud of. Lawrance has a good career in the Civil Service and has inherited some of my sporting talent. As a boy, he was an excellent footballer. He might well have gone on to be a professional but understandably got fed up with people continually comparing him with his dad and decided to turn his attention to other sports. He played a lot of football when he was at school, though, not just with proper teams but also with his friends in the street.

When Hibs reached the Coronation Cup Final in 1953, we were each given smaller versions of the trophy as mementoes of our achievement. One day, when Lawrance was at primary school, I noticed that my Coronation Cup trophy wasn't in the display cabinet. I looked out the window and saw that Lawrance and his pals were engaged in a full-scale game. Hanging on the garden fence was my trophy. I went out and asked Lawrance what it was doing there. He told me that he and his friends were playing a challenge match and the winning team was going to get my trophy to keep.

I soon put him right on that one, reclaimed my treasured Coronation Cup memento and returned it to its usual place behind glass in the living room. Lawrance changed his games to rugby and cricket and played for his school at both. He still plays a bit of cricket now and coaches one of the cricket teams at Stewart's Melville. He is also pretty useful on the golf course. He is a lifelong Hibee and rarely misses a game at Easter Road.

Like me, Lawrance loves the Hibs and is delighted when we win. Like his dad too, he gets down when we lose. I'll never forget how disappointed he was when Hibs played Celtic in the League Cup semi-final in 1965. I took him to Hampden and with five minutes to go, Hibs were leading 2–1. We left at that point to beat the traffic. The car I had then didn't have a radio, so we didn't know the score when we got home. Lawrance was sure that Hibs were in the final and was really excited about going back to Hampden and seeing his team win the cup. I didn't get the full-time score till the morning. It was after midnight when we got home and all the radio and television stations were closed down for the night by that time in those days. I didn't phone anyone to check the result, either, as it was too late to bother anybody.

When I turned on the radio in the morning, I was sickened to hear that Bobby Lennox had scored a last-minute equaliser for Celtic. When I broke this news to Lawrance he was devastated. He was only nine and a Hibs fanatic. It took him a long time to get over that particular disappointment.

I was fortunate enough to be awarded a number of honours when I finished playing. Two newspapers, the *Daily Record* and the *Herald*, held competitions, a few years apart, to give their readers the chance to choose the greatest ever Scotland team. I was privileged to be selected in the final eleven on both occasions. The players who were picked to play alongside me included Jimmy Cowan, Davie Mackay, Jim Baxter, George Young, Gordon Smith and Denis Law, so you can see that I was in the very best of company. It's interesting that the SFA Selection Committee ignored Gordon more often than not, but the Scottish footballing public fully recognised his worth.

The *Herald* arranged for a portrait or photograph of each player in the all-time great Scotland team to be hung in the National Portrait Gallery in Queen Street in Edinburgh. Iris and I were delighted to go along with the other players and their wives to the unveiling ceremony at the gallery. It was a memorable occasion.

As will have been evident throughout this book, playing for Scotland meant an awful lot to me. I am a proud Scot and I was always pleased to lead my country's attack at a time when Scotland was a force to be reckoned with in international football. I was tremendously honoured, therefore, to be inducted into the SFA Hall of Fame.

I received this honour at Hampden in 2005 and my pleasure was increased when I was presented for induction by my good friend and all-time Hibs great Pat Stanton. A bonus of being a member of the Hall of Fame is that I can visit the Scottish Football

Museum and bring guests with me at any time and our entrance will be complimentary!

At the induction dinner, I sat close to another Scotland centre forward called Reilly. This one was Rose Reilly, who is also a member of the SFA Hall of Fame. She was very pleasant company and from what I've seen of her on film she was a pretty good centre forward as well.

When David Taylor was SFA Chief Executive and Walter Smith was Scotland team manager, they took the time to write me a joint letter congratulating me on my scoring record against England. That was a nice touch which I appreciated. Taylor's successor in the top job at Hampden was of course Gordon Smith, the former Rangers player and media pundit. Gordon was an excellent player but every time I saw him, I wanted to tell him that, as a player, he wasn't a patch on his more famous namesake who played with me at Hibs. My natural good manners stopped me from doing so of course!

Hibs people didn't forget me when my playing days came to an end, either. In 2006, I was invited across to Belfast to receive a beautifully inscribed mirror from the Northern Ireland Hibernian Supporters' Association. Pat and Jackie MacNamara accompanied me on that trip. The inscription acknowledged my 'exceptional service' to Hibs, which was nice. The Hibs Former Players' Association organised a dinner for me at Easter Road in the same year and they presented me with a superb wall clock which is now on my living room wall. The mirror from Ireland is up in my dining room.

I regularly attend the Former Players' Association meetings. It's great to keep in touch with the lads – and the Association, with people like Paul Kane at the forefront, do great work in looking after ex-Hibs players who need a bit of support and helping good causes generally.

I also act as a match-day host at Hibs' home games. Pat Stanton does this too when his SFA delegate duties allow him to be available. Pat and I each host a table before the game. It's great to meet so many of the club's supporters. We join them again at half-time and after the match and the conversation is always lively and enjoyable. We usually find time to sign autographs and pose for photographs too.

The fans always seem delighted to spend time with me and I enjoy discussing the match with them. Mind you, it's not only older supporters who show me respect. Recently, as I came out of my house, I saw three youngsters looking at me. Eventually one of them said, 'Is it true that you're Lawrie Reilly?' When I confirmed that I was indeed that man, they all bowed before me in an extravagant gesture of homage. That was nice. I fared slightly better than my old teammate Sammy Kean. One day when Sammy came out after training, a young lad asked him for his signature. Sammy said to the boy, 'Did I not give you my autograph yesterday?'

'Aye,' said the young supporter, 'but I can swap two of yours for one of Gordon Smith's.'

Pat and I watch the game from the row of seats immediately behind the directors' box. We sit beside Grant Stott and his dad and the craic is first class. Grant does a great job of hosting the corporate hospitality at Easter Road and, with his dad and brother John, is a real dyed-in-the-wool Hibee. Sitting where we do also allows me to have a chat with anyone I know in the directors' box just below us.

I attended another Hibs-related function in 2007. This one was a bit different. After I retired, I found out that the supporter who always started off the 'Gie the ba to Reilly' chant at Easter Road was called Charlie Anderson. If there is a town crier around with a louder voice than Charlie I am yet to meet him. When Charlie celebrated his ninetieth birthday in the Dockers' Club in Leith, Iris and I were delighted to attend.

Charlie's catchphrase is, of course, immortalised in song. One of the songs most closely associated with our club is 'Glory, Glory to the Hibees'. In the verse on the Famous Five, the singer, Hector Nicol, shouts 'Gie the ba to Reilly.' As this song is played at most Hibs' home games, Charlie's words are never likely to be forgotten.

Finally on the Hibs front, I was hugely honoured when the club recently decided to set up its own Hall of Fame and invited me to be one of the inaugural nominees. Of course I was delighted to accept and it means a great deal to me to be accorded such recognition by the team which I have supported all my life.

One career which never appealed to me is that of football manager or coach. That may surprise people but it just wasn't for me. To be a successful manager, you have be consumed by your job. It takes over your whole life. I have always loved football and still do but I have also always had lots of other interests. Managing Hibs might have been a possibility for me, but I can honestly say that it was a possibility which I never seriously entertained.

Two of my old teammates took on the job of Hibs manager, of course, and they were Eddie Turnbull and Willie Ormond. Willie's spell in charge was a short one due to ill health but Eddie was at the helm for nine years. Willie also had a spell as manager of Hearts. That's a job which certainly wouldn't have appealed to me. Round about the time that Willie was in charge at Tynecastle someone asked me how I would react if I was offered the job of Hearts' boss. With my tongue firmly in my cheek, I said that I would take it and make sure that they were relegated within a season.

When Turnbull took charge at Easter Road in 1971, the Famous Five were reunited for the first time for many years before one of the pre-season friendlies against the German team Schalke. One of the pressmen pointed to us that Hibs hadn't won a trophy since the Five had broken up. I assured him that Eddie would soon put that right and of course he did. Ned's team – known as Turnbull's Tornadoes – won three trophies between 1972 and 1973.

People often ask me which was the better team, the one I

played in or the Tornadoes team which Pat Stanton led. If the two teams had taken each other on at their respective peaks, it would have been a classic match and very close indeed. I have to say, though, that I think we would have come out on top. If you asked Pat (and I never have), he might see it differently, but I base my judgement on one criterion. If I was told that I could choose any member of the Turnbull's Tornadoes side to put into the Famous Five team, I would only make three changes to the team which won three league titles. I would pick Pat of course and also John Blackley. I think I would probably include John Brownlie too, although Jock Govan might have had something to say about that. The rest would be the team which I was so proud to be part of. The only other player since I retired that I would have to find a place for in a best post-war Hibs team would be Joe Baker. Mind you, deciding which member of the Famous Five to leave out to accommodate Joe would be virtually impossible.

I still cheer the Hibs on at every home game although I don't get to too many away matches these days. I stopped going to Easter Road for a while when David Duff owned the club. I wasn't sure how things were going at that time so I stayed away. I've been back ever since Sir Tom Farmer stepped in to ensure the club's survival in 1990. It's hard for us to compete with the Old Firm now because every time we find some top players, bigger clubs come along and entice them away with higher wages. I am often asked whether I would have left Hibs if I had played after the abolition of the maximum wage and an English club had offered me thousands of pounds a week to sign for them. That is a hard question and, as the situation never arose, one which I have never had the need to answer. I will simply say this. I was born a Hibee and I will die a Hibee. There's nothing else to add.

So, there you have it. It's been a great pleasure looking back over my career and remembering so many great players and wonderful matches. Writing this book has brought back a lot of very happy memories.

You might wonder why I left producing my autobiography so

late. Well, I wasn't called Last Minute Reilly for nothing, you know. I would like to end by expressing the hope that everyone who buys this book gets as much enjoyment from reading it as I have had from writing it.

Oh, one last thing. By the time this book is published, it will be almost 109 years since Hibs last won the Scottish Cup. That's just ridiculous, isn't it? Surely our Scottish Cup hoodoo can't go on much longer?

I would like to end with a wish. That wish is that Hibs will lift the cup in the near future. If they do, no one will be more delighted than me. I will be first in line to congratulate the manager and shake the captain's hand.

So, come on Hibs. Go for it – and please don't leave it to the last minute!

Appendix – Tribute to Eddie Turnbull

I feel privileged to have been part of Hibernian's Famous Five. Gordon Smith, Bobby Johnstone, Eddie Turnbull, Willie Ormond and I didn't just combine successfully on the field, we were good friends off it too. Eddie's recent sad passing is a real blow. It also leaves me as the last surviving member of Hibs greatest forward line and that is a very poignant feeling indeed.

Eddie Turnbull joined Hibs when he was in his early twenties. Eddie came late to the game because of his war time service in the Royal Navy. The action he had seen had matured him and everyone at Easter Road was immediately struck by his self assurance.

Eddie's first game in green and white was a reserve match against Queen of the South. He scored with a header from a corner taken by yours truly. Eddie soon became a vital member of our team and contributed greatly to our success through his consistent performances. He never stopped working, tackled hard and used the ball intelligently. He got more than his fair share of goals too. Not many of his finishes were of the side foot variety. He liked to leather the ball past the goalkeeper. We nicknamed him the Cannonball Kid after a comic book character of the time.

Eddie became our penalty taker. He once scored four goals, including a hat trick of penalties, in a 4-1 win against Celtic. There is only way to describe how Eddie struck a spot kick. He absolutely blootered it! It took a lot of nerve to score three penalties in the same game but that was something Eddie never lacked. When you've dodged torpedoes in the Arctic, taking a penalty is a dawdle.

Eddie was a strong man with forthright views. When he became captain, he drove his team mates on and we all knew exactly where we stood. Eddie's talents were also recognised at international level but he deserved more caps than he got. It was great to see him do well for Scotland in the 1958 World Cup Finals at the age of thirty-five.

Eddie and I played a lot of golf together when he retired. His golf, like his football, was of high quality. If anything our friendship deepened after our respective retirements.

When Eddie became Hibs manager, he built a great team. I can still recall sitting in the stand at Tynecastle on New Year's Day 1973 taking great pleasure in counting the goals as Eddie's Tornadoes put seven past Hearts.

Eddie always said that there was 'class, first class and then Hibs class'. Well, old chum, you were class as a friend and colleague, first class as a player and manager and Hibs class in everything you did.

Rest in peace.

Lawrie